Global Power Shift

Ample empirical evidence points to recent power shifts in multiple areas of international relations taking place between industrialized countries and emerging powers, as well as between states and non-state actors. However, there is a dearth of theoretical interpretation and synthesis of these findings, and a growing need for coherent approaches to understand and measure the transformation. The central issues to be addressed include theoretical questions and empirical puzzles: How can studies of global power shift and the rise of 'emerging powers' benefit from existing theories, and which alternative aspects and theoretical approaches might be suitable? How can the meanings, perceptions, dynamics, and consequences of global power shift be determined and assessed? This edited series will include highly innovative research on these topics. It aims to bring together scholars from all major world regions as well as different disciplines, including political science, economics and human geography. The overall aim is to discuss and possibly blend their different approaches and provide new frameworks for understanding global affairs and the governance of global power shifts.

All titles in this series are peer-reviewed.

More information about this series at http://www.springer.com/series/10201

Ursula Werther-Pietsch

Transforming Security

A New Balance-of-Power Doctrine

Springer

Ursula Werther-Pietsch
University of Graz
Graz, Austria

ISSN 2198-7343 ISSN 2198-7351 (electronic)
Global Power Shift
ISBN 978-3-030-87096-6 ISBN 978-3-030-87097-3 (eBook)
https://doi.org/10.1007/978-3-030-87097-3

This Springer imprint is published by the registered company Springer Nature Switzerland AG
The registered company address is: Gewerbestrasse 11, 6330 Cham, Switzerland

"We see the beginning of a new movement".

Antonio Guterres

United Nations Secretary-General,
September 2020

Preface

Power, autonomy, state responsibility, and human beings; international law and relations are made up of those ingredients. They essentially build part of the Global Peace Mechanism and, in their complex interfaces, are to be taken into account in International Crisis and Conflict Management under new geostrategic constellations.

Roland Paris, the advisor to the Canadian Prime Minister, speaks of a deeply felt foundering of the Pax Americana, which, both internally and externally, was only fuelled by four years of republican volatility. The Australian World Affairs Council simultaneously warned of an upcoming Cold War II as tensions between the two antagonists in world leadership, the United States of America and the People's Republic of China, evolve in the South Chinese and Indian Sea. Syria and the Middle East remain hot spots of the protracted crisis of our days. Data sovereignty is at risk through geo-technological clusters and the continued expansion of the "non-state". To this adds that de-globalisation happened in wide areas as a result of the COVID-19 pandemic. The argument for "clash of civilisations" (Huntington, 1999) has been re-evolved, but it came and lasts in very different facets of injustice and discrimination than forecast.

The resilience of states and societies is deeply undermined whereas multilateralism unfolds strategically poor results. Therefore, accelerated by COVID-19, the paradigm of equidistance and human-centrism is in the making. Possibly, this process will end up in a global trilateralism, demonstrating increased levels of strategic autonomy of the regions.

And indeed, in times of hard realpolitik and growing autocracy, as UN Secretary-General Antonio Guterres puts it, "We need a new world order" (Nelson Mandela Commemoration Lecture 2020, New York, 18 July 2020), an order shaped by Multilateral System Thinking. We do have to think about anticipatory democratic global governance able to face frontier risks.

The aim is to define and form building blocks in order to set up a new model.

Vienna, Austria/Munich,
Germany/Luzern, Switzerland
March 2022

Ursula Werther-Pietsch
Lecturer of International Law and
International Relations

Acknowledgements I would like to thank Allen Tawanda Mandevhana for proofreading, Burhan Ilhan for his courageous technological evacuation on 6 June, Jaime Bayer from the Austrian Ministry for European and International Affairs for forgiving me for delaying our coffee on the day of submission, Vijay Kumar Selvaraj and Sindhu Sindar for perfectly navigating the manuscript on its way to publication, Johannes Glaeser for his excellent editorial support and the kind acceptance of my thoughts by Prof. Xuewu Gu, Director of the Center for Global Studies Bonn, to be brought to the public.

Contents

About the Author

Ursula Werther-Pietsch Born in Graz/Austria.

Academic career: Studied law, French, and architecture. Post-graduate courses in Cambridge/UK and Bruges. Editor at MANZ publishing house, founder of the scientific journal "Juristische Ausbildung und Praxis (JAP)". Assistant and lecturer at the Universities of Graz and Vienna. From 2012, holder of a Ph.D. (Habilitation), venia in International Law and International Relations at University of Graz.

Positions: Federal Chancellery Constitutional Service, Federal Ministry for European and International Affairs, Bureau of the Legal Advisor and Development Section, most recently Deputy Director and Senior Adviser. Co-founder of Austrian 3C Net.

Further academic affiliations: 2019/20 Visiting Senior Fellow at the Institute for Peace-building and Conflict Management of the National Defence Academy. From 2020 onwards, Lecturer at the Bundeswehr University Munich. 2021 Masterproject "Sustaining Peace" at University of Graz.

Memberships: Member of the Austrian and German Society of International Law. Scientific Commission of the Federal Ministry of Defence. Scientific Advisor to the Academic Forum for Foreign Policy. Member of the Editorial Board of the Austrian Military Journal. Member of OECD International Network on Conflict and Fragility and several other epistemic circles. Visiting Lecturer and Assessor of academic works at several High Schools such as Vienna Diplomatic Academy or FH Burgenland.

Research fields: International law, international organisations, human rights, human security, multilateral system thinking, UN reform, EU foreign and security policy, geopolitics, international crisis and conflict management, resilience, anticipatory democratic governance, and human-centrism.

Recent books and articles: Powering Universalism. Future Global Governance (Klein 2021), Kollektive Sicherheit, 2030 (NDA 2020), Women as Drivers for Peace (Blue Helmet Forum/UNIS 2020), Global Peace and Security (MANZ 2017), Human Rights and Inclusive Societies (intersentia 2014); EU Security Structure Key for Strategic Autonomy—A Proposal. In AIES Yearbook (Springer 2021), Gender Equality. In Handbuch zur österreichischen Außenpolitik (Springer 2022), Global Pandemic and the Regionalisation of Security (The Hague Yearbook of International Law, Jan 2022). **YouTube**: Videos UWP, interviews, roundtables and guest lectures.

New Autumn lecture: Globalisation and Law, Institute of System Sciences, Innovation and Sustainability Research, University of Graz.

New scientific journal: The Defence Horizon Special Edition, Co-Editor (since 2021), www.thedefencehorizon.org.

Abbreviations

3C	Coordination, Complementarity, Coherence
A4P	Action for Peacekeeping
AI	Artificial Intelligence
ASEAN	Association of Southeast Asian Nations
AU	African Union
BAKS	Federal Academy for Security
BICC	Bonn International Center for Conversion
BRICS	Brazil, Russia, India, China, South Africa
BTI	Bertelsmann Transformation Index
CA	Comprehensive Approach
CCCM	Cooperative Crisis and Conflict Management
cf.	Compare
CFSP	Common Foreign and Security Policy
CHS	Commission on Human Security
CIFP	Country Indicators for Foreign Policy
CIMIC	Civil-Military Cooperation
COE	Centre of Excellence
CPA	Comprehensive Peace Agreement
CPCSC	Civil, Political, Economic, Social, and Cultural (human) rights
CPIA	Country Policy and Institutional Assessment
DAC	Development Assistance Committee
DDR	Disarmament, Demobilisation, and Reintegration
DFA	European Defence Agency
DFID	Department for International Development
DFS	United Nations Department of Field Support
DPKO	United Nations Department of Peacekeeping Operations
DRC	Democratic Republic of the Congo
e.g.	example given
EC	European Commission
ECLAC	Economic Commission for Latin America and the Caribbean

ECOSOC	Economic and Social Council
ECOWAS	Economic Community of West-African States
EDT	Emerging of Disruptive Technologies
EPON	Effectiveness of Peace Operations Network
ESC Rights	Economic, Social, and Cultural Rights
EU	European Union
EUFOR	European Union Force
EU-GSVP	Common Security and Defence Policy
EUTM	European Union Training Mission
EUV	Treaty on European Union
FAC	Foreign Affairs Council
FM	Foreign minister
FRD	Friendly Relations Declaration
FS	Festschrift
GCC	Gulf Cooperation Council
GDP	Gross Domestic Product
GPG	Global Public Goods
HDP(S)	Human Development Peace Security
HIPPO	High-level Independent Panel on Peace Operations
HLP	High-level Panel
i.a.	Inter alia
i.c.w.	in conjunction with
i.e.	that is
ICC	International Criminal Court
ICCM	International Crisis and Conflict Management
ICISS	International Commission on Intervention and State Sovereignty
ICJ	International Court of Justice v International Court of Justice
ICRC	International Committee of the Red Cross
ICTY	International Criminal Tribunal for the former Yugoslavia
IDA	International Development Association
IDP	Internally Displaced Person
IFI	International financial institutions
IGAD	Intergovernmental Authority on Development
IHL	International Humanitarian Law
IICP	Center for Peace Research and Peace-building
IL	International Law
ILC	International Law Commission
ILT	International Law of Transition
IMF	International Monetary Fund
INCAF	International Network on Conflict and Fragility
INEF	Institut für Entwicklung und Frieden
INF	Intermediate-Range Nuclear Forces Treaty
INSCT	Institute for National Security and Counterterrorism
IOC	Organisation of Islamic States

IR	International Relations
IS / ISIS	Islamic state
ISS	Institute for Strategy and Security Policy
JHU	Johns Hopkins University
JUSCANZ	Japan, United States, Canada, Australia, New Zealand
KAIPTC	Kofi Annan International Peacekeeping Training Center
KFOR	Kosovo Force
LATAM	Latin America
LAWS	Lethal Autonomous Weapon System
LICUS	Low-Income Countries Under Stress
MD(O)	Multi-domain (operation)
MDGs	Millennium Development Goals
MENA	Middle East and North Africa
MINURSO	UN Mission for the Referendum in Western Sahara
MINUSMA	Multidimensional Integrated Stabilisation Mission in Mali
MINUSTAH	United Nations Stabilisation Mission in Haiti
MRR	Human Rights Council
NAM	Non-aligned Movement
NATO	North Atlantic Treaty Organisation
NGO	Non-Governmental Organisation
NPO	Non-Profit Organisation
NZZ	New Zurich Newspaper
OC	Organising Committee
OCHA	United Nations Office for the Coordination of Humanitarian Affairs
OD	Outcome document
ODI	Overseas Development Institute
OECD	Organisation for Economic Cooperation and Development
ÖFSE	Austrian Research Foundation for International Development
OIC	Organisation for Islamic Cooperation
ONUCA	United Nations Observer Group in Central America
ONUMOZ	United Nations Operation in Mozambique
OSCE	Organisation for Security and Cooperation in Europe
PBC	Peace-building Commission
PBSB	Peace-building and State-building
PCIJ	Permanent Court of International Justice
P-COEs	Peace-Centres of Excellence
PESCO	Permanent Structured Cooperation
PK	Peacekeeping
PKO	Peacekeeping operation
POC	Protection of Civilians
PSC	Peace and security Council
PSG	Peace-building and State-building Goals
R2P	Responsibility to Protect
RPF	Regional Protection Force

SADC	Southern African Development Community
SDG	Sustainable Development Goal
SHIRBRIG	Standby High-Readiness Brigade
SOFA	Status of Forces Agreement
SPA	Sustaining Peace Agenda
SRSG	Special Representative of the Secretary-General
SSR	Security Sector Reform
SWOT	Strengths and Weaknesses, Opportunities and Threats
TDHJ SE	The Defence Horizon Journal Special Edition
TCC	Troop Contributing Country
UK	United Kingdom
UNDOF	United Nations Disengagement Observer Force
UNDPO/UNDPKO	United Nations Department of Peacekeeping Operations
UNEF	United Nations Emergency Force
UNGA	United Nations General Assembly
UNICEF	United Nations International Children's Emergency Fund
UNIFIL	United Nations Interim Force in Lebanon
UNISDR	United Nations International Strategy for Disaster Risk Reduction
UNMISS	United Nations Mission in South Sudan
UNMOGIP	United Nations Military Observer Group in India and Pakistan
UNO	United Nations Organisation
UNOCHA	United Nations Office for the Coordination of Humanitarian Affairs
UNOSOM	United Nations operation in Somalia
UNPROFOR	United Nations Protection Force
UNRIC	United Nations Regional Information Centre
UNSAS	United Nations Standby Arrangements System
UNSC/UNSC	United Nations Security Council
UNSCR	United Nations Security Council Resolution
UNSG	United Nations Secretary-General
UNTAC	United Nations Transitional Authority in Cambodia
UNTSO	United Nations Truce Supervision Organisation
UNUSG	United Nations Under Secretary-General
US/USA	United States of America
USAID	United States Agency for International Development
USSR	Union of Soviet Socialist Republics
VCLT	Vienna Convention on the Law of Treaties
vs.	versus
WDR	World Development Report
WFP	World Food Programme
WPS Agenda	Women, Peace, and Security Agenda
YPG	Kurdish People's Defence Units

List of Figures

Chapter 1
Prologue

The Interplay of Geopolitics and Law

1.1 Is This the End of the UN?—Geostrategic Streams and Influencers

In 2020, the globe was haunted by the coronavirus (COVID-19) pandemic, which turned a series of policy axioms upside down. In the field of peace and security, a factual contraction in the course of the pandemic met with a geostrategic trend of regionalisation. The world of today needs a new balance-of-power doctrine. In this picture, the intertwined vision of equidistance and human-centrism may serve as a guiding principle for new global regulatory frameworks in the spirit of the rule of law, human security, and human rights to govern allocation of natural resources including the use of outer space, and steer a human-centred management of new technologies. (Gu, *TDHJ #03 21;* Werther-Pietsch, 2019: 446) Together, they build a potential axis for renewal.

International Crisis and Conflict Management at the same time face new conditions, and this is not only because of the COVID-19 pandemic. The international domain is latently exposed to a prevailing big deal mentality, protectionist thinking, autocracy, and populism in both the East and the West, and faced with augmented cyber vulnerability. The climate of cooperation and established multilateralism in the long run are in a process of change. A range of actors, among them three dominant players shape today's security landscape: the USA, China, and Russia against the background of the big liberal-autocratic challenge—a significant departure from the constellation under the UN Charter and, later, the Cold War. What is more, we find ourselves in a fomented arms race.

On the political agenda, failed fight for freedom in the "Arab Spring" from 2011 onwards, China's rise to 20 percent of the world population at the end of the decade, the chaotic decline and stagnation of Latin America, discord in the follow-up of Brexit, and consequences of an unexpectedly volatile US leadership are only symptoms which obscure an ongoing fundamental reorganisation of the world order. All these phenomena hide basic antagonisms of power and diplomacy, sovereignty and self-determination, realism versus idealism as they must be balanced in their own

U. Werther-Pietsch, *Transforming Security*, Global Power Shift,
https://doi.org/10.1007/978-3-030-87097-3_1

way and answered anew at every stage of global strategic thinking. The real challenge lies in adapting models and concepts of global coexistence and integration, which have become far more complex and multi-level since 1945 and must open up to a shift in geopolitical postures.

In undergoing those changes, international relations experienced an uneasy crisis: The dwindling consensus of values, the erosion of the "universal human rights age", the agony of the old order and creeping suppression of democratic forms of decision-making are consequences of a deep-rooted backlog of reforms that hamper effective international cooperation. So, there is the newly sparked "*great power competition*" with a centre of gravity in the Indo-Pacific region, a severe confrontation about the global spreading of the "Chinese virus", intensified lines of confrontation in access to resources by sea and trade routes such as the dispute over the South Chinese Sea, the race for Arctic passages, Mars landing, or exploiting rare earth metals. All these take place against the background of still growing inequality worldwide and a large part of disappointment about the "*blessings of globalization*" (Stiglitz, 2018). Against this background, political problem solving had been increasingly pushed into *adhocism.* Nevertheless, with the newly installed US-Biden Administration, a restart under changed conditions is again in sight, with still open dynamics on the regional level. One speaks of a probable disintegration of the West and the emergence of new structures on the one hand, revitalising democracies and a revival of multilateralism and diplomacy, on the other.

1.2 Do We Embark on a World of Regions?

When identifying trends to understand the current backlash of the rule of law and progressive regionalisation, security-loaded realpolitik, hybrid threats in still under-regulated cyberspace, the irrationality of non-state actors, new methods of warfare in outer space and by Artificial Intelligence (AI), weaponisation of many domains, economic sanctionism, and nuclear power struggles come to mind. This study examines the impact of phenomena in all fields of action, and subsequent transformation of concepts and institutions as well as International Crisis and Conflict Management (ICCM) actors under the auspices of the United Nations. The path taken from its founding moment to the "Sustaining Peace Approach" (UNSCR 2282/2016) has, despite many obstacles, dynamic traits and the potential to reinvent key principles of intervention in order to adjust to geopolitical reconfiguration.

Peacekeeping has undergone a series of evaluations from the early 2000 Brahimi to the 2015 HIPPO Report and the latest 2017 management reform to remain relevant in a fast-changing world, lived up to recommendations to a certain extent, and experienced a substantive enlargement, with the "Triple Nexus" as its current top work mode. Lessons learned in the realm of military engagement in fragile environments were translated in a soft law consensus "Declaration on Action for Peacekeeping" by the United Nations General Assembly (UNGA) under the apt chairmanship of

United Nations Secretary-General (UNSG) Antonio Guterres in 2018 and offer a common ground to restart profound change.

1.3 Geopolitical Reconfiguration—The Desired End State

A mixed picture remains, given the ambiguous past experiences of peacekeeping operations, new geopolitics, new challenges, and increasing signals of non-compliance to rules-based world order. Must we expect these dynamics to undermine action in UN peacekeeping and peace-building and in which ways? Has the UN peace architecture already embarked on a "culture of prevention" (World Bank, and UNDP 2018)? What other ways promise to be successful, how about a progressive interpretation of "principled pragmatism" (EU Global Strategy 2016)? And, does the Action for Peacekeeping Declaration and the Sustaining Peace Approach necessitate a move towards a renewed joint International Crisis and Conflict Management (ICCM) of the UN?

An analysis of "milestones", combining peace and security, development and human rights as interlinked pillars (2005 UN reform summit), such as the Agenda for Peace, the Human Security Agenda, the Agenda for Humanity, and the Agenda for Sustainable Development, shall enable to draw conclusions for shaping future engagement along refocussed lines of universalism and the resilience of regions. The Peace and Security Agenda of tomorrow will look indeed differently.

Guiding tools for transforming security, a "new world consensus on peace and security", in the twenty-first century could comprise:

- Joint fight for humanity approach ("human-centrism");
- A Two-tiered peacekeeping model in a world of regions ("principle of equidistance");
- A comprehensive approach of the International Community as a whole (revised "Key Principles of Cooperative Crisis and Conflict Management").

The book is here to prove these theses.

1.4 Methodology and Arts

On the basis of the identification of "milestones", the book critically analyses whether these three guiding tools can be regarded as a new guideline for future intervention logic and is thus sufficient as a reform step in the framework of the UN to be fit for the twenty-first century.

Part I lays the foundations for a closer liaison of theory and practice in the formation of peaceful and inclusive societies as reflected in the Sustaining Peace Approach. The famous reform year 2015 has brought a package of impulses to be processed by 2030 (Basel Peace Forum 2019). In order to be able to react adequately to the aforementioned trends, these impulses—to be described in Part II—should be incorporated in a new peace and security agenda. What is learned from the pandemic and multilateral agenda setting at large is a new form of systems thinking and key principles for joint engagement in fragile situations (Appendix 1, Chap. 8). Political "milestones" taken into consideration occurred chronologically from the end of the Cold War:

- 1992 Agenda for Peace (concept of peace-building);
- 2000 Brahimi Report (peacekeeping reform; MDGs, ICISS Report);
- 2005 UN Reform Summit (Peace-building Commission, Human Rights Council, R2P);
- 2008 Capstone doctrine (Integrated Missions in fragile contexts);
- 2015 HIPPO Report (Peacekeeping II, Global Study 1325, peace-building);
- 2015 Agenda 2030 (Sustainable Development Goals, SDGs);
- 2016 Agenda for Humanity and Sustaining Peace Approach (Triple "HDP" Nexus);
- 2018 Action for Peacekeeping (A4P) Declaration;
- 2030 Sustaining Peace Agenda (UNSCR 2282/2016).

The analytical approach chosen follows a list of characteristics for significant agendas in periods viewed in order to increase comparability: The stages identified are broken down according to the below-mentioned criteria. This makes it easier to grasp trends and draw conclusions about future developments:

- Integration into the geopolitical framework;
- Trigger/cause;
- Objectives: Characteristics and new elements;
- Trends for the intervention logic;
- Operationalisation in the mandate;
- Balance sheet, further development;
- Global political commitment and readiness to reform ("mood");
- Acting UNSG.

Overall conclusions on how geopolitics interacts with International Law (IL) in general, which may be embedded in a global trilateralism of USA, China, and the supposed "third", regional entities dedicated to multilateral systems thinking, will be derived from this assessment of the international agenda and projected into future. Part III, which deals with the paradigms of human-centrism and the principle of equidistance as founding pillars of a new balance-of-power doctrine between collaborative regions, finally picks up insights and findings to offer a new institutional and normative set-up for global peace and security under changed conditions.

References

EU Global Strategy. 2016. https://europa.eu/globalstrategy/en/global-strategy-promote-citizens-interests. Accessed 8 Aug 2021.

Gu, Xuewu. Eine G3-Weltordnung. *TDHJ Special Edition #03 21*: 22–26. https://www.thedefencehorizon.org/special-editions?lang=dett. Accessed 8 Aug 2021.

Stiglitz Joseph, E. 2018. *Globalisation and its discontents revisited. Anti-globalisation in the era of Trump*. New York/London: W. & W. Norton & Company.

Werther-Pietsch, Ursula. 2019. Innovative military high technology—Do we need a new warfare ethic? *Austrian Military Journal* 04: 438–447.

World Bank, and UNDP. 2018. *Pathways for peace. Inclusive approaches to preventing conflict*. Washington DC: World Bank. https://openknowledge.worldbank.org/handle/10986/28337. Accessed 8 Aug 2021.

Part I
Collective Security and its Inherent Failures

Chapter 2
Intertwined Pillars in a World of Change

"Peace and security, development, and human rights"

Peace and security, development, and human rights build a triangle of three interacting pillars of the System of Collective Security of the United Nations (paragraph 9 Final Document of the UN Reform Summit 2005; Rensmann in Simma et al. 2012: 67). This triad perfectly represents the greatest global effort ever to achieve collective, peaceful, and inclusive conflict resolution and settlement (Ipsen 2018). It is not only the basis of today's understanding of the International Crisis and Conflict Management (ICCM) but also of the broader notion of Sustained Peace.

Interconnectivity of these pillars has intensified along each reform step of the United Nations, yet the institutionalisation of a holistic approach cannot disguise the mixed record of UN peacekeeping missions in total. The shaping of the UN Charter by the victorious powers of WW (World War) II, followed by the end of the East–West conflict in 1989, the multistakeholder evolvement, followed by a new democratic–autocratic antagonism as well as a deeply felt, broadening "*non-compliance*" such as the engagement of the USA and its allies in Iraq in 2003, the provocative refusal of a seat in the Security Council by Saudi Arabia in 2013, or the interim termination of disarmament treaties in 2019 have extremely challenged the capability for the progress of the system over time. But in its 75 years of existence, the UN has finally survived the fragility of its own underlying assumptions.

The path embarked upon with the "Agenda for Peace" of 1992 is a multilateral response based on a state-driven and secular model of equilibrium, grounded in a balance-of-power model which over the past decades has produced the foundations for today's dealings with fragile situations. Decisive for this evolution is the guiding principle of human security and a perception of responsible sovereignty that comes with human rights (Deng, Luck, Peters, Sorrano, Thürer, Kaldor et al.), as well as the depiction of the post-WW II political interplay in the Collective Security System (Werther-Pietsch 2013).

U. Werther-Pietsch, *Transforming Security*, Global Power Shift,
https://doi.org/10.1007/978-3-030-87097-3_2

An era of disengagement after an ambitious start?

This process, however, lost speed and merely collapsed. No new peacekeeping mission has been mandated by the UNSC since 2017. The concept of responsible sovereignty has suffered setbacks in the application (Libya, Syria, Ukraine, and Myanmar). Tactical mobility according to "*principled pragmatism*" based on an interest-driven raison d'être increased (EU Global Strategy 2016). The slowing down of multilateralism, a "shutdown" of reform, divergent action by the superpowers including a calculated breach of international law regarding Crimea in 2014, and a series of deeper autocratisation of governance, e.g. in Belarus, Hungary, or Myanmar, evoked widespread uncertainty and engendered a loss of mutual trust. Sandwiched from both sides, capitalism and autocracy, networks of reliable information and partnerships for progress diminish. The continued discrediting of the UN by the heated climate between the world powers are signs of a gradual turning away from global multilateralism and the "human rights age".

Against this backlog, the International Community is equipped with a type of peacekeeping to fence power at the global level in a classical way: Predominantly active in most remote areas and developing countries faced with fragility, challenges go far beyond the original interposition of forces in a given conflict scenario, as was intended by Charter's "blue helmets". The task is thus huge, as, for example, the two Sudanese countries after the independence of the South Sudan in July 2011, the massive withdrawal of the USA from Syria in December 2018 and from Afghanistan in August 2021, developments between India and Pakistan around the province of Kashmir from August 2019, onwards or the military putsch in Myanmar in February 2021 and its lasting consequences rightly show.

Through dynamic interpretation of Article 39 of the UN Charter, according to which the United Nations Security Council (UNSC) must identify a threat to world peace before activating Chapter VII and/or VIII, the prohibition of the use of force in Article 2 (4) in conjunction with the principle of non-intervention of Article 2 (7) of the UN Charter and thus the basis for robust action was expanded in three respects:

- Broad understanding of what a global peace and security threat is or might be
- Extending enabling conditions in the framework for intervention
- Expanding strategic potential and technical advice for action.

Peacekeeping, a term that is not anchored explicitly in the UN Charter leads—in Antonio Guterres' words—to a "*review of peacekeeping missions in order to develop a comprehensive, modern, and effective operational peace architecture*"(Vision Statement of the UNSG, 4 April 2016).

The reference to a "global peace and security architecture" to be developed by the UN in the broader sense entails tasks of peace-building and demonstrates that this respective field of action similarly has given way to a broader meaning.

These insights were incorporated in the 2016 "Sustaining Peace Approach" of the UN with a focus on conflict prevention (UNSCR 2282). Together with the Action for Peacekeeping Declaration of 25 September 2018, the approach finally replaced the traditional term of "post-conflict peace-building" as enshrined in the Agenda for Peace of 1992. With these new instruments, the UN, after seven decades of experience in practice, is ripe for renewal. Elements are there, preparations of the UNSG's reform programme signal a perfect time for a restart.

2.1 "Principled Realpolitik"[1]

Huge movements

Pacifist, human rights activist, globetrotter, and first female Nobel Peace Prize winner Bertha von Suttner, an Austrian, was an early visionary of the "United Nations". (Ziegerhofer in Werther-Pietsch, 2017: 15–19) Her commitment can be summed up in the well-known dictum "*Die Waffen nieder!*".

"The Weapons Down", which means the overall prevalence of peaceful conflict resolution and conflict prevention is a fundamental peace movement thought that today seems to have lost influence on broad security thinking compared with the post-WW II period. However, in the upswing after the polycrises decade from 2010 to 2020 where new phenomena occurred and humanity had to learn its lessons in many ways, the dawn of a new era begins to glow.

Along with the "One Belt One Road Initiative" of Chinese President Xi Jinping inaugurated in 2013, the Crimean occupation by Russian President Vladimir Putin in 2014, and the ballots of Donald Trump for US President in 2017, we witnessed a dark paradigm shift in world politics. Signs of deep restructuring became denser. Wolfgang Ischinger, the architect of the Munich Security Conference, spoke of an "epoch break" (Ischinger 2018). To date, driving forces behind the erosion of multilateral mechanisms that occurred have not been sufficiently taken care of in International Law (IL): The world was undergoing profound change as a result of a few phenomenons, strengthening of self-interest, the revival of realpolitik, and new forms of autocracy against the background of still growing and new inequality agendas such as digitalisation. Matthias Herdegen called this emerging ambiguity a competition of two systems, the open democratic society versus a repressive world of autocratic leaders and elites (2019: 52, 219; Werther-Pietsch 2021: 127–151).

Whereas the swift shifting to populist "Trumpism" tightened egocentrism in a global style, both the US-Biden administration and the European Union (EU), the latter despite lacking a supranational nature with still complex procedures of decision-making, turned to a somewhat "principled realpolitik"—The EU/EC especially could play a far more conscious role and foreseeably gain weight in global affairs (Biscop 2006).

A reconfigured world of interests and values

The latest ante-COVID-19 "*big dealism*" and post-pandemic "*big idealism*" arrangements of the USA, Russia's solo efforts in its "near abroad", and China's steady

[1] Elements are taken from an analysis provided in Ursula Werther-Pietsch. 2022 (forthcoming). Global Pandemic and Regionalisation of Security, *The Hague Yearbook of International Law*.

global economic expansion stimulated the dominance of unilateral action. Resulting in a constant undermining of the rules-based international system, these instability factors, aggravated by the pandemic, illustrate how new impulses could impact the post-WW II balance-of-power doctrine. What characterised the decade from 2010 to 2020 were the following facts:

- Repositioning of world powers and probable collapse of NATO protection shield over Europe;
- Erosion of the European integration by Brexit, a temporary but deep unease for both sides;
- Aspirations and volatile competition among "newcomers" such as Turkey and India and "freelancers", mostly smaller states in the environment of strong alliances;
- A remaining series of "down-unders" including non-state actors feeling hurt by an unjust old order like Libya, Malian, or Somali fighters.

To this adds an oscillating picture, drawn against the background of an intensifying arms race, by the global health crisis. Some anticipated heavy disruptions of the world economy that will further unfold as a consequence of the biggest "lockdown" since 1945 and the supposed end of neoliberalism. (Schulmeister, YouTube, 28 March 2020; Bayer, YouTube 12 April 2020) Others, more cautiously, called for lessons to be learned from today's feeling of a world in isolation. (Nannt, "The World after COVID-19", LinkedIn, 22 March 2020).

This reconfigured world in geopolitical terms entails the effects of instability.

Part of this instability is the above-mentioned distorted consensus of values worldwide. As today's System of Collective Security stipulated in the UN Charter shows, value-driven factors like human rights protection had increasingly enlarged the original stabilisation task of UN peacekeeping. This, however, created lasting tensions between a UN as a loose clearing house mechanism to avoid armed conflict and a dedicated community for positive peace under the Agenda 2030 that have led the UN into a dilemma of opposing expectations. Moreover, progressive climate and technological change, digitalisation, fragmented societies, and confrontational extremist ethics confirm the thesis that the constructive search for commons at the international level has clearly been replaced by multipolar rivalry and hard-won compromises between changing partners (Werther-Pietsch 2017: 97). This culminated in a deeper consciousness of otherness. Diversity concepts partly shifted to confrontational positioning in multilateral fora, a fact counterbalanced so far by Chinese smart affirmative diplomacy and Russian-style affiliation to IL doctrine, filling this fragility gap of accepted common values and weak multilateralism.

"Our relations to technology in the twenty-first century"

Technically speaking, the world is changing, reflecting the dual face of technological progress. On the one hand, this fact comprises not only hybrid threats, but also totally unprecedented settings. Military scenarios include electronic warfare, the use of cyberspace and outer space for military purposes, lethal autonomous weapons systems based on AI, and irrational tactics of non-state actors in the net provoking randomly high-risk situations (Werther-Pietsch, 2019b, 445–447; LinkedIn 4 June 2021). It became "normal" that cyberattacks on critical infrastructure increased (Austrian Ministry of Defence 2019). Research, testing, and production of Lethal Autonomous Weapon Systems (LAWS) make clear that big powers compete to be the first (Hammer in Werther-Pietsch 2021: 225–237). All in all, the climate of self-restraint, trust, and global responsibility has progressively disappeared in security policy. This observation applies in particular to the relationship between the three big powers.

On the other hand and in a similar vein, and energised by social media, radicalisation and violent extremism arise to widespread threats with high scores of probability everywhere. The "9/11" attacks on the World Trade Center (2001) marked a turning point in both the use of force and tactics: The vulnerability of modern societies reached a global scale. Sven-Bernhard Gareis and Johannes Varwick, building on Mary Kaldor and Herfried Münkler, forecast that in the twenty-first century, "war" as a separate condition of society would vanish. COVID-19 is only an echo effect of this hypothesis and reveals massive failures to coordinate quickly and efficiently. The factual contraction in the course of the pandemic stimulated a process of fragmentation already under way and geostrategic regionalisation. As will be elaborated in this book, new trends in conflict and fragility require a reconfiguration of the International Community's engagement in crisis and conflict regions.

These challenges made progressively evident in many places that multilateralism suffers from strategic weakness, which severely impacts the international system. (Werther-Pietsch, YouTube, 13 August 2020; Werther-Pietsch 2022; Gareis and Varwick 2014: 122).

Future international crisis engagement

Wither this strategic weakness, it is, therefore, wise to start from "principled realpolitik" taking into account geostrategic calculations and real-time positioning alike. A game-changer may be seen in the Afghan case 2021. Given this fact of more interest-led multilateralism, the question arises whether parameters of ICCM should also be fundamentally re-assessed. That is equally true for IL to be efficient in securing peace.

Why does ICCM always seem to lag behind evolutions, even in the framework of the UN and its broad wisdom for sustaining peace strategies? The answers are multi-fold. In addition to current leading military strategies, a mix of deterrence and escalation dominance, the qualitative change in theatres produced far-reaching consequences and were to a certain extent reflected in permanent modifications of peacekeeping instruments (Werther-Pietsch 2020a: 47, 51ff). A main game changer in the last decades was the shift from intergovernmental to internal and domestic forms of violent and armed conflicts. Consequently, both force protection of the UN troops and inclusive peace processes are subject to respective adaptations. Although not yet fully reflected in ICCM, the line between domestic and external security matters is blurred. In this context, it is interesting to note that, despite the many steps for progress in multistakeholder decision-making in the international sphere and the overall UN reform initiative of UNGS Antonio Guterres, there has been no real integration of non-state actors into international law with the early exception of IHL (Common Articles 3 Geneva Conventions).

In response, humanitarian aid especially to vulnerable groups in the context of flight and migration, efforts to localise mediation for peace and support state-building processes, fostering sustainable development shaped by the digital era, and the role of women as drivers for peace ("Women, Peace, and Security (WPS)" Agenda; Werther-Pietsch 2020b) were unified in the so-called "Triple HDP (Humanitarian–Development–Peace-building) nexus", demanding a new culture of joint engagement.

2.2 Relocation of Policy and Legal Discourses

There is much uncertainty over external action in fragile and high-risk environments. A good example is a controversial debate on peace forces in North Syria between German Foreign and Defence Ministers in October 2019. New tools are constantly discussed and developed; however, usually, they end up unsatisfactorily coordinated or unimplemented (Bertelsmann, and CEPS 2020: 371–374). A similar assessment, as Sven Biscop puts it, can be demonstrated regarding the status of EU-CSDP on the whole: As learned from many hesitant moments in the past, and certainly from COVID-19, a "*coherent full spectrum force package*" is not yet in force (2018: 191–195; FAC Video conference, 6 April 2020).

In the meantime, the UN continues providing the framework for global peace and security which stems from a phase of balance-of-power politics after WW II (Kissinger 2014: 361–374) and reflects a corresponding world order. As argued above, the organisation was later substantially enriched by the emergence of value-driven agendas, especially the human rights regime. Thereby, the UN has developed from its core task of peacekeeping (Cede and Sucharipa-Behrmann 1999: 14) to a much broader forum for global problem analyses and solution. Today, it has a bridging function and is the centre of an extended multilateral flow of information, a catalyst and venue for negotiations, monitoring the implementation of treaties and compliance with commitments, as well as continuously assessing expectations about the stability of international agreements (Gareis and Varwick 2014: 70, 76). This means that it simultaneously acts as a negotiation platform, knowledge hub, and implementation agency.

Over the years, the security policy discourse has thus changed the UN 's "essence, especially in the 'way in which international affairs are managed'" (UN 2000: 9). Despite high flexibility and adaptive openness, new technology, fundamentalisms, and regional developments ask for strategic rearrangement. Against this background, what are the big constitutional antagonisms and features of the security discourse at the beginning of the twenty-first century along which the debate is moving?

Forms of political governance

The principles of sovereignty and self-determination frame the old dispute of who is a legitimate member of the International Community. On the one hand, we witness a worldwide emphasis on state sovereignty. This can easily be derived from the behaviour of states in the multilateral arena (Schneckener 2016). On the other hand, self-determination movements are equally experiencing an upswing grounded either in increased polarisation, demarcation, radicalisation, or perception of scarcity of resources. Catalonia, Scotland, Kosovo, or Kurdistan all reflect distinctive scenarios, factually and normatively decoupled from earlier colonial context. *International development law* shaped by independence movements on the African continent in the past with the relative exception of South Sudan predominantly originated from a black and white model of suppression. Sovereignty has thereby kept to play a severely restrictive barrier for intervention in favour of smaller parts of a country's population. The principle of self-determination today may, therefore, have to be differentiated, reinterpreted from a "society as driver" perspective, and accorded a higher status than was previously the case (Werther-Pietsch 2018: 7).

This leads to the modern form of irregularity in power-balancing, creating new "proxies of the future" according to the dichotomy of democratic and autocratic regime-types. The one half will follow Chinese or Russian models, the other the US, the EU, and its member states. An underlying feature of this new rivalry that is related to a lifestyle moment of societies is the question of consumerism versus productivity. Parallel to governance models, this aspect influences the well-being and behaviour of the majority, national growth rates, and global power at large.

Irregular power formats—power diffusion

Emerging diffusion of power structures, the renaissance of national interests, and the changing role of diplomacy painted a rather mixed picture during the last years. Over time, it became obvious that the categories of the Cold War in the periphery faded away and were replaced by what is perceived as "vicinity", alliances, clubbing, or large ungoverned spaces occupied by non-state armed groups. Power and state diplomacy are increasingly falling apart.

Hence, the broad dichotomy of war and peace evaded, creating a dynamic of relative (in)security, as reiterated by Herfried Münkler in a lecture at the National Defence Academy in March 2019. Responding to that very challenge and in addition to the rules of IL for the immediate stabilisation, elements of a longer-term "ius post bellum" were designed (de Brabandere, 2010: 119–149). Possible legal scenarios for the transition from fragility to peace were identified. (May in Stahn et al. 2014: 15) But what really happens in this "midfield", a term borrowed from Inge Kaul regarding the SDGs, exposed to hybrid threats and radicalisation is still under-researched and, therefore, remains unregulated at present. We speak of power diffusion in fragile contexts in which diplomacy, trying to rally with parties to the conflict, is faced with non-state actors, armed groups, and autocratic elites.

Moreover, since the entry into force of the UN Charter, communication and exchange as important power factors expanded and accelerated many times over.

This has induced processes that are more transparent with the aim of access for all, new forms of policy digitalisation, and constitutional inclusion. All levels of life have been permeated by information floods, strongly underpinning the need for rules-based control mechanisms from which may emanate new means of assessing societal behaviour and needs (e.g. COVID-19 apps) or participation in early stages of democratisation.

Adaptivity, contextuality, and localisation

From the proclamation of a "culture of prevention" in 1999 by the then UNSG Kofi Annan to the "Action for Peace Initiative (A4P)" of the current office holder Antonio Guterres, two decades of struggling for prioritising preventive measures passed (UN HLP 2015). Conflict prevention undoubtedly appears to be the most cost-effective option in the spectrum of international action for peace. This was recently confirmed by a World Bank study in 2018 (World Bank, and UNDP 2018). In doing so, realistic ICCM activities in response to outbreaks of violence were complemented by idealistic approaches focussing on prevention in latent conflict and a high degree of adaptation. Global crises such as COVID-19 reveal limits and, as already pointed out, detect desperately weak disaster risk reduction preparedness.

Sustainable conflict prevention includes intervention in the cultural sphere and thus, a courageous concept of mutual rapprochement between intervenors and the population on the ground. Localisation can be a way out (Santner in Werther-Pietsch 2021: 270–280), a new era of local awareness can help establishing new perspectives and solutions. This goes far beyond merely technical "securitisation" in the short-term horizon, i.e. the intervention from the protection perspective. In fact, if not balanced by policies of enlightened self-interest protection of human rights and promotion of the vulnerable groups, it can quickly crash into the altruistic (Barnett and Finnemore 2004: 39–41). Therefore, demand for preventive action in the light of lessons from the past, and the overwhelming present, is on the rise.

Resilience of international norms[2]

Building on this, and perhaps most importantly with regard to the framework of International Relations (IR), changes are taking place in the normative sphere: Firstly, stagnation in law-making dominated for long, due to years of widespread permanent shrinking space and a climate of intense public repression—as can be observed in the domain of universally recognised human rights and the broader *soft law* created by the UN General Assembly (UNGA) and tougher ultra-conservative stances. An outstanding example for systematically watered-down high-ranking policy documents is the Agenda 2030 for Sustainable Development Goals (SDGs), a potential world governance programme, which, however, lacks political weight. During the recent COVID-19 crisis, little international echo was indeed made to the SDGs. Secondly, International Law (IL) has undergone a manifest dismantling, for instance, by the US opting out from the Paris Climate Agreement or the Medium-Range Weapons Treaty. And thirdly, the unresolved question of manifold poverty still affects

[2] The remarks on paths of progress in IL follow an article I wrote for The AIES Yearbook 2021.

the normative order. A number of economists like Nobel laureate Joseph E. Stiglitz (Keynote, Political Days of the European Forum Alpbach, 25 August 2018) anticipate a collapse of international rules perpetuating inequality, isolated protectionism, and neoliberalism practice.

"*Do ut des*" as the reborn guiding principle of IR—a final disillusionment of Koskenniemi 's universalism (2005)—is the resulting formula for foreign policy, which, therefore, is in acute crisis insofar as it totally loses legal predictability and thus much of its original raison d'être. Accordingly, reactions to even small irritations have become more rigid, less contextually flexible, and are to escalate rapidly. In this sense, COVID-19 seems to reactivate a certain will of cooperation among actors that had already started to act competitively (G-7 Declaration of 26 March 2020). As early as 2016, Georg Nolte and Heike Krieger of Freie Universität Berlin early stated that in a permanent fluid general IL had lost much of its visionary weight, overall significance, and compliance effectiveness.

According to Daniel Thürer (2016), IL faced a period of fragmentation provoked by a process of specialisation and disintegration such as the special normative framework for climate protection. By concentrating on very detailed ramifications in self-contained regimes albeit legalising some sensitive areas (e.g. UN Migration Compact 2018), standard-setting for a irreversibly slipped into a dead end. Initially, well-intentioned concrete recommendations such as the monitoring of complicated implementation processes by indicator systems resulted in increasingly complex exercises causing high administrative burdens while creating a climate of incomprehension, refusal, and denial. Today, in turn, this was again gradually giving way to bilateral agreements, hence a step towards lack of transparency. Between these shifting powers, the UN finds itself pushed into the role of a globally active NGO with little political reach, which may further discredit the organisation. The UN indeed remains quite apart from its major reform projects that could not have been completed for decades. This is true, for example, for a reconfigured UNSC to better represent the world's population and enhance the resilience of the whole system. A permanent loss of credibility counts as a dangerous side-effect.

What is needed to make the international order resilient is to critically face realities, detect chances of regionalisation, and identify a small set of guiding rules for global peace and security that reflect today's human condition.

2.3 Between Realism and Idealism

But where does IL stand in relation to these developments? What was gained and what was neglected? Has mutual learning between IL and IR been utilised enough?

If one considers the dynamics since the founding of the UN, one will find a solid set of rules for world security. And indeed, despite blatant weaknesses, the post-WW II world organisation made substantial contributions that helped avoid major escalations several times in the past. There can be no doubt that the rules-based approach reached a temporary peak with the signing of the UN Charter by 51 states at the San Francisco Conference on 26 June 1945. At that time, on the basis of the then existing world political constellation of victorious powers and the experiences from two world wars, a global Collective Security System including a sanctions regime was created, the implementation of which, however, remained largely with the member states. That is why the subsequent reality-check of the Charter as a "flexible constitution of the world community" (Ress in Simma et al. 2012: XLV-LXV, XL VIII)—with its principles of self-determination, sovereign equality of states, and the general prohibition of the use of force and non-intervention—turned out to be enormously challenging. (Dubler and Kalyk 2018: 574–597; Paulus 2001).

In the course of this slow but infinite adjustment, the UNSC and peace missions at its heart have built up numerous links between the various fields of action in conflict and fragility. UNSC's broad understanding of the provisions of the UN Charter became the organisation's most effective method of progress. The Westphalian tradition of universalism creating step-by-step instruments like human rights principles, protection of civilians, or the Responsibility to Protect (R2P) have thus—as some believe to its negative—come close to a universally applicable "humanitarian foreign policy" (Kissinger 2014: 124).

Dynamics of interpretation

- **"Threats to peace", an open and adaptive norm**

Action lines in the Capstone Doctrine 2008 established a broad interpretation of threats to peace: UNSCR 1325/2000 and subsequent resolutions on the role of women in armed conflicts, but also UNSCR 1612/2005 on children affected by conflict and (1674) 1894/2009 on the protection of civilians were included in the list of tasks ("mandates") of peacekeeping missions which significantly changed their original objective. In UNSCR 2086/2013, these "cross-cutting issues" were combined in the model of integrated mission—the "Comprehensive Approach" within the UN framework. Further important impulses came from UNSCR 2250/2015 (Youth4Peace) and, most importantly, UNSCR 2282/2016 ("Sustaining Peace Approach"): Over time peacekeeping operations, at least in terms of mandating, became full-fledged "peace support operations" (Bothe in Simma et al. 2012: 1182)—a term that could not take the lead but is reflected in regional organisations such as NATO, EU, or the OSCE. However, in general, "*the assumption of a threat to peace (Article 39 of the UN Charter) [was] perpetuated [...] until the peaceful reappraisal of a violation of international law*" (Herdegen 2016).

Following the concept of human security, the term "threat to peace" was increasingly used to describe a concern about the threat to the security of populations, overriding the sphere of state security under certain conditions. Accompanied by the recognition of a broad area of action and actors, this poses difficult and unresolved operational questions for local command structures.

- **Readjusting and precising criteria for intervention**

Criteria for intervention further illustrate the development of the human security concept prevailing in a series of UNSC resolutions. UNSCR 688/1991

(Kurds), 794/1992 (Somalia), 940/1994 (Haiti), 771/1992 (Bosnia and Herzegovina), 1070/1996 (Sudan), 1203, 1244/1999 (Kosovo), 1272/1999 (East Timor), 1368 and 1373/2001 ("9–11"), 2249/2017 (terrorism), and others can be used to justify a second thesis. These resolutions dealt with the question of "internationalisation" of war and conflict zones, i.e. the cross-border dimension and the linking of security interests identified as global, which subsequently enabled the UNSC to intervene.

In the 1960s and 1970s, the sanctions against the colonial policy of Southern Rhodesia and the apartheid regime in South Africa had already prepared the ground for this argumentation. Mandates of peace operations got even more broader in the 1990s, reaching their climax when almost "adopting" the entire running of state structures in fragile or post-conflict contexts by international administration. This holistic approach amounted to a near takeover of state affairs by the international presence. What adds to this picture is the broad interpretation of the concept of "crimes against humanity" under IL that took place at first instance between 1991 and 1998. Questions of transitional law, the establishment of sustainable institutions, and peace in the sense of justice and reconciliation were given more attention in the UN ICCM framework. It became clear that the older but still valid occupation regulations of the Hague Law (1908) had proven too narrow and partly outdated. Subsequently, approaches for a new IL of Transition (ILT) appeared in literature after 2012 (e.g. May in Stahn 2012).

Finally, there are open questions concerning the involvement of non-state armed actors as part of the ICCM. Resolutions such as UNSCR 2254/2015 (Syria Road Map to Peace) already show the possible contours of an "all-inclusive" peace effort. An extension of conditions for intervention against such groups is reflected in the debate around the definition of "armed attack" since 9–11 (New York 2001), international criminal law, and in the analogous application of IHL: Common Articles 3 of the 1949 Geneva Conventions at least ensure the responsibility of armed groups such as inhumane treatment of prisoners of war without making these actors full and equal parties to the conflict, entitled to negotiate. Despite a respective UN convention, a "culture" of resolutions, and the Tallinn Handbook, comprehensive clear lines of action against terrorist attacks and those carried out in cyberspace are still pending.

- **Streams of progressive individualisation**

International law and its direct effect on individuals have been an ever-growing topic for scholars. The expansion of the potential for action in internal conflicts is an aspect linked to the previous point of enlarging the collective response capacity through the inclusion of non-state actors. While UNSCR 1701/2006 actively engages, for instance, Hezbollah on an exceptional basis, the prevailing control theory of the Tadic case (ICTY vs. ICJ) directly addresses executive persons or groups. Historical steps of substantial individualisation in IL, which has so far been dominated by mediating legal effects at the level of states, can be traced back to complex legal questions:

- International criminal law (ICC, Rome Statute 1998);

- Expansion of sanction's regimes by "targeted" or "smart sanctions" against rulers from Libya to North Korea and Iran (2011–2018);
- Legitimised reaction to terrorism which entails collective action on the legal basis of the various assistance clauses (Article 51 of the UN Charter; Article 5 NATO Treaty; Article 4(h) AU Charter; Article 42 of the TEU);
- Extraterritoriality of human rights norms anchored in ECHR jurisprudence during the Iraq intervention of US forces but still controversial today (Case of Al-Jedda and United Kingdom, Application no 27021/08 and Case of Al-Skeini and Others and UK, Application no 55721/07, 7 July 2011);
- Evolution of ius cogens—a certain window of opportunity to be detected in the following (especially in Part III Chapter 8).

As Georg Nolte puts it, the consequent incorporation of a system of values [here: the human rights regime] into multilateral relations has provoked a shift regarding the prohibition of the use of force (zaörv 59. 1999: 943.) in Hersch Lauterpacht's central thesis (Institut de Droit International, Aix-en-Provence 1954, Yearbook 45-II, 292): "*The scope of this field [reserved field] depends on international law and varies according to its development appeared to be in need of revision in case of defending common values and the community itself*" (Tams 2009: 393). However, is keeping the peace thus finally subject to a success criterion it cannot meet? (Peace-keeping Ministerial 22 March 2019[3]) And, is Article 39 of the UN Charter already overstretched in the limits of its content? Do missions have to refocus in order to remain intact and be able to continue making constructive operational contributions to peace and stabilisation? Has the discourse on human security led to an overload of the UN's core security tasks of stabilisation or can/should peacekeeping rightly be understood as human rights protection, under the precondition of activating the notion of a "vital core of IL"?

- **Regulating new spaces**

"Cyber-war" at Deutscher Bundestag in 2015–2017, or in 2020, the Austrian Ministry for European and International Affairs, has already started. The malicious use of Information and Technology (IT) including AI, the dark side of the coin, actually figures in all security, liberty, sovereignty, democracy, and space debates. Task Forces have been installed, for instance, the Global Partnership on Artificial Intelligence (GPAI), the Council of Europe's Ad hoc Committee on AI (CAHAI), the EU Digital Compass, the European way for the Digital Decade, or the Global Coalition for a High Seas Treaty Initiative. One of the areas of utmost priority is the field of artificial intelligence weapons. According to the Future of Humanity Institute (2018), its dual use in the civilian and military sphere calls for a new order. The Finnish Center of Excellence produced the "Tallinn Manual 2.0" on cyber responsibility (NATO CCDCOE 2017) similar to the 2001 Draft Articles of State Responsibility.

---

[3] https://peacekeeping.un.org/en/2019-peacekeeping-ministerial-conference-event. Accessed 1 April 2014.

Furthermore, many interlinkages with IHL shed light on problems of applicable rules that a multilateral cyber security treaty should answer, for instance, the analog application of the Martens Clause, a probable ban of Lethal Autonomous Weapon Systems (LAWS), or better containment of collateral damage, following Article 51(4)c of the Additional Protocol 1977 to 1949 Geneva Conventions and the argumentation of the ICJ in his opinion on nuclear weapons of 1996 (Werther-Pietsch, 2019b: 440).

How far does the normative global peace and security order, as established after WW II, cope with the above analysed new conditions and preliminary answers? Let us review some important basic principles and definitions to frame the picture before revisiting these questions.

References

Barnett, Michael, and Martha Finnemore. 2004. *Rules for the world, international organizations in global politics*. London: Ithaca.

Bertelsmann Stiftung, and Centre for European Policy Studies (CEPS). 2020. *Europe's coherence gap in external crisis and conflict management: Political rhetoric and institutional practice in the EU and its member states*. Brussels: Bertelsmann Stiftung.

Biscop, Sven. 2006. Courage and capabilites for a "More Active" EU. Report from the 1PstP European Strategic Forum, Warsaw. In Internationale Politikanalyse, Friedrich Ebert Stiftung, ed. Stefanie Flechtner. http://www.egmontinstitute.be/papers/06/sec-gov/Biscop_Report%20Warsaw.pdf. Accessed 8 Aug 2021.

Biscop, Sven. 2018. PESCO, Strategic Autonomy, and Ambition. In Security and Peace. 4/2018, 191–195.

Bothe, Michael. 2012. Peace-keeping. In *The charter of the United Nations*, ed. Bruno Simma, Daniel-Erasmus Khan, Georg Nolte and Andreas Paulus, 3rd edition. Oxford: Oxford University Press.

Cede, Franz, and Lilly Sucharipa-Behrmann. 1999. *The United Nations, law and practice*. Vienna: MANZ.

De Brabandere, Eric. 2010. The responsibility for post-conflict reforms: A critical assessment of Jus Post Bellum as a Legal Concept. *Vanderbilt Journal of Transnational Law* 43: 119–149.

Dubler, SC, R., and M. Kalyk. 2018. *Crimes against humanity in the 21st century—Law, practice and threats to international peace and security*. Boston/Leiden: Brill.

Gareis, Sven Bernhard, and Johannes Varwick. 2014. *The United Nations. Tasks, instruments and reforms*, 5th edition, Opladen/Toronto: Publisher Barbara Budrich UTB.

Hammer, Susanne. 2021. A short story of LAWS. In *Powering universalism*, ed. Ursula Werther-Pietsch, 225–237. Vienna: Klein Publishing.

Herdegen, Matthias. 2016. *International law*, 15th edition, Munich: C.H. Beck.

Herdegen, Matthias. 2019. *Der Kampf um die Weltordnung*. München: C.H. Beck.

High-level Panel (HLP) on Threats, Challenges and Change, "A more secure world: our shared responsibility", UN-Dok A/59/565 as of 2 December 2004. http://www.un.org/secureworld/report.pdf. Accessed 8 Aug 2021.

Ipsen, Knut. 2018. *International law*, 7th edition. Bochum - Munich: C.H. Beck.

Ischinger, Wolfgang. 2018. *World in danger*. Berlin: Econ Verlag.

Kaldor, Mary, Mary Martin, and Sabine Selchow. 2007. Human security and the European Union. *International Affairs* 83 (2): 237–288.

Kissinger, Henry A. 2014. *World order*. Penguin Random House UK.

Koskenniemi, Martti. 2005. *From apology to Utopia*. Cambridge: Cambridge University Press.
May, Larry. 2014. Jus Post Bellum, Grotius, and Meionexia. In *Just Post Bellum, towards a law of transition from conflict to peace*, ed. J. Stahn, J.S. Easterday and J. Iverson. The Hague: T-M-C Asser.
Nolte, Georg and Krieger, Heike. 2016. The International Rule of Law–Rise or Decline? KFG Working Paper, No. 1
Rensmann, Thilo. 2012. Reform. In Simma, Bruno, Khan, Daniel-Erasmus, Nolte, Georg and Paulus, Andreas (Ed.) 2012. The Charter of the United Nations, 3rd edition. Oxford: Oxford University Press, 25-69.
Ress, Georg. 2012. Auslegung der Charta, In *The charter of the United Nations*, ed. Bruno Simma, Daniel-Erasmus Khan, Georg Nolte and Andreas Paulus, 3rd edition, XLV-LXV. Oxford: Oxford University Press.
Santner, Friedarike. 2021. Localisation as a principle. In *Powering universalism*, ed. Ursula Werther-Pietsch, 270–280. Vienna: Klein Publishing.
Schneckener, Ulrich. 2016. *Fragile statehood. "States at Risk" between stability and failure*. Baden-Baden: Nomos.
Thürer, Daniel. 2009. Völkerrecht als Fortschritt und Chance - Grundidee Gerechtigkeit. 2 Vol. Zurich/St. Gallen: Dike publishing house AG.
UN High-level Panel (HLP) on Threats, Challenges and Change, "A more secure world: our shared responsibility", UN-Dok A/59/565 as of 2 December 2004. http://www.un.org/secureworld/report.pdf. Accessed 8 Aug 2021.
Werther-Pietsch, Ursula. 2013. *Selbstbestimmung, Gewaltverbot und Friedenssicherung heute*. Habilitation. Vienna/Graz: Neuer Wissenschaftlicher Verlag.
Werther-Pietsch, Ursula. 2017. *Global peace and security. International crisis and conflict management*. Vienna: MANZ.
Werther-Pietsch, Ursula. 2018. The impact of SDGs on international law—A nucleus of a right to peace. *Austrian Political Science Journal* 47 (1).
Werther-Pietsch, Ursula. 2019a. Comprehensive approach 3.0: "Triple Nexus." *Austrian Military Journal* 02: 155–166.
Werther-Pietsch, Ursula. 2019b. Innovative military high technology—do we need a new warfare ethic? *Austrian Military Journal* 04: 438–447.
Werther-Pietsch, Ursula. 2020a. *Women as drivers of inclusive peace*. Blue Helmet Forum Series, National Defence Academy.
Werther-Pietsch, Ursula. 2020b. *Kollektive Sicherheit 2030. UNO Friedenssicherung im Wandel*. Vienna: National Defence Academy. Series Volume 3/2020.
Werther-Pietsch, Ursula. 2021. *EU Security Structure. Key for Strategic Autonomy—A proposal*. Vienna: AIES Yearbook 2021.
Werther-Pietsch, Ursula. 2022 (forthcoming). *Global pandemic and the regionalisation of security. The Hague Yearbook of International Law*. The Hague.
World Bank, and UNDP. 2018. *Pathways for peace. Inclusive approaches to preventing conflict*. Washington DC: World Bank. https://openknowledge.worldbank.org/handle/10986/28337. Accessed 8 Aug 2021.
Ziegerhofer, Anita. 2017. Tribute to Bertha von Suttner. In *All human rights for all. Vienna guidebook on peaceful and inclusive societies*, ed. Manfred Nowak and Ursula Werther-Pietsch, 15–19. Vienna– Graz – Antwerp: nwv – intersentia.

Chapter 3
New Ways to Tackle Global Peace and Security

3.1 The Emergence of Human-Centrism

Harmonising differing terms

Various prismatic terms around crisis and conflict appeared over time and should be aligned in a new conceptual picture.

The term "crisis" often interpreted in opposing ways (Kaldor et al. 2007) may be the most comprehensive basis calling for external intervention by the International Community or parts of it. "*Urgent threat(s) to the core values of polity*" were mainly perceived as crises when human action is involved. However, this is by no means characteristic of all situations of threats. The concept of human security has contributed to strongly relativise this limited perception and expanded the concept of security. Natural disasters that can be countered with civilian and military forces (basic supplies, transport, logistics, sanitary tasks, securing access to the crisis area, maintaining security and order, etc.) do not involve the same questions of lawfulness under IL regarding actions or omissions of persons and regimes in a context of violence. Mali, Côte d'Ivoire, Nigeria, Yemen, Syria, Sudan, and South Sudan belong to this category: This reiterates that for reasons of the narrower field of peace and conflict research, only those cases of "insecurity" caused by the use of violence in combat are considered.

Similarly, the terms "risk", "vulnerability", and "violence" build a spiral of increasing uncertainty to which IL links different legal consequences. Thus, the phenomenon of violence is to be understood comprehensively today. Of course, it is no longer limited to inter-state wars as it was the reading of Article 2 (4) of the UN Charter and in UNGA Resolution 3314/1974 as well as in the jurisprudence of the ICJ and of international special criminal courts at the beginning (cf. for instance, Additional Protocol II 1977 to the Geneva Conventions 1949, the definition of aggression of the ICC Conference of the Parties, 17 June 2010 in Kampala/Uganda, or the ILC Report 2019, A/74/10 as of 20 August 2019). Today it also includes non-state forms of physical threat with weapons, such as organised crime and terrorism with cross-border regional and global effects even when still attaching to it different sanction

U. Werther-Pietsch, *Transforming Security*, Global Power Shift,
https://doi.org/10.1007/978-3-030-87097-3_3

regimes. In particular, "crime" as a form of originally "private" violence is increasingly causally associated with the appearance of fragile situations at the state level, as shown by the later classification of terrorist acts as international criminal offences. An imminent threat such as the possession of weapons of mass destruction or the formation of terrorist networks has also given rise to interpretative extensions of the prohibition of the use of force (UNSCR 2249/2017). The term "protection of civilians" or "responsibility to protect" is specifically linked to armed conflicts and thus to a narrower concept of security (UNSCR 1894/2009).

"Human security", a twentieth-century metaphor of utmost efficacy for political thinking, therefore remaining inconclusive from 1994 till now, may be replaced by an upcoming techno-political paradigm, the intertwined paradigm of the "principle of equidistance", "human-centrism" and "multilateral system thinking" as a human rights-oriented global strategy which tends to overcome traditional differentiations of internal/external security dimensions. The "human rights approach in fragile situations" offering the most holistic common understanding for all actors may, in this upcoming framework, remain a central starting point for a revised international intervention logic. The attempt of a diplomatic initiative to derive a "right to peace" from the SDGs or a deduction of a right to a dignified existence in an international context from the human rights regime equally inspires future concepts (Werther-Pietsch 2018; Gunnarsson et al. 2019).

To draw this new conceptual picture, we first will turn to an assessment of underlying basic principles, and in a second step, advance to assess terminology in factual situations.

3.2 Multilateral System Thinking

3.2.1 History of Thoughts

As an introduction, it may be mentioned that the systemic fundamentals in viewing today's condition of humanity in this book lay in a holistic the multilateral systemic perspective as the overall guiding theory of change. Multilateralism in the twentieth century has its own origins, axioms, and derivations and builds a separate forceful knowledge basis and scientific approach, within the realm of historical and political sciences research. Solemnly created in 1945, with the inherent goal of building for peace, both the term "global peace and security" and underlying formative power relations shifted from narrow to broad, from rules between states to expanding to all-inclusive armed groups, and from a focus on East–West confrontation to dealing with new world issues of violence. And trends show again back, from multipolar to future liberal-autocratic antagonism. In this sense, from the founding moment of the UN Charter onwards, **multilateral system thinking** coined meta socio-political streams:

- **Universalism** (UN Charter 1945);
- **Individualisation** (Sen, Ogata, Axworthy; ICC);
- **Securitisation** (Buzan, Daase; APM Convention);
- **Developmentalisation** (Buur, Brock, Sachs, Stiglitz; SDGs);
- **Human rights-based approach** (Thürer, Ermacora, Nowak, Arbour, Alston);
- **Constitutionalisation** (Kant, Verdross, Koskenniemi, Frowein, Simma);
- **Humanitisation, resilience, and fragility** (Meron, Dahlmann; EU Global Strategy, ICISS, IDPS);
- **Human-centrism, subsidiarity and anticipatory governance** (Krastev, ILC, Werther-Pietsch).

3.2.2 Future Conceptualisation

These currents can be seen as having had a prismatic impact, particularly on the enrolment of the rules-based international order. What is relevant for modern cooperative ICCM at different levels is that attention to both inclusion of individual expectations and the need of the population concerned as a fragmented but cohesive collective is given. Furthermore, based on lessons from the COVID-19 pandemic, aspects of crisis prevention were strengthened.

An outflow of the human security paradigm (Amouyel 2006) and the correspondingly emerged responsiveness of governance models (accountability) are characteristics of today's peace-building and state-building endeavours under the aegis of *human-centrism* (see Fig. 3.1).

3.3 From Fragility to Resilience

3.3.1 Fragile Contexts

Possible failure of polity and the moral or legal obligation to intervene when societal organisation collapses has basically been subject to philosophical thinking since antiquity. ICCM concepts including humanitarian aid, conflict prevention, peacekeeping, peace consolidation, and the establishment of local authorities are comparably relatively young in their current understanding. Fields of action as such may not only have broadened but also been enriched in character. Accordingly, their terminology is in flux (Werther-Pietsch and Ritzer 2012: 25–64; Werther-Pietsch 2020: 66–79).

While the International Community is striving to develop joint concepts for risk and resilience, vulnerability, and armed violence, there remains still some room for manoeuvre at the operational level due to the multitude of different players in the ICCM (UN, NATO, EU, civil society). A generally valid and accepted definition of fragility and a consistent assessment of the situation would certainly help to

Key priorities of international Agenda setting in Peace & Security		
Mainstream	**Seminal driving events**	**Selected key insights & multilateral responses**
Poverty focused development	End of Cold War 1989/90 Monterrey Consensus on Development 2009 Paris Aid Effectiveness Agenda 2005	• MDGs • Failed states as a development threat • Protecting development from "securitisation"/"politisation"
Conflict prevention and Peace-building	Balkan Wars 1992-2001 Rwandan Genocides 1994 UN Missions in West Africa, Mozambique, East Timor, etc.	• Strategic (enlarged, politicised) Peace-building • Conflict sensitivity • Preventive action/diplomacy • Human security as raison d'être for intervention
Security and development	Kosovo 1999 Terrorist Attacks of 9/11 Afghanistan engagement post 2001 Iraq since 2003	• Failed states as a security threat – State-building (institutionalism/ structuralism school) • Link to Security Sector Reform • Enhanced civilian-military relations
Post-hegemonic joint engagement **Fragility and resilience**	Iraq post-Hussein 2006 Afghanistan post-2014 Ukraine from 2014 onwards Libya 2011 "Arab Spring" 2011-2014 Syria/Middle East hot spot 2011-today	• End of humanitarian intervention • Effective multilateralism and non-indifference • R2P and POC (UN Summit 2005, UNSG Report, 2009) • Normative shape of human security (Krasner, 2010) • PSGs/SDGs • Compliance to rule of law
Post-COVID-19 world **G2 confrontation** **Multilateral System Thinking** **Human-centrism**	Cyberattacks (Germany, AT, UKR, USA 2015-2020…) Withdrawal of US in N Syria 2018 Targeted killing, provocations World powers in change (Russia 2021, China 2049, USA 2030)	• Effect-based Comprehensive Approach • Differentiated responsibilities • Principled approach • COVID-19 contraction of external engagement • G2 or quadripolar power system • *Regionalisation of security*: Model of collaborative resilient regions paired with core universalism / fight for humanity approach • Anticipatory governance
Fig.1 Own source		

Fig. 3.1 Own source

make engagements more coherent and clarify which tasks should be managed by which actor. Consequentially, this would also facilitate international coordination and division of labour.

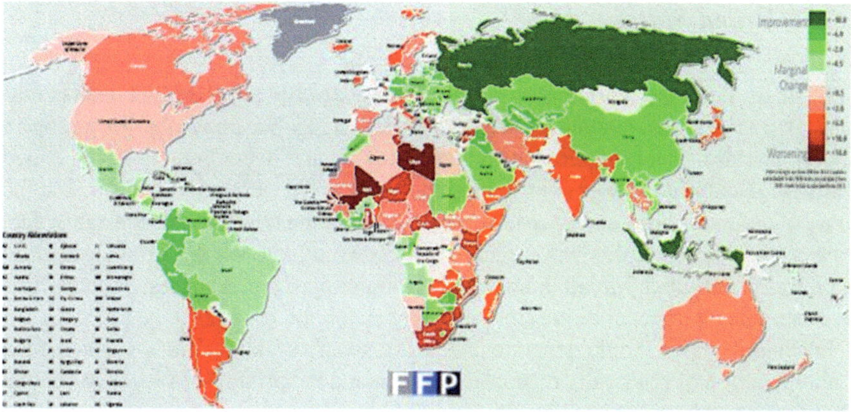

Fig. 3.2 "The fragility landscape". *Source* Fragile States Index, Fund for Peace (accessed 8 August 2021)

To understand the phenomenon, the OECD in its latest research published a fragility framework with six dimensions. To the economic, environmental, political, security, and societal dimensions, the human dimension was added in 2021, which puts different states under the top-twenty of fragility (OECD States of Fragility Report 2016, statement on ongoing analytical work, OECD INCAF Meeting on 18 May 2021). All forms of fragile contexts are viewed as causing societal backlog and conflict.

State fragility in a more normative understanding is made up by authority, service, and legitimacy failures (Stewart and Brown 2009), which can to be broken down in measurable criteria along several leading indices (Altmann in Werther-Pietsch and Ritzer 2012: 42–46; Fig. 3.2).

Definition Fragility

In the scholarly work of Frances Steward and Graham Brown of Oxford University (2009), deficits in the expectations of citizens regarding state functions and capabilities of the state become the focus of attention. Three categories serve as criteria of state fragility in this people-centred view:

- *Authority failures (survival functions of the state)*
- *Service failures (expected functions of state engagement)*
- *Legitimacy failures (political functions of legitimate government).*

In this concise summary, the survival functions and provision of public goods such as security, protection, and preservation of the environment; distributive justice; and a strong civil society for maintaining a dialectic political fabric are considered decisive for sustainable state stability.

3.3.2 Failed States

The state as the modern organisation of social life steadily oscillates between conditions of fragility and resilience. Weak or failed states became hubs for action in modern warfare. Changed geostrategic constellation and overall relocation of armed conflicts are external factors contributing to that fact. This also put failed states at the centre of defence policy and doctrines, particularly of the USA, which constantly feel threatened by state fragility worldwide. The main argument was that arms smuggling and terrorist activities spread unhindered through ungoverned spaces. Whether this over-estimates the global dimension of failing statehood remains to be seen.

In general, states should generate prosperity, security, and legitimacy to serve the double function of politically responsible action and the principle of legality (Debiel 2003):

1. *Security governance*: Ensuring collective and individual security;
2. *Political governance*: Political decision-making subject to horizontal and vertical power control;
3. *Judicial governance*: Institutionalised conflict resolution and law enforcement;
4. *Administrative governance*: Legally binding implementation of legislative decisions that handle public resources responsibly and are accountable;
5. *Social governance*: Basic social services and distributive justice;
6. *Economic governance*: Infrastructural and legal prerequisites for the development of economic activities.

In this sense, still in the narrow state-centred view of the beginnings of this century and following first emanations of the discourse such as Rainer Tetzlaff (1999), fragility processes can be expressed in progressive dimensions:

- State capacity to shape governance areas declines (functional dimension);
- State authority has less and less legitimacy (normative dimension);
- Erosion of state institutions (institutional dimension);
- Control over the territory is successively lost (spatial dimension).

Equally, depending on the extent to which the collapse of the ability to govern has progressed, categories can be formed:

- Partially consolidated statehood;
- Unstable statehood, weak/strained states—states under stress;
- States at risk/failing states;
- Collapsed statehood (WDR 2011; OECD 2012; Schreiber and Abendroth-Dias, TDHJ #02 2021).

The COVID-19 crisis, however, clearly demonstrated what risks lay in the competitive behaviour of world powers themselves as well as subversive action by armed groups and networks, such as Daesh in the Maldives to profit from weaknesses of NATO (NATO SG Stoltenberg, 17 April 2020). In the big controversy between democracies and autocratic regimes, V-dem has put forward several critical theses in 2020 that favour democracies as the comparatively more prosperous and effective forms of governance (2020).

Definition Failed States

State erosion is a process that takes place in apparent contradiction to globalisation, whereby the "failed" aggregates have been given different names such as "*warlord states, parallel states, shadow states, neo-patrimonial states, quasi states, phantom states*" (McLoughlin 2010; Faria 2011).

A number of indices compare state parameters and attempt to categorise them on an objective basis. De facto, however, this analysis of fragility factors remains exposed to political considerations regarding the functionality of statehood and diplomatic relations between states, which lead to more or, as context imposes, less intensive ICCM engagement.

The phenomenon of "failing states" in the ICCM became internationally relevant through their assessment as a security risk, regionally and globally. From the point of view of development policy, it was clear that development cannot take place without lasting "pacification" of social upheavals, thus opening the avenue for the International Community to build peace beyond immediate stabilisation. Since 2005, donor programmes for fragile states, e.g. DFID/United Kingdom, have increased by up to 40%. This has recently been reaffirmed by the OECD in defining its fragility assessment framework (2016).

In response, new doctrines diminish the importance of territorial aspects, seeking checks and balances in inclusion and identity, a *more societal approach*. Furthermore, responsibility for individuals present in a state rather than formal citizenship and extraterritorial effects are emphasised. Only hybrid threats with cross-border dimensions remain in the regional or global sphere where the use of force is lawfully possessed by the UN as the only universally legitimate representative of the International Community.

3.3.3 Resilient Societies

Grounded in a broad societal understanding, the International Network on Conflict and Fragility (INCAF) of the OECD published a non-binding State-building Guidance (2010; OECD/g7+) and is a pioneer of a combined state–society approach which underpins leading policy documents like the EU Global Strategy (2016):

> By the OECD/DAC's own definition ,States are fragile when its structures lack political will and/or capacity to provide the basic functions needed for poverty reduction, development and to safeguard the security and human rights of their populations' (OECD/DAC 2007). [...] We propose modifying the OECD/DAC definition of a fragile state, simply as one unable to meet its population's expectations, manage changes in expectations and capacity

through the political process. [...]. Fragility arises from substantial disequilibrium in state-society relations. [...] There are extreme events of shocks that might produce fragility in even apparently resilient states; our greater concern is with chronic fragility, which renders states less resilient to shocks. (OECD/DAC Concepts and Dilemmas of State-building in Fragile Situations 2008: 16)

Definition Resilience

Resilience is a control and decision-making tool used to react to risks that can lead to or have led to increased volatility of a system [in this case state structures]. Strategic focus on resilience has, therefore, a preventive and remedial role.

In the field of ICCM, resilience is a visionary guide to restore the social fabric and bolster social cohesion. It should be kept in mind that resilience must be complemented by values, norms, and legitimacy since the concept cannot be equated with codes of conduct such as sustainability or human rights. Democratic governance, in contrast, leads to more peace, gender equality, and wealth (V-dem 2020; Freedom House 2021, Carnegie Endowment, 4 June 2021, High Level Forum on Civil Society). Rigid forms of autocracy may appear temporarily resilient when they serve stabilisation, but they are by no means flexible sustained orders underpinning liberal, inclusive, and prosperous change in the long run. The prosperity that comes from high scores of long-standing democratic governance equally depends on whether a country lies in a region that is dominated by democratic regimes.

Achievement of resilient systems of socio-political order combined with a regionalisation of security can thus be described as the integral guiding principle of global peace and security today. It, therefore, can be introduced as the desired end state of intervention (Werther-Pietsch 2020: 158).

3.4 External Intervention

There is an intrinsic link between the broader concept of ICCM and international relations.

Inspired by respective policies as well as strategic experiences of the twentieth century, the prevailing IL doctrine has produced a legal figure of "intervention to preserve international peace and security"—not a matter of course if one considers the many diverse motives and political layers that underlie any intervention regime.

From a status of global peaceful equilibrium for all follows the supreme mission of the UN: Protection of world peace in the common interest. However, to fulfil this task, the UN makes generally use of state capacities to operationalise this responsibility in a decentralised manner—a clearly recognised enforcement deficit of IL. But first, the question should be answered what this common interest of maintaining global peace and security in the sense and by the means of the UN signifies and how this common interest is defined. In which ways do the concept of human security, the principles of self-determination, and state sovereignty contribute to shaping it? To what extent is the protection of human rights embedded in this structure? What powers of action exist in the framework of IR and for whom? What effects does the geopolitical power constellation have on normative order and the established mechanisms of peacekeeping?

With the founding of the UN in 1945, a renunciation of the use of force to assert one's own interests in favour of a joint peaceful conflict resolution crystallised as a driving narrative of transformation. This formal restriction of sovereignty builds on the ideas of the League of Nations of 1920 and the Briand Kellog Pact of 1928. At the same time, this explains why sovereign equality of partners and the principle of non-intervention were subsequently enshrined in the Charter, building important axioms from the very beginning.

But the whole system of the UN is currently based on the sovereignty between equal partners on the one hand and special treatment of certain members on the other, namely the five veto powers (permanent five, P-5) in the UNSC. Nevertheless, the question arises whether this balance-of-power doctrine still hits the facts today and is able to continue to serve as the *rationale* behind an effective system of collective security. What is the situation now? Mandating collective peacekeeping measures is increasingly not based on the requirements of the conflict, but on the degree of commitment of potent intervention states (Gareis and Varwick 2014: 117). Clearly, modern peace missions concentrate capacities. For this reason, they can be carried out only by a few states beyond their own defence necessities and in their total complexity in favour of only a few beneficiary states either. This leads to an interest-driven policy of elicitation, which undermines the claim for universalism.

To the contrary, methods of warfare and damaging potential, such as cyberattacks on critical infrastructure, are no longer reserved solely for the great powers who played a decisive role in 1945 but an opportunity for smaller states and all non-state actors to become centres of gravity of global reach (al-Qaida and IS groupings around Osama bin Laden or Abu Bakr al-Bakhdadi). Furthermore, the willingness of terrorists to give up their own lives constitutes a difficult element of irrationality to combat. This phenomenon counters any rational international action and certainly the intentions of the "founding fathers" of the UN.

In this sense, ICCM today principally reflects a value-oriented implementation of what is meant by the human security challenge of sovereignty and non-intervention. Lastly, it seems that challenges of the big powers today, in one or the other way, involve themselves far more directly than in comparably earlier stages of IR, when "proxies" were to act instead.

3.4.1 Genesis

External intervention in its modern conceptualisation with roots in heroic epics of Herodot and Homer has an eventful past but has been an oscillating phenomenon at all stages of history alike (Gombrich). If we look 50 years back, one can discern this evolution: The concept of intervention under the framework of the UN in the 1970s was initially very narrow, based on the understanding by the *Friendly Relations Declaration* (FRD), UNGA Resolution 2625/1970 replacing the older classical view in the nineteenth century. Just 10 years later, the pendulum was again swinging to the other side: A declaration on large admissibility of intervention in UNGA Resolution 36/103 (1981) was brought to the attention of the UNSC and failed because primary subjects of IL preferred to uphold the principle of sovereignty.

In parallel, focussing on concepts, various interdependence models in political science, such as the centre–periphery model, examined any kind of interaction as intervention, be it of political, economic, or cultural nature. However, these comprehensive theories were again relativised by the constructivist approach in the mid-1990s: More recent approaches were based on the assumption that only in a closer process of "*arguing and bargaining*" of all actors, conflict resolution can really be concretised, focussing on local conditions ("contextualisation"), independently of the given macro socio-economic factors. This ultimately led to the birth of the "Friedensdiskurs" and to the foundation of the interventionist active peace engagement in Germany, Switzerland, and Austria (Daase, Bonnacker, Goetschl, Truger).

The effects of this political sciences debate finally reached IL, which following another logic missed the essential turning point of social sciences, as Tobias Debiel and Goede (2009; Debiel et al. 2009) of the German Institute for Development pointed to. Operational military conflict management, for its part, initially remained unaffected as well. Robust strategies could only slowly free themselves from a lack of sensitivity to local conditions. Development cooperation, for its part, in recent years acknowledged the interaction between development and security and accordingly took up the long-ignored principle in the debate on fragility: "Every peace operation is political" (Schöndorf, 2011: 328), and relies on it to increase engagement in fragile situations. On the whole, findings of the resilience discourse (World Bank [WDR] 2011; World Bank, and UNDP 2018) suggest a holistic approach.

The views in IL on the scope of intervention, therefore, seem ambivalent: restrictive in connection with the prohibition of the use of force according to the UN Charter and extensive with reference to the support for special international regimes such as the protection of human rights on the basis of treaty law's limitations put on sovereignty. Overall, robust deployments with and without a UN mandate have declined in the meantime as a result of the repositioning of world powers and presumably in the follow-up of the COVID-19 crisis. This slow withdrawal from joint action reflects the response to lacking overall consensus and capacity, in the face of the UN's blatant failures and inability to counter with effective reforms.

The millennium's reconfiguration of NATO as a self-defence community with the aim of actively contributing to global peace and security (transition to offensive self-defence) fell into this mixture of intervention concepts. In this phase, the well-known NATO-supported international mission in Kosovo took place on 26 March 1999. According to a declaration by the NATO Council, this was based on "compelling humanitarian reasons". Operated without a UN mandate, a new era of humanitarian intervention seemed to start. The UNSC in turn did not condemn the operation itself; the real problem, therefore, lay in the action taken outside the UN Charter. From the point of view of the affected states of Serbia and the then autonomous province of Kosovo, cooperative international law had resulted in the end in a clear-cut down-turn of the regulatory competences normally reserved for states to implement their sovereign "*choice of political, economic, social, and cultural system and formulation of foreign policy*" according to the FRD.

The trend towards unilateral intervention continued to rise after these formative events in South-East Europe but was successfully reinterpreted as a proactive strategy of lawful responsibility to protect. The framework of intervention became more pronounced subsequently, in particular in the famous 2001 report of the *International Commission on Intervention and State Sovereignty* (ICISS): Criteria of *recta auctoritas, recta intentio, iusta causa*, immanence, proportionality, and suitability provided non-UN-based alliances with objective benchmarks. This is also due to a growing understanding that populations, rather than states, are the real sovereign (and thereby offer an alternative interpretation of the FRD). However, against the background of the terrorist attack on the *Twin Towers* ("9–11") in New York 2001, the question arose who, in response to large-scale aggressive acts—states and/or terrorists—could legitimately be attacked in exercising self-defence by military means.

Still an oscillating endeavour

The current *concept of intervention* is characterised by a comprehensive understanding of the connections and interplay between globalisation, de-globalisation, and fragility. In legal circles, the debate focussed on normative values and their implementation following Kant's universalist constitutionalisation project, as well as regarding the military field, coordination requirements and interoperability, technical innovation, counter-terrorism and de-radicalisation, as well as interaction with civil engagement.

The more recent intervention practice from 2000 onwards—with various lessons of the military, political, financial, and result-oriented nature above all in Iraq and Afghanistan—has prompted leading players like the USA to rethink their engagement and most recently led to a phase of stronger integration into the multilateral system. Interestingly, collective resistance of developing countries against intervention, e.g. in the formation of the Non-Aligned Movement (NAM), had also been reversed by a focus on the non-colonialist protection of civilians (see Article 4 (h) AU Charter).

The British and French UNSC members on this stage were rather driving forces behind the model of the International Community's responsibility to protect. This was demonstrated by the active role of French President Nicolas Sarkozy during the

2008 war in Georgia, the French position in the run-up to the UNSC's decision in the case of Libya 's liberation 2011 or old francophone ties, manifest in the West-African Economic Community like the high-risk deployment in Mali until now, or the solo attempt of France to intervene after the military coup in Côte d'Ivoire in the same year. French President Macron continued this tradition and played the West-African card to demonstrate power within the EU. In this context, the counterproposal to PESCO and the French reluctance to establish a European Defence Fund in the second half of 2018 may be reiterated.

As a former imperial world power, the UK with critical military potential, especially in the air force, likes to appear arbitrary and determined—Libya and Syria are examples of this attitude on the international stage. But as a consequence of Brexit on 31 January 2020, UK will in the future be more bound to the strong Anglo-Saxon axis than to European partners if there will not be complementary action. The alignment shows an in-depth joint decision-making and alliance.

In the case of Syria, Russia, as an ally of the Assad regime, sent out proactive signals soon after the "rebellion" for a democratic political turnaround and the outbreak of violent conflict in the Northern parts of the country on 15 March 2011. The Russian view of the situation was later addressed and demonstrated by its (own) "no-fly zone" in 2018 by means of the Russian air force and, finally, its political engagement for a "protection zone" in North Syria in 2019. Similar to the 2014 Crimea annexation, the protracted conflict in Eastern Ukraine, and the earlier 2008 Georgia war, Russia obviously cares for its citizens in spheres of influence in its immediate neighbourhood (the "near abroad ").

China did and does not (yet) go that far, but major global economic projects such as the Silk Road are increasingly placing the Peoples Republic in a security dilemma. China arranges progress and alliances without direct confrontation, by "occupying" Bhutanese territory in its fortification against India or banking up rocks in the South Chinese Sea, officially to build military bases "in defence of their trade routes" or collecting "pearls" of harbours along the coasts to Europe. In the run-up to an enhanced engagement in UN peacekeeping under President Xi, there were already interesting signs of relativisation of the concept of non-intervention ("positive non-intervention", e.g. South Sudan for rescue action). The position of China remains open till 2049. Apart from its international intervention stance, China altogether remains an unprecedented rising star.

3.4.2 Responsibility to Protect

"Responsibility to Protect" (R2P) (Verlage 2009; Hilpold 2006, 2011; Janik 2020) is understood as a mandatory intervention of the International Community in the case of massive human rights violations, which is only permitted and under distinct conditions obligatory when the state concerned commits a "*widespread or systematic attack directed against any civilian population*" see Part III Sect. 8).

The UN Charter provides the framework of resolving armed conflict by the system of collective security through military intervention by the UNSC in the event of a threat to peace &andsecurity pursuant to Article 39 of the UN Charter. The principle of non-intervention and state sovereignty as well as the prohibition of the use of force with the exception of

- individual self-defence pursuant to Article 51, and
- collective security according to Chapter VII of the Charter

frame such UNSC decisions.

Moreover, in the case of self-determination, tensions between the principle of sovereign equality of states and, as a result, the conservative attitude of IL vis-à-vis new entities in order to preserve the existing order become particularly evident: the softening of the prohibition of the use of force in the course of the decolonisation process from 1960 onwards (legitimate use of force by liberation movements under certain conditions) is a recognised exception, but has not yet seen further expansion.

The concept of R2P can only refer primarily to fragile situations involving human action. Older doctrine predominantly pursued the legal opinion that, as a complementary instrument for maintaining global peace and security in humanitarian missions, a right or a duty to intervene by military means in natural catastrophes does not make sense. Intervention to secure peace in the narrower sense, therefore, deals only with the presence of the International Community as a reaction to politically caused disasters. While not fundamentally rejecting a concept that also encompasses natural disasters, this could become more used in the future, for instance, in complex climate change scenarios. Given this state of play, one can summarise that R2P has already "emerged", but dimensions remain controversial.

Building Blocks of "Intervention"
AU Charter, Article 4—Principles

"The Union shall function in accordance with the following principles:

(h) the right of the Union to intervene in a Member State pursuant to a decision of the Assembly in respect of grave circumstances, namely: war crimes, genocide and crimes against humanity; …".

Responsibility to protect; R2P according to paragraph 139 SD of the 2005 UN Reform Summit:

"We stand ready to take timely and decisive collective action through the Security Council, in accordance with the Charter, notably Chapter VII, in individual cases and in cooperation with the relevant regional organisations, if peaceful means prove insufficient and national authorities manifestly fail to protect their populations from genocide, war crimes, ethnic cleansing and crimes against humanity" (para 139 of the Final Document).

UNGA/RES/60/1 of 24 Oct. 2005 (Final Document of the UN Reform Summit 2005, paragraph 138)

The International Community, through the United Nations, also has the responsibility to use appropriate diplomatic, humanitarian and other peaceful means, in accordance with Chapters VI and VIII of the Charter, to help to protect populations from genocide, war crimes, ethnic cleansing and crimes against humanity. In this context, we are prepared to take collective action, in a timely and decisive manner, through the Security Council, in accordance with the Charter, including Chapter VII, on a case-by-case basis and in cooperation with relevant regional organizations as appropriate, should peaceful means be inadequate and national authorities are manifestly failing to protect their populations from genocide, war crimes, ethnic cleansing, crimes against humanity.

UNSG Report on Implementing the Responsibility to protect, A/63/677, 12 Jan. 2009, paragraph 10 lit c

While the scope should be kept narrow, the response ought to be deep, employing the wide array of prevention and protection instruments available to Member States, the United Nations system, regional and sub-regional organisations and their civil society partners. To that end, in paragraph 138 of the Summit Outcome, States were called on to use "appropriate and necessary means" to prevent such crimes and their incitement, and the International Community was called on to "encourage and help" States to exercise their responsibility and to "support the United Nations in establishing an early warning capability". In paragraph 139 of the Summit Outcome, reference is made both to "appropriate diplomatic, humanitarian and peaceful means" under Chapters VI and VIII of the Charter and to "collective action" under Chapter VII. Our approach to the responsibility to protect should therefore be both narrow and deep; …

Important links:

—"Action for Peacekeeping" Declaration of Shared Commitments on UN Peacekeeping Operations: https://peacekeeping.un.org/sites/default/files/dpko-dfs-declaration-shared-commitments-unpeacekeeping-1812605e.pdf

—ICISS Report "Responsibility to Protect" 2001: http://www.iciss.ca/report2-en.asp

—UNSCR 1973/2011 – Establishment of the No Fly Zone over Libya: http://www.un.org/News/Press/docs/2011/sc10200.doc.htm.

—UNSCR 1894/2009 – Protection of Civilians: http://www.humansecuritygateway.com/documents/UNSC_SRES1894_ProtectionCiviliansArmedConflict.pdf

—ILC Report 2019: https://legal.un.org/ilc/

In these constellations, peace operations included the following tasks (UN Handbook on United Nations Multidimensional Peacekeeping Operations 2003; New Horizon 2010):

- military protection of aid supply chains;

- military enforcement of sanctions;
- establishment of No-fly zones;
- administration of security corridors;
- air strikes;
- extensive occupations and whole invasions;
- mediation;
- early warning;
- security sector (system) reform, including protection advisers;
- protection against violence against women, including protection advisers;
- protection of children in armed conflicts, including protection advisers;
- protection of civilians, including protection advisers;
- state-building tasks, such as setting up or supporting Rule of Law institutions
- ("*tool-/scenario-based future of PKOs*", Haery 2010).

Accordingly, at the operational level, the responsible department in the UN Secretariat sees robust missions as "*a posture by a PKO that demonstrates willingness, capacity and capability to deter and confront, including through the use of force when necessary, an obstruction to the implementation of its mandate*" (UNDPKO and DFS concept note 2009; Belgian non-paper 2021). In line with that, peacekeeping goes along the offensive position outlined by the UNSC for the protection of civilians, which can quickly bring international forces close to a conflict party. (Abdelkérim Ousman, Royal Military College of Canada, Sudan and South Sudan, National Defence Academy, 5 December 2011) Pioneering in the intervention based on humanitarian motives, the fundamental orientation of IHL reflects the slowly maturing of external engagement towards human rights in the 2010s. Although the associated "individualisation" helped to widen the concept of intervention—especially to extend it to complex crises—the final answer to the clash of idealism and realism is yet to be found: It can be assumed that the human rights regime must also be adjusted and differentiate weighted in order to identify the core of IL that can be regarded as compulsory law, the realm of *ius cogens*, in the words of Ian Brownlie "the Ferrari which so far remained in the garage" (Simma 2009: 273). A non-negotiable *ius cogens* (Article 40 of the Draft Articles for State Responsibility, 2001; Article 53 Vienna Convention on the Law of Treaties), which requires a mandatory reaction in case of violation, would mean a departure from the amorphous structure of human rights and thus form two classes within one regime that many human rights activists had long feared and vehemently tried to avoid. The most important reason for rejecting a separation of a narrow core "and the rest" was the fight for equality between ESC and CP rights—a struggle the development hemisphere in the meantime won (1993 Vienna World Conference on Human Rights Declaration and Action Plan). This fundamental question should, however, be resolvable within a larger framework of global peace and security as suggested in Chap. 9.

Wars today are no longer won on the battlefield, but by sustainable peace (Nye 2004: 5–11, Lederach 1998: 77). Or they get stuck in the harsh "*no peace to keep*" zone of protracted crises, without a beginning or end, in the low-threshold confrontation in the cyber and IT sector. Even "real winners" can no longer dictate peace as they see it (Schmunck, Brussels, European Development Days in June 2010). This has become even clearer in the age of increasing interconnectivity (Sachs 2017), which emanates from the global SDG policy. However, this worldwide initiative to deepening the dilemma between peace policy, military action, economic interests, climate change, and development cooperation has so far found little stance in the behaviour of major players. Methods of warfare changed to "weaponisation" of all kinds of the infrastructure of the society and misinformation in the cyberspace, operated by China or Russia especially (Galeotti 2019: 52). That is why the former quest for a broad or narrow understanding of intervention gives way to a holistic notion.

3.4.3 Holistic Approach

Indeed, intervention in fragile situations cannot be reduced to classical dispute resolution. Perfidious intervention such as the shielding of hospitals (forum on EJIL 30/2019 No. 2) needs every counterbalancing by targeted foreign and development policy instruments, including health, environmental, trade, and economic measures. In the dual view, the monitoring of cyberspace can also fulfil a socio-political task of sustaining peace if freedom of information and access for all is threatened and, therefore, becomes anchored in the mandate of the respective mission. Security policy is interdependent with activities that contribute to the development of a society in the broadest sense.

What is resulting is first of all the perception of a *mediator role* of the International Community that may arise during and after the end of hostilities, along a peace process following a conflict-transforming approach, the maximum rapprochement to civil conflict resolution methods in a situation that, of course, the parties to the conflict, perpetrators, and victims must solve themselves. This is all best done from a local or regional level and needs "grounded" expertise. From this one end of the scale to robust military intervention with the aim of stabilising an escalated situation, the challenge remains always the same: How far should an existing conflict or a post-conflict situation be influenced from the outside? If one follows the view that peace processes are processes of increasing realisation of self-determination (Cassese 2005; Nowak and Werther-Pietsch 2014; Paffenholz et al. 2017), one comes to the conclusion that pursuing sustainable development essentially depends on "procedural justice" with an opened state, as the entity defines itself, the strict observance of which must be monitored and, if necessary, supported externally. In a positive sense, can this holistic notion contribute to a more rules-based approach, a normative way of ending conflicts, and to more legal certainty of sustaining peace?

Internationalisation and societal transformation

Once critical point in this endeavour is the following: Is it possible to stay neutral when internal armed conflict becomes internationalised or is external intervention necessarily associated with a transformation of the local society?

An example of intrinsic change in dominant conflict resolution patterns in societies is the Sahel zone. Where the cohesion of clan societies is not based on territorial claims, ethnic, religious, and political ideas may clash with the normative order created and perpetuated by the *Uti possidetis* principle and the strategy of "*divide et impera*". In large parts of the North African and Central African regions, according to Traub, this divergence is resulting from colonisation. The evolutive historical process, however, contradicts the normative postulate that the core of the principle of self-determination guarantees the formation and recognition of states according to the "*free will of the people*". It is still controversial and subject to steady re-conceptualisation to what extent the right of self-determination as stipulated in the UN Charter can actually be exercised and under which (narrow) conditions an exception of the prohibition of the use of force can be claimed lawfully (Weller 2007).

The close relationship between Lauterpacht's absolute ban on the armed force for the protection of individual life (Lauterpacht 1950) and the Cassesean principle of self-determination for the development and promotion of communities and entities (Cassese 2005) raises tensions requiring clear demarcation. Any fair balance between the legal use of force and the principle of self-determination must take into account not only the particularities of collectives, marginalised and vulnerable groups, and minorities, but also the dominant majority which puts pressure on the respective parts of the population. The social dimension, in which the well-being and interest balancing between societal groups flourish, reveals prerequisites for peaceful conflict resolution. In this sense, *peace is a structural consequence of functioning internal mechanisms of social balance.* This includes respect for legitimacy rules and the protection of diversity.

When this network of relations is disrupted, for example, by the experience of massive injustice, disadvantage, or discrimination, and if the established institutional mechanisms for political balance are no longer sufficient, the stability of a society is at risk. If latent willingness to engage in conflict and framework conditions that promote the outbreak of armed conflict comes together—for example, the availability of weapons when security bodies are weak—a fragile situation arises that, according to today's understanding, may require intervention. Through this negative spiral, in a climate of growing hostile fragmentation between parts of society, potentially innovative phenomena such as migration may become a threat to security and development. (V-dem, 17 May 2021, fact sheets; Ursula Werther-Pietsch, Democracy forever, Wiener Zeitung, 20 Jan 2021).

With this assumption, intervention and the debate on fragility penetrates two dominant spheres on the ground, security on the one hand since it assesses security threats by long-term criteria, and development on the other by including fragility in the sustainable development agenda.

References

Altmann, Stephanie. 2012. How fragility is measured. In *Failed states—Statebuilding as conflict prevention*, ed. Ursula Werther-Pietsch and Thomas Ritzer, 41–46. Vienna - Berlin: nwv Verlag

Amouyel, Alexandra. 2006. What is human security? *Human Security Journal* 1.

Cassese, Antonio. 2005. *International law*, 2nd ed. Oxford: Oxford University Press.

Debiel, Tobias. 2003. *UN peace operations in Africa.* World Domestic Policy and the Reality of Bruges Wars. Bonn.

Debiel, Tobias, and Nils Goede. 2011. Military interventions and stabilization operations—A critical interim balance. *Peace Report*, 194–207. Berlin: Lit Verlag.

Debiel, Tobias, Nils Goede, Holger Niemann, and Robert Schütte. 2009. From "New Interventionism" to R2P. *Die Friedens-Warte* 84 (1): 60–80.

EU Global Strategy. 2016. https://europa.eu/globalstrategy/en/global-strategy-promote-citizens-interests. Accessed 8 Aug 2021.

Faria, Fernanda. 2011. Fragile states: A fluid concept for peacebuilding and statebuilding. Norwegian Peacebuilding Resource Centre (NOREF) Policy Brief No. 3.

Freedom House. 2021. Freedom in the world 2021: Democracy under Siege. https://freedomhouse.org/report/freedom-world/2021/democracy-under-siege, accessed 6 March 2021. Accessed 8 August 2021.

Galeotti, Mark. 2019. *We need to talk about Putin.* How the West gets him wrong, London/New York: Penguin.

Gareis, Sven Bernhard and Varwick, Johannes. 2014. The United Nations. Tasks, instruments and reforms, 5th ed. Opladen–Toronto: Publisher Barbara Budrich UTB

Gunnarsson, Logi, Ulrike Mürbe, and Norman Weiß. 2019. The human right to a dignified existence in an international context. Legal and philosophical perspectives. Series of publications of the MenschenRechtsZentrum der University of Potsdam No. 46. Baden-Baden: Nomos.

Haery, David. 2010. *UNDPKO/DFS briefing paper*. New York: United Nations.

Hilpold, Peter. 2006. Duty to protect. In *10*, ed. Max Planck United Nations Yearbook. No, 34–69. Leiden/Boston: Martinus Nijhoff.

Janik, Ralph. 2020. *International law and the use of force. Cases and materials.* London: Routledge.

Kaldor, Mary, Mary Martin, and Sabine Selchow. 2007. Human security and the European Union. *International Affairs* 83 (2): 237–288.

Lauterpacht, Elihu. 1950. *International law and human rights.* Cambridge: Cambridge University Press.

Lederach, John Paul. 1998. *Building peace—Sustainable reconciliation in divided societies.* Washington DC: United States Institute of Peace.

McLoughlin, Claire. 2010. Topic guide on Fragile States, Governance and Social Development Resource Centre (GSDRC), https://www.gsdrc.org. Accessed 8 Aug 2021..

Nye, Joseph. 2004. *Soft power: The means to success in world politics.* New York: Public Affairs.

OECD Statebuilding Guidance. 2010. https://www.oecd-ilibrary.org/development/supporting-statebuilding-in-situations-of-conflict-and-fragility_9789264074989-en. Accessed 8 Aug 2021.

OECD/g7+. 2011. New deal. https://www.pbsbdialogue.org/en/new-deal/new-deal-principles/. Accessed 8 Aug 2021.

Paffenholz, T., A. Hirblinger, D. Landau, F. Fritsch F., and C. Dijkstra. 2017. "Inclusion and the Prevention of Violent Conflict." Thematic paper for the United Nations–World Bank flagship study, pathways for peace: Inclusive approaches to preventing violent conflict. Washington DC: World Bank.

Schöndorf, Elisabeth. 2011. From traditional peacekeeping to complex statebuilding operations, status and further development of international peace insets. In *Strategie und Sicherheit,* ed. Johann Pucher and Johann Frank, 323–334. Vienna: böhlau.

Schreiber, Dan, and Kulani Abendroth-Dias. 2021. Unpacking the black box of fragility. *TDHJ Special Edition #02 21*: 13–22. https://ca9d3787-8643-4d85-9af7-d052377ac9b8.filesusr.com/ugd/0d3ede_e7c96c4fd93945a9bfe58c6c564427c2.pdf. Accessed 8 Aug 2021

Simma, Bruno. 2009. Universality from the perspective of a practitioner. *EJIL* 20 (2): 273ff.
Stewart, Frances, and Graham Brown. 2009. Fragile States, Center for Research on Inequality, Human Security and Ethnicity (CRISE). University of Oxford, Working Paper No. 51.
UN Handbook on United Nations Multidimensional Peacekeeping Operations. 2003. New York United Nations.
V-DEM Institute. 2020. Autocratisation surges—Resistance grows. Democracy report 2020. https://www.v-dem.net/media/filer_public/de/39/de39af54-0bc5-4421-89ae-fb20dcc53dba/democracy_report.pdf. Accessed 6 Mar 2021.
Verlage, Christopher. 2009. Responsibility to protect. *Jus Internationale et Europaeum* 29, ed. Thilo Marauhn and Christian Walter.
Weller, Christoph. 2007. Civil conflict transformation. *INEF Report* 85: 9–18, Universität Duisburg.
Werther-Pietsch, Ursula, and Thomas Ritzer. 2012. *Failed states—Statebuilding as conflict prevention.* Vienna/Graz: nwv - Berliner Wissenschaftsverlag.
Werther-Pietsch, Ursula. 2018. The impact of SDGs on international law—A nucleus of a right to peace. *Austrian Political Science Journal* 47 (1).
Werther-Pietsch, Ursula. 2020. Kollektive Sicherheit 2030. UNO Friedenssicherung im Wandel. Vienna: National Defence Academy Series Volume 3/2020.
Werther-Pietsch, Ursula. 2021. Democracy forever, Wiener Zeitung, 20 Jan 2021.
World Bank, and UNDP. 2018. *Pathways for peace. Inclusive approaches to preventing conflict.* Washington DC: World Bank. https://openknowledge.worldbank.org/handle/10986/28337. Accessed 8 Aug 2021.
World Bank. 2011. Conflict, security, and development. World Development Report. Washington DC: World Bank. https://wdr2011.worldbank.org/. Accessed 8 Aug 2021.

Chapter 4
Who, Why and When—The Normative Framework

4.1 Prevalence of the UN Charter

In Article 1 (1) of the Charter, member states agreed,

> To maintain international peace and security, and to that end: to take effective collective measures for the prevention and removal of threats to the peace, and for the suppression of acts of aggression or other breaches of the peace, and to bring about by peaceful means, and in conformity with the principles of justice and international law, adjustment or settlement of international disputes or situations which might lead to a breach of the peace.

The overall goal of the UN System of Collective Security is the preservation and maintenance of peace and security by an internationally agreed obligation to settle disputes peacefully, which is intertwined with the principle on the prohibition of the use of force in Article 2 (4) of the UN Charter. This basically refers to the exercise or threat of state military force. The prohibition was formulated and specified in the preamble, Article 51 of the UN Charter (exceptions), the 1970 "Friendly Relations Declaration" (FRD) and UNGA Resolution 3314/1974 (definition of aggression by the UNGA; ICC reform conferences from 2010 onwards till now, ILC Report 2019) as well as in the Nicaragua judgement of the ICJ 1986 (see also Activités armées sur le territoire du Congo [République démocratique du Congo c. Riz'andu], ordonnance du 21 Octobre 1999, C. I. J. Recueil 1999, 1025], and current border disputes handled by the court[1]).

After 1945, in view of the failure of the League of Nations to prevent a second World War, the time seemed ripe for a global mechanism with the aim of maintaining and restoring international peace and security. The UN, as the universal prototype of a collective security system, was, therefore, endowed with the powers and means to respond actively to a threat to peace, a breach of peace or an act of aggression. Equipped with ultimate decision-making capabilities, the UN Charter assumes the status of a "constitution of the International Community". In principle, coercive measures of such a model apply to members only, which distinguishes the collective

[1] https://icj.org. Accessed 8 August 2021.

U. Werther-Pietsch, *Transforming Security*, Global Power Shift,
https://doi.org/10.1007/978-3-030-87097-3_4

system from a defence alliance solely directed against "the outside" (Heintschel von Heinegg in Ipsen 2018: 1178).

Adaptability and flexibility of the UN Charter over decades were praised in many places (Paulus 2001), but in its almost eight decades of existence, a constant "*fire-fighting rather than a grand design*" in reform matters was also noted (Rensmann in Simma et al. 2012). This culminated in the dictum of the former UNSG Kofi Annan that included and is particularly true for the peace and security pillar: "*The United Nations is by no means a perfect instrument, but it is a precious one*" (Speech before the UNGA on 23 September 2003, UN Doc. A/58/PV.2003, UN Doc. [2003]4). This evolution results from the fact that the UNSC's interpretation has always been dynamic so that the purpose of the International Community's action under the Charter has widely been seen to resolve threats to peace in a sustainable way.

4.2 Broad Conceptualisation of the Peace and Security Agenda

The basic understanding of the UN as an international organisation to serve as an overarching long-term peacekeeper has only come with an extensive interpretation of these normative foundations, paving the way for a broad concept of peace. Such broad conceptualisation reconciles the competing imperatives of security and development that created tensions from the very beginning in terms of goals and capabilities. In turn, the Agenda 2030 for Sustainable Development adopted in 2015 (Sustainable Development Goals; SDGs) makes reference to and integrates at the highest level possible explicitly aspects of fragility and resilience in the development hemisphere (SDG 16).

Policy documents such as the Guidelines of the German Federal Government "Preventing Crises, Managing Conflicts, Promoting Peace" (2017), the New Deal between the OECD and the Group of 7 + states (2011) in the spirit of the UN reform summit 2005 (paragraph 9 of the Outcome document) have finally been able to transfer this binary view combining security and development in the national domain. These policies focus, in harmony with the Sustaining Peace Approach, on a comprehensive picture of building peace as the generic goal. A path that corresponds in particular with the central function of law according to Immanuel Kant:

> No Treaty of Peace Shall Be Held Valid in Which There Is Tacitly Reserved Matter for a Future War; Otherwise a treaty would be only a truce, a suspension of hostilities but not peace, which means the end of all hostilities – so much so that even to attach the word „perpetual" to it is a dubious pleonasm. (Kant, Article 1 ‚Preliminary Articles' 1795)

In the following, a brief description of the UN's main institutions in the field of global peace and security, their powers and modes of interaction as a framework of geostrategic action is provided.

4.3 Interfaces Between the Organs

In between the four cornerstones in international relations—prohibition of the use of force, sovereignty, non-intervention as well as human rights and self-determination—the *Security Council* (UNSC) is established as the ultimate authority for deciding peace and security matters: The responsibility for determining a threat to peace, a breach of the peace and acts of aggression in a given situation lies with the UNSC (Krisch in Simma et al. 2012: 1272ff). The Council consists of five permanent members (the "P-5") and further ten members rotating every two years (Oosterom, IPI New York 23 July 2020). Article 12. in conjunction with Article 39 and Chapter VII of the UN Charter equip the UNSC as the primary authority responsible for the maintenance of international peace and security beyond its originally intended "short term crisis" management function. As an instrument of the P-5, the UNSC in its composition and decision-making is the centre of a rather political system of collective security (Kissinger 1996: 845; critical Eitel 2008: "*institutional sclerosis* "; Ischinger 2018) Article 24 regulating the competences of the UNSC (see Must Know text in the resume) refers to Chapter VI (non-binding decisions on peaceful settlement of disputes; cases of application in Article 34), Chapter VII (cases of application in Article 39) and Chapter XII.

In contrast, the *General Assembly* (UNGA) bears comprehensive competence for all UN activities, including world peace (Article 11). However, this competence is only a subsidiary one insofar as it depends on the action taken by the UNSC (Certain Expenses Opinion, 1962 ICJ Rep 151, 163). According to mainstream doctrine, and in search for an urgent peaceful conflict resolution between the two Koreas against the background of the Cold War, decision-power to maintain world peace was transferred to the General Assembly in 1950, when the UNSC was blocked ("secondary competence", legally non-binding, does not include coercive measures or the authority to decide on peace operations). Article 12, stating that the UNGA may not make any recommendations as long as the UNSC is dealing with a matter, has thus lost importance in practice (cf. expert opinion on the construction of the wall 9 July 2004 [2004] ICJ Rep 136, Paragraph 27 and 28). The UNGA, for instance, expressed its views on the violent action of Syrian President Bashar al-Assad against opposition forces, apart from emergency meetings of the UNSC in February 2012 (A/RES/66/253 of 16 February 2012). Notwithstanding that bias in power, the UNGA decides independently on budgetary matters. Furthermore, the UNGA was also able to establish the UNEF I mission (Suez Canal/Sinai) under Article 14 as early as 1963, which established the UN's classic peacekeeping principles. From that time onwards, however, all missions were deployed by the UNSC.

The *UN Secretary-General* (UNSG) and the *Secretariat* play a central role in agenda setting and implementation with far-reaching tasks of analysis, initiatives and their implementation, which are regulated in Article 97–99 of the UN Charter. The UNSG usually appoints Special Representatives to lead operations and functions like the head of the command structure, supported by the UNDPO, a separate department of the UN Secretariat headed by a special UN-USG for peacekeeping.

Issues of rights and obligations in the host country of missions are governed by the 1946 United Nations Convention on Privileges and Immunities and the 1994 United Nations Convention on the Safety of Personnel and Associated Personnel (Ipsen 2018: 1188). In principle, only the overall command is transferred to the UN; the national troop-providing states retain the personnel administration, disciplinary and criminal powers. Permanent peacekeeping structures pursuant to Article 43, i.e. troops made available bilaterally to the UN or a separate force as a rapid reaction capability, although intensively discussed since the founding of the UN such bilateral agreements were never negotiated and do not (yet) exist.

4.4 Chapter VI—Peaceful Settlement of Disputes

The principle of *peaceful settlement of disputes* is governed by Article 2(3) of the UN Charter. The UN Charter is supplemented by the Manila Declaration on the Peaceful Settlement of Disputes of 15 November 1982, which is still very near to the originally broad understanding of the principle of sovereignty and the Declaration on the Prevention and Elimination of Disputes and Situations which May Threaten International Peace and Security of December 1988. At the same time, peaceful settlement of disputes is anchored in customary IL (ICJ, Military and Paramilitary Activities in Nicaragua, judgment of 27 June 1986, ICJ Rep. 1986, 14 (290) and is closely connected with the prohibition of the use of force and non-intervention in Article 2 (1) and (4) of the Charter.

The UN Charter has in principle adopted and further developed the statutory dual system of collective security of the League of Nations, namely: (1) efforts to prevent the outbreak of a conflict and (2) measures in the event of the failure of a peaceful solution. The additional "cooling off" mechanism provided for by the League of Nations, which subordinated latent conflict situations to a "preliminary procedure" to create a time buffer for appeasement, was not transferred. The intended mechanism, however, at that time, regulated the matter inefficiently to the extent that hostilities below the war threshold were excluded. This lesson identified appears to be inspiring in rethinking established peace and security instruments.

According to Article 33 (1) of the UN Charter, the means of dispute resolution include (not exhaustive):

- **Negotiations, good services, mediation**
    - "Diplomatic means" comprise direct negotiations *between* two or more parties ("*negotiations*"). The oldest "negotiated" peace agreement known to us refer to trade relations in Mesopothamia (Vienna, Kunsthistorisches Museum). These include all forms of talks between the parties to the dispute aimed at resolving the conflict, separate bilateral meetings, in international organisations or at multilateral conferences, in principle without the participation of third parties. According to Volker Epping (in Ipsen 2018: 1232), the prerequisite is a

fundamental willingness to compromise (minimum flexibility) on one's own position.
- "Good offices" are not explicitly mentioned in the texts, but they represent an important (passive) form of diplomatic dispute resolution carried out in the background by the UNSG, such as establishing contacts or providing places for mediating. Examples comprise Syria talks in 2016 and 2019 in Vienna or tanker incidents Gibraltar and Strait of Hormus 2019 with USA, Germany, Iran, and UK involved.
- "Mediation" by third parties (states, international organisations or private individuals) can actively lead to positive negotiation results. Nevertheless, even when proposals are made, the role of the mediator must remain neutral, what makes the UN an ideal peace-broker.

- **Inquiry, fact-finding and reconciliation**

  - Promotion of the settlement of disputes through impartial fact-finding by local, equally staffed or purely external parties with a non-binding character
  - Reconciliation proceedings as a kind of mixed form of investigation and mediation, ad hoc or contractually (e.g. Bogotà Pact, European Convention for the Peaceful Settlement of Disputes, Convention on the Law of the Sea, Vienna Convention on the Law of Treaties).

- **Arbitration, recourse to universal or regional judicial regulation**

  In these cases, the parties to the dispute voluntarily accept arbitration in good faith according to Article 37 (I) of The Hague Convention for the Peaceful Settlement of International Disputes. Complementary to this, the ICJ as one of the six main organs of the UN can exercise a judicial competence on the basis of its Statute in accordance with Article 7 of the UN Charter, with the right and obligation to interpret the Charter authentically, including acts of the UNSC or regional bodies or agreements. The scope of the latter is, however, controversial insofar as the legal significance of resolutions of the UNSC which are binding for member states must be taken into account.
- **Other peaceful means** such as cultural exchange, sports events, etc. provided they are intended to contribute to a peaceful settlement and can actually make a contribution to achieving this goal.

4.5 Chapter VII—Blue Helmets and Robust Action

On the basis of Article 1 Z 1, Article 2 (5), Article 34 and Article 39 et seq. of the UN Charter, the UNSC may, in the event of a threat to or breach of world peace, use a series of repressive or preliminary collective measures. This includes political recommendations, interim measures, and—if a situation threatens to escalate or breaks out in armed conflict—non-military and military coercive measures.

4.5.1 Non-military Coercive Measures

Article 41 of the UN Charter offers a broad spectrum of possibilities for the UNSC to react to latent conflict situations, which in principle should not be seen as a punitive measure but exert political pressure. Exactly for that reason, it has become smart to turn to "sanctionism" as a less risky method of calling for compliance. In practice, both lines are blurred; if not, in the age of social media, the former dominates.

According to the logic of Article 25 of the Draft Principles of State Responsibility, non-military measures are legally binding. Their effectiveness is based on:

- the assumption that states are rational actors, so that negative effects impact their behaviour
- the ascertainment of developing political pressure in the country.

Nevertheless, economic sanctions are considered to be "last resort" as they mostly affect civilians for government actions. Already, the 1990s were described as the "decade of sanctions" (Cortright and Lopez 2000). This is experiencing a renaissance under the 2019 "trade war" between the USA and China. Other recent cases of the sanctions regime include Iran, Iraq, Ex-Yugoslavia, Serbia, Ethiopia, Angola, Liberia, Sierra Leone, Somalia, Haiti, Libya, Afghanistan and Sudan. As an outstanding example following the unlawful annexation of the Crimea in 2014 and a questionable referendum on self-determination, embedded in a covert action of pro-Russian "para-military" forces during the Olympic Games in Sochi, economic sanctions and travel restrictions were imposed on the entourage of the Russian president Putin for breach of IL and failure to respect Ukrainian sovereignty.

Far-reaching consequences of sanctions such as serious humanitarian consequences, loss of legitimacy, and effects of economic nature (isolation of states through landing bans, etc.) have constantly given rise to further discussion. To resolve this problem, a fund to compensate the affected population could be established. The sanction regime has therefore been progressed by embargo provisions with "targeted" or "smart sanctions". The freezing of accounts represents a substantial intervention in individual rights. They were already imposed e.g. against close relatives of the Libyan ruler Col. Gaddafi 2011 or ban on importing luxury watches for the ruling dynasty into North Korea. What is questionable though, is that no appeal can be lodged against this "naming and shaming", especially when the person concerned has been placed on a watch list (UNSC decision). More than 20 sanctions committees monitor currently implementation by member states.

According to Article 40 of the UN Charter, provisional measures are also possible; this form of a call to end hostilities or other peace-threatening behaviour has often been used. So, apart from economic sanctions, the establishment of the Criminal Tribunal for the former Yugoslavia with its famous cases of inconsistency with ICJ jurisdiction (UN Doc. S/RES/827 [1992] of 25 May 1993; see, for example, the Tadic case) has also been considered an effective non-military coercive measure. Those tribunals with far-reaching powers act in politically sensitive areas since an international arrest warrant in case of allegations of war crimes of leaders regularly attracts international attention.

4.5.2 *Military Coercive Measures*

Peacekeeping—The legal framework

Military coercive measures in accordance with *Article 42* of the UN Charter serve as "ultima ratio"; the scope for discretion is large. Special agreements pursuant to Article 43 for the provision of air forces (Article 45) and planning (Article 46) by a General Staff Committee (Article 47) have never been concluded. In practice, however, "coalitions of the willing" regularly established themselves for this task (Chapter VIII). There is a difference between mandated ("blue helmets") and authorised missions. The former stand under UN authority and are bound to UNDPO Rules of Engagement. The latter are not under the operational command of the UNSG. These are subject to the respective national rules of engagement. Consequently, in this configuration, the UN is not responsible for operation command or control. In addition, the law applicable to each peacekeeping force is governed by the Model Status of Forces Agreement (SOFA, UN Doc. A745/594 of 9 October 1990), which guides the UN, the state of residence and the TCCs. In the case of a mandated deployment, the 1994 Convention on the Protection of UN Personnel also applies, except hostilities cross the threshold of armed conflict.

It is particularly principles and rules of IHL that come into play when a particular situation is classified as armed conflict. The principles of warfare methods, intensity of armed actions, collateral damage, beginning and end of armed conflicts, but also responsibilities towards prisoners of war and civilians are regulated in it (Haslinger in Werther-Pietsch 2017: 99). Complementarily, individual acts of violence can be asserted under the human rights regime, which presupposes the exercise of *jurisdiction*. When effective control over a territory is exercised, violations are then attributable to the home state. The ECHR has, however, denied using this justification in the case of Behrami and Saramati for UNMIK and KFOR in Kosovo (ECHR, Behrami and Behrami vs. France, 31 May 2007, Application no. 78166/01; Saramati and France, Germany and Norway, 2 May 2007, Application no. 78166/01).

Within the mandate, the UNSC decides not only on the deployment of a mission, but also on its tasks and staffing levels. In everyday missions' life, troops were assisted by experts of the *standby register* introduced in the 1990s on the basis of the Brahimi report. Member states from "Level 1 to 4" have the capacity for a rapid response by a multilateral force of brigade size, Jordan and Uruguay are the only countries to date to have made entire quotas available for deployment within 30–90 days. So-called "*on-call lists*" additionally allow team building with military and civilian experts on a smaller scale within 7 to 14 days.

Basic principles of peacekeeping

Principles of peacekeeping are based on practice established by the UNEF I mission (Suez Canal) but have undergone an interpretative change since then. Original characteristics are:

1. Consensus of the parties to the conflict is paramount ("*There is no peacekeeping if there is no peace to keep*", UN-USG Guehenno, 2010)
2. Leadership responsibility lies with the UN
3. Strict impartiality and use of weapons is lawfully executed only for self-defence (Sinai 1956–67 and II 1973–79; the robust component was defined in ONUC (Congo) 1960).

Due to the experiences in Somalia, in 1995, and the former Yugoslavia in the early 2000s, and slightly deviating from the original consensus principle, the wording "*to use all necessary means*" or "*to take the necessary action/measures*" is chosen in recent mandates. This includes the use of military means beyond self-defence to fulfil the purpose, similar to the "implied power" rule in IL, with a remaining grey area which undoubtedly requires additional consideration in the concrete situation.

Schematic sequence of a UN mandated engagement

1. Identification of a threat to or breach of world peace or of an act of aggression pursuant to *Article 39* of the UN Charter by nine members of the UNSC, among them all P-5; this threat/breach may be induced by states, bilaterally, regionally or globally for instance through illegal existence of weapons of mass destruction, it further includes to a limited extent domestic sources of conflict as well as non-state threat scenarios such as large-scale acts of terrorism; or, notwithstanding the legal character of the actor involved, massive violations of human rights or international humanitarian law which are to be given halt for humanitarian reasons.
2. Recommendations or measures that can be imposed: *Recommendations* are addressed to all members in accordance with Article 24 in conjunction with Article 48 and 49 of the UN Charter, whereby there is no duty to be followed by the addressee state as well as other states. In practice, this led to its easier application. *Measures* under Article 41 and 42 are individual or abstract in nature, such as international terrorism in UNSCR 1373/2001 or the proliferation of weapons of mass destruction by non-state actors in UNSCR 1540/2004 as a "threat to peace". From a legal point of view, both are justifications for action by the member states. As mentioned above, the UNSC does not refer to single articles, but regularly uses the formula "*Acting under Chapter VII*" in order to signal the willingness to use robust means ("ultima ratio").
3. There is wide scope for the choice of coercive measures. However, the UNSC is not *legibus solutus* in decision-making. There are absolute however not clear enough precised term of "crimes against humanity" such as genocide or slave trade which according to Article 53 VCLT cannot be tolerated by the International Community. This does not apply to IHL or human rights in general, but the

scope of *ius cogens* is dynamic and remains to date controversial in substance and outreach (ILC Report 2019). According to Heintschel von Heinegg (in Ipsen 2018: 1184), for example, the UNSC cannot authorise direct attacks against civilians or individual civilians, indiscriminate attacks or arbitrary killings of persons (Osama bin Laden, May 2011; al-Baghdadi, October 2019, Qasem Soleimani, January 2020). According to Article 103 of the UN Charter, the obligations of the members, however, take precedence over contractual and customary obligations under IL, which is why the UNSC is, within the described overall limits, free to decide "*in the sense of the high importance of the goals of protection of world peace and international security*" (Heintschel in Ipsen ff; see Fig. 4.1; with the exception of ICJ ruling) (Fig. 935).

Typology of missions

It is a matter of fact that the tasks of UN missions have grown from their original observer and monitoring function to entire state-building processes. The following categorisations have emerged:

- *Phases along Gareis and Varwick*: Origin 1948–56, assertion 1956–67, slumber 1967–73, "resuscitation" 1973–78, maintenance 1948–88, expansion 1988–93 and shrinking phase since 1993. (Gareis/Varwick 2014: 126)
- *Qualitative criteria according to* Debiel (2003): consensus-oriented peacekeeping, multidimensional peacekeeping, robust peace missions, military peace enforcement in medium- and high-intensity wars.
- *"Four generations" theory*: traditional blue helmet missions, broadening the range of tasks, merging peacekeeping with peace enforcement and responsibility to civil administrative functions.

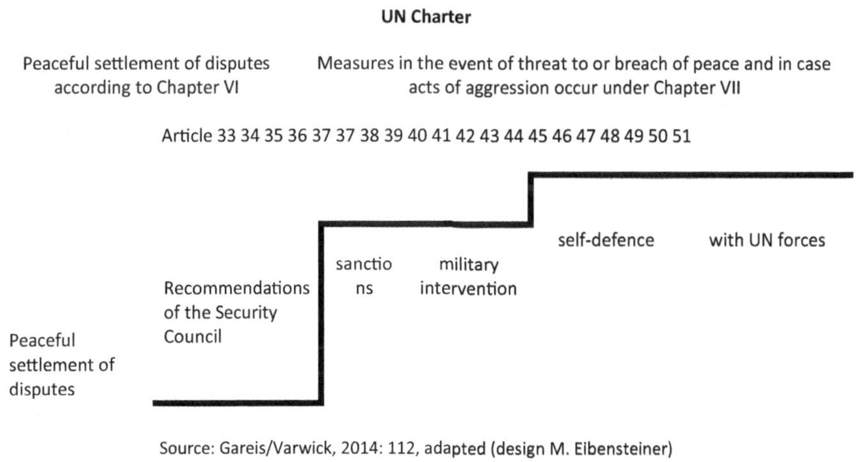

Fig. 4.1 Sequence of a UN mandate

- *"Agenda for Peace" categories*: preventive diplomacy, peacekeeping, peacebuilding and peace consolidation, still prevalent today.
- *Different subtypes according to Bellamy and Williams* (2010): preventive deployments, traditional peacekeeping, extended peacekeeping, peace enforcement, transition assistance, transition management, *peace support operations* (including political missions) (Fig. 4.2).

Peace Support Operations—"missions other than war"

Today's functions of peacekeeping according to Michael Bothe (in Simma et al. 2012: 1182) are:

- Transparency and confidence building: observer missions (UNMOGIP, UNTSO, ONUCA)
- Separation of conflict parties: "(military) interposition forces" (UNEF I and II, UNDOF, UNIFIL)
- Maintaining order in *failed states, post-conflict* peace-building (UNTAC, ONUMOZ, UNOSOM II)
- Humanitarian aid or protection of aid operations (UNOSOM, UNPROFOR)
- Verification as part of *post-conflict* engagement
- Local DDR programmes, demining (ONUMOZ)
- Support for the reconstruction of state structures, e.g. elections (MINURSO, Haiti, "village policing" in Mali and Kosovo).

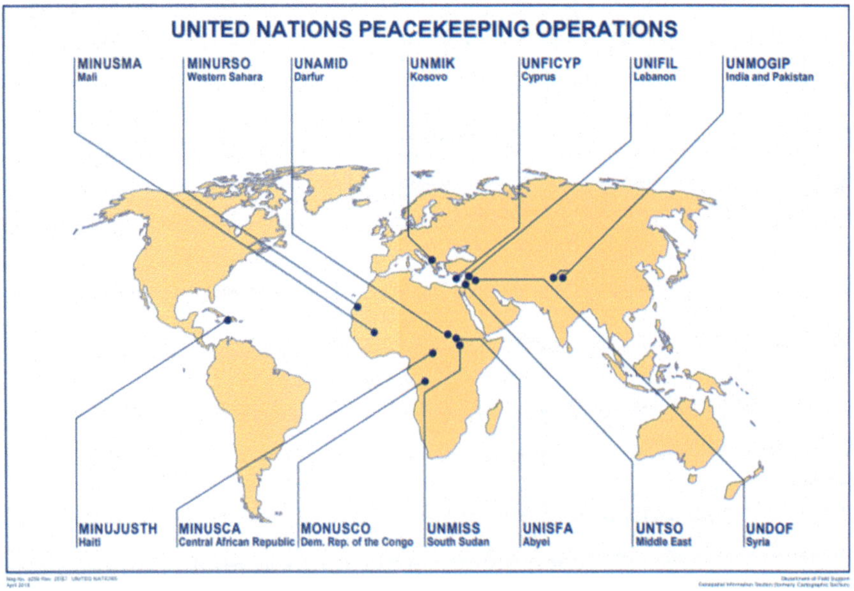

Fig. 4.2 Peacekeeping operations landscape. *Source* UNDPO, https://www.un.org/en/peacekeeping/operations/current.shtml. Accessed 8 August 2021

Recent UNSC post COVID-19 activities encompass matters of security and environment, an initiative of Germany during the UNSC presidency in July 2020 that may require further innovations. Moreover, new forms of warfare and changing threat patterns require modified components in the military arm of peacekeeping. Equally, alternative, hybrid models of peacekeeping have emerged which remain within the objectives of the Charter but do not run counter to the principle of sovereign equality as well as the interests of the P-5. This is reflected in the behaviour of world powers: US-led "*We call you if we need you*"-wars, as mentioned, developed quickly (anti-terror missions since "9–11"), with the exception of the UK, which was usually involved in the planning of operations to a higher degree. As the second largest contributor of troops, China has shown increased interest in *Peace Support Operations* since 2011 (Libya), 2015 (South Sudan), and especially under President Xi and the new Chinese military doctrine of 2017. These movements, as well as Chinese impulses for a renewed multilateralism, may, however, have been driven by geostrategic intentions.

To resume successes and failures in UN peacekeeping in a nutshell, it may be recommendable to resort to the "phased" approach: As Sven-Bernhard Gareis and Johannes Varwick (2014) emphasise, the concentration on "conflict calming" was the decisive success of peacekeeping in the first phase. Following the two authors, this is based on the "conception of restraint, strategic wisdom and limitation to what is feasible". The 1960–64 Congo mission (ONUC), the "Vietnam of the UNO" (William Durch of the Stimson Center, New York) showed that the state-building tasks and the arming of the troops as recognised today (holistic approach, R2P) originally did not correspond to the peacekeeping principles of UNEP I.

With the end of the East–West conflict and the resulting rapprochement between the USA and the USSR, UN peacekeeping boomed. Legitimacy, however, suffered considerably from "*seminal events*" such as the Iraq/Kuwait war in 2003, unresolved African conflicts (consequences of the Somalia mission in 1995, the non-prevention of the genocide in Rwanda in 1994) and incidents and occurrences in South-East Europe (warlike disintegration of Yugoslavia, powerless "watching" of ethnic cleansing in Srebrenica). From 1948 to 1988, 16 missions were present globally, from 1988 to 1992 only 14 and from 1993 to 2017 again 16 missions deployed—as listed in the following table.

"Mission creep", indiscernible expansion of mandates, had thus internationally led to an erosion of readiness for peacekeeping missions. Despite the "A4P" Declaration 2018, annual ministerial meetings, warnings on the part of the UNSG due to increased risks and sharpened constellations, the International Community seems to "withdraw" partly from its all-encompassing vision. This has taken place against the background of excessively high demands of world public opinion and expectations of the populations concerned about what the UN can do or not. In the past, there were found other ways to address this "gap", like the establishment of the Peace-building Commission, critically reviewed in the following (Fig. 4.3):

LIST OF PEACEKEEPING OPERATIONS **1948 - 2019**

ACRONYM	MISSION NAME	START DATE	END DATE
UNTSO	United Nations Truce Supervision Organization	May 1948	Present
UNMOGIP	United Nations Military Observer Group in India and Pakistan	January 1949	Present
UNEF I	First United Nations Emergency Force	November 1956	June 1967
UNOGIL	United Nations Observation Group in Lebanon	June 1958	December 1958
ONUC	United Nations Operation in the Congo	July 1960	June 1964
UNSF	United Nations Security Force in West New Guinea	October 1962	April 1963
UNYOM	United Nations Yemen Observation Mission	July 1963	September 1964
UNFICYP	United Nations Peacekeeping Force in Cyprus	March 1964	Present
DOMREP	Mission of the Representative of the Secretary-General in the Dominican Republic	May 1965	October 1966
UNIPOM	United Nations India-Pakistan Observation Mission	September 1965	March 1966
UNEF II	Second United Nations Emergency Force	October 1973	July 1979
UNDOF	United Nations Disengagement Observer Force	June 1974	Present
UNIFIL	United Nations Interim Force in Lebanon	March 1978	Present
UNGOMAP	United Nations Good Offices Mission in Afghanistan and Pakistan	May 1988	March 1990
UNIIMOG	United Nations Iran-Iraq Military Observer Group	August 1988	February 1991
UNAVEM I	United Nations Angola Verification Mission I	January 1989	June 1991
UNTAG	United Nations Transition Assistance Group	April 1989	March 1990
ONUCA	United Nations Observer Group in Central America	November 1989	January 1992
UNIKOM	United Nations Iraq-Kuwait Observation Mission	April 1991	October 2003
MINURSO	United Nations Mission for the Referendum in Western Sahara	April 1991	Present
UNAVEM II	United Nations Angola Verification Mission II	June 1991	February 1995
ONUSAL	United Nations Observer Mission in El Salvador	July 1991	April 1995
UNAMIC	United Nations Advance Mission in Cambodia	October 1991	March 1992
UNPROFOR	United Nations Protection Force	February 1992	March 1995
UNTAC	United Nations Transitional Authority in Cambodia	March 1992	September 1993
UNOSOM I	United Nations Operation in Somalia I	April 1992	March 1993
ONUMOZ	United Nations Operation in Mozambique	December 1992	December 1994
UNOSOM II	United Nations Operation in Somalia II	March 1993	March 1995
UNOMUR	United Nations Observer Mission Uganda-Rwanda	June 1993	September 1994
UNOMIG	United Nations Observer Mission in Georgia	August 1993	June 2009
UNOMIL	United Nations Observer Mission in Liberia	September 1993	September 1997
UNMIH	United Nations Mission in Haiti	September 1993	June 1996
UNAMIR	United Nations Assistance Mission for Rwanda	October 1993	March 1996
UNASOG	United Nations Aouzou Strip Observer Group	May 1994	June 1994
UNMOT	United Nations Mission of Observers in Tajikistan	December 1994	May 2000
UNAVEM III	United Nations Angola Verification Mission III	February 1995	June 1997
UNCRO	United Nations Confidence Restoration Operation in Croatia	March 1995	January 1996

Fig. 4.3 List of peacekeeping operations. *Source* UNDPO, https://peacekeeping.un.org/sites/default/files/unpeacekeeping-operationlist_3_1_0.pdf

ACRONYM	MISSION NAME	START DATE	END DATE
UNPREDEP	United Nations Preventive Deployment Force	March 1995	February 1999
UNMIBH	United Nations Mission in Bosnia and Herzegovina	December 1995	December 2002
UNTAES	United Nations Transitional Administration for Eastern Slavonia, Baranja and Western Sirmium	January 1996	January 1998
UNMOP	United Nations Mission of Observers in Prevlaka	February 1996	December 2002
UNSMIH	United Nations Support Mission in Haiti	July 1996	July 1997
MINUGUA	United Nations Verification Mission in Guatemala	January 1997	May 1997
MONUA	United Nations Observer Mission in Angola	June 1997	February 1999
UNTMIH	United Nations Transition Mission in Haiti	August 1997	December 1997
MIPONUH	United Nations Civilian Police Mission in Haiti	December 1997	March 2000
UNCPSG	UN Civilian Police Support Group	January 1998	October 1998
MINURCA	United Nations Mission in the Central African Republic	April 1998	February 2000
UNOMSIL	United Nations Observer Mission in Sierra Leone	July 1998	October 1999
UNMIK	United Nations Interim Administration Mission in Kosovo	June 1999	Present
UNAMSIL	United Nations Mission in Sierra Leone	October 1999	December 2005
UNTAET	United Nations Transitional Administration in East Timor	October 1999	May 2002
MONUC	United Nations Organization Mission in the Democratic Republic of the Congo	November 1999	June 2010
UNMEE	United Nations Mission in Ethiopia and Eritrea	July 2000	July 2008
UNMISET	United Nations Mission of Support in East Timor	May 2002	May 2005
MINUCI	United Nations Mission in Côte d'Ivoire	May 2003	April 2004
UNMIL	United Nations Mission in Liberia	September 2003	March 2018
UNOCI	United Nations Operation in Côte d'Ivoire	April 2004	May 2017
MINUSTAH	United Nations Stabilization Mission in Haiti	June 2004	October 2017
ONUB	United Nations Operation in Burundi	June 2004	December 2006
UNMIS	United Nations Mission in the Sudan	March 2005	July 2011
UNMIT	United Nations Integrated Mission in Timor-Leste	August 2006	December 2012
UNAMID	African Union-United Nations Hybrid Operation in Darfur	July 2007	Present
MINURCAT	United Nations Mission in the Central African Republic and Chad	September 2007	December 2010
MONUSCO	United Nations Organization Stabilization Mission in the Democratic Republic of the Congo	July 2010	Present
UNISFA	United Nations Organization Interim Security Force for Abyei	June 2011	Present
UNMISS	United Nations Mission in the Republic of South Sudan	July 2011	Present
UNSMIS	United Nations Supervision Mission in Syria	April 2012	August 2012
MINUSMA	United Nations Multidimensional Integrated Stabilization Mission in Mali	April 2013	Present
MINUSCA	United Nations Multidimensional Integrated Stabilization Mission in the Central African Republic	April 2014	Present
MINUJUSTH	United Nations Mission for Justice Support in Haiti	October 2017	October 2019

Find out more on, peacekeeping.un.org
and follow us on social media

UN United Nations Peacekeeping

Fig. 4.3 (continued)

4.6 Peace-Building Commission

4.6.1 *Wither an Institutional Gap*

Aims and goals

With the steady broadening of the peace and security agenda, the whole peace-building and state-building business expanded more and more. In the 1990s, transitional administrations with quasi-state functions developed along operations in Cambodia, East Timor and Kosovo. By massive international presence, these engagements de facto suspended national sovereignty and the governing power of the state concerned. However, it follows in principle from the logic of the collective security system as established that, once the conflict has been resolved, its mandate ends. From this fact stems the practice of annually extended missions. Prolonged post-war contexts, as well as protracted crises, could only be subsumed under this responsibility in a broad interpretation of intervention to counter fragility. The Peace-building Commission (PBC) was founded in 2005 to institutionally fill this gap between peace-keeping and long-term commitment. Originally intended to play a far-reaching role in conflict prevention, the PBC is a subsidiary organ of the two main organs, the UNSC and the UNGA to which it reports once a year. With the number of fragile states figure on its agenda, the Peace-building Fund has allocated nearly 1.47 billion US dollars to 62 recipient countries from 2006 to 2020.[2]

Genesis

A number of UN agencies already contributed to various aspects of post-conflict reconstruction: The 2000 Brahimi Report mentions the following administrative units: "*UNDP, UNICEF, the High Commissioner for Refugees, the Office of the High Commissioner for Human Rights, UNDPKO, UNDPA and the Department for Disarmament Affairs*" (Panel on UN Peace Operations, 21 August 2000, UN Doc A/55/305-S/2000/809, paragraph 44f). To further increase the coherence of the UN peace-building activities, UNSG Kofi Annan first defined the role of coordinating peace-building at the UNDPA (1997 Review), which was mandated to convene the Executive Committee for Peace and Security. Later, the UN-USG for Political Affairs was designated focal point. It slowly became clear that a new body of its own would be needed to summarise these agendas, as the HLP on Threats, Challenges and Change 2004 states:

> "[W]hat is needed is a single intergovernmental organ dedicated to peace-building, empowered to monitor and pay close attention to countries at risk, ensure concerted action by donors, agencies, programmes and financial institutions, and mobilize financial resources for sustainable peace."

The establishment of the PBC can, therefore, be seen as a major step forward in terms of implementation of the comprehensive approach (see Part I Section 4.3),

[2] https://www.un.org/peacebuilding/fund, accessed 27 July 2021.

since after numerous internal conflicts, from Angola, Rwanda, Sierra Leone to Haiti, East Timor, etc. the necessary international instruments for the transition from the end of violent acts to lasting peace were either not used at all, used too late or uncoordinatedly, and around half of the countries affected fell back into war and violence within five years (Annan 2006). In 2004, therefore, the HLP also proposed to identify countries that could collapse and to that extent to work with the UNSC in a preventive way. Obviously, this proposal did not find a majority in 2006 for political reasons.

In the first decade of its existence, the PBC underwent two reviews to address initial and ongoing weaknesses and criticisms. Ongoing discussions aim at integrating the HDP nexus in the interface between UN peace-building and peacekeeping (EU-wide Belgian Initiative on Strengthening EU multilateral action in the areas of Peace-building and Peacekeeping, 27 April 2021).

4.6.2 Founding Mandate and Audit

Task portfolio

As an intergovernmental advisory body, the PBC pursues three main objectives:

- *"bringing together all of the relevant actors, including international donors, the international financial institutions, national governments, troop contributing countries;*
- *marshalling resources; and*
- *advising on and proposing integrated strategies for post-conflict peace-building and recovery and where appropriate, highlighting any gaps that threaten to undermine peace."* (UNSC 1645/2005, 1646 and the GA 60/180 of 30 December 2005, UN Doc. A/RES/60/180[3]).

In order to achieve these objectives, the PBC should, on the one hand, develop a coordinated and coherent comprehensive approach and, on the other hand, respond to specific country needs. It, therefore, meets in different formats, in the form of the organising committee and in country-specific configurations.

Short profile

The organising committee consists of 31 members and is mainly concerned with procedural issues (regulations of 23 June 2006): 7 members are appointed by the UNSC, 7 by ECOSOC and the other members from the "top ten" financial and military donors. Members are appointed for two years and can be re-elected. Geographical balance must be taken into account, the P-5 practically in all cases being represented in this mechanism (Berdefy 2019: 6, 11, 13).

The country configurations additionally take care of:

[3] www.unorg/securityconcil/content/subsidiary-bodies.

- the country concerned;
- a regional component: neighbouring countries involved and partners in political dialogue, sub-regional organisations such as the OIC or the EU (based on an agreement of 19 December 2007);
- the strongest financial, troop contributing and civilian (police) actors engaged in the reconstruction process;
- the highest UN representative in the country and other high-ranking UN diplomats; and
- regional organisations and IFIs.

Other UN-SRSGs, team leaders of the World Bank and the IMF as well as other donors may be invited. Depending on the configuration, the PBC can count about 50 to 60 participants—with the result of limited flexibility in favour of inclusivity. Important consultations with civil society, NGOs and the private sector are also provided for in § 21 of the regulations.

Country formations were predominantly started in African countries:

- BINUB—United Nations Integrated Office in Burundi
- BINUCA—United Nations Integrated Office in the Central African Republic
- UNMIL—United Nations Mission in Liberia
- UNIPSIL—United Nations Integrated Peace-building Office Sierra Leone
- UNOWA—United Nations Office for West Africa
- UNIOGBIS—United Nations Integrated Peace-building Office in Guinea Bissau (UNPBC 2011).

The agenda shall include countries proposed by the UNSC or UNSG, or at the request of ECOSOC or the UNGA or the country itself, if it is not on the agenda of the UNSC. All the Commission's activities and statements are based on the consensus of its members and its proposals are non-binding in nature.

Financing, especially in the early stages, is provided by the Peace-building Fund, founded on 11 October 2006, supported by an advisory body since 2008. This construction is supported by the Peace-building support office with a small staff in New York and the working group on lessons learned.

By its purely consultative role, the PBC is extremely dependent on the UNSC and its political priorities (International Peace Academy, The UN PBC: Benefits and Challenges, 6 June 2006, 3). The close dynamic between the UNSC and the PBC has already been critically taken up ("*does not necessarily always help maximize the impact on the ground*", 5th Special Research Report 33).

Further points of criticism are:

(1) Failure in its key role to bring all actors together in an integrated, comprehensive approach to avoid overlap and redundancy
(2) Lack of local ownership; high economic market standards were implemented rather than domestic capacities sought
(3) Incapable to surmount the "conflict trap" in regions with systemic crises. (Curtis/Adebajo, 2012: 140–157).

Peace-building in the sense of support for political processes enabling local societies to get out of the crisis thereby remains "*under-recognized, under-prioritized and under-resourced*" (Santner in Werther-Pietsch 2021) and represents only a step towards a capability-driven comprehensive approach. Again, there is much post COVID-19 potential for reform (OECD DAC High Level Forum on Civil Society, 4 June 2021).

4.7 Chapter VIII—Regional Organisations

Legal basis

As a consequence of post COVID-19 contraction of external engagement worldwide, a retreat of donors and "first-aid" actors from the global scene and certain "withdrawal" from geopolitics at the forefront for reasons of resilience ("geotechnical ensembles", David Criekemans, IPSA, 15 July 2021, Brussels) and the easier handling of challenges in smaller units (subsidiarity) was to be observed. In this sense, regionalisation as a model of handling peace and security issues came up. The UN Charter had already prepared for this: In fact, it established regional organisations as implementers in Chapter VIII of the Charter. Realisation and use of this implementation chain until now remained, however, incomplete.

Chapter VIII clarifies that the universal System of Collective Security does not exclude the existence of regional systems of collective security as well. The purpose of this "subordinate level" is the supposed homogeneity of its players and their proximity as well as intertwined willingness and capability to end the causes of conflict.

As to the relationship between the global, regional (and local) peace and security mechanisms, the goals and principles of the UN Charter must be observed. That means that military force, with the exception of self-defence as inherent in the Charter, is only permitted when the regional organisation is authorised to do so by the UNSC. Furthermore, there is lacking consensus on what exactly is meant by "regional arrangements or institutions".

The most important regional players between the many recognised as Chapter VIII organisations are only on an exemplary basis listed here:

- African Union (AU); Economic Community of West-African States (ECOWAS); SADC (Southern African Development Community (SADC)
- Association of Southeast Asian Nations (ASEAN); Shanghai Cooperation Organisation (SCO); or QUAD (Afghanistan, the Central Asian country of Uzbekistan, Pakistan, and the US)
- Economic Commission for Latin America and the Caribbean (LATAM); Comunidad de Estados Latinoamericanos y Caribeños (CELAC)
- Arab League; Gulf Cooperation Council (GCC); Organisation of Islamic Cooperation (OIC)

- North Atlantic Treaty Organisation (NATO); Organisation for Security and Co-operation in Europe (OSCE); European Union (EU).

Potential of the regional level as part of the proposal in this book will be subject to analysis in Part III, Sect. 9.

Appendix—Relevant Articles of the Charter of the United Nations

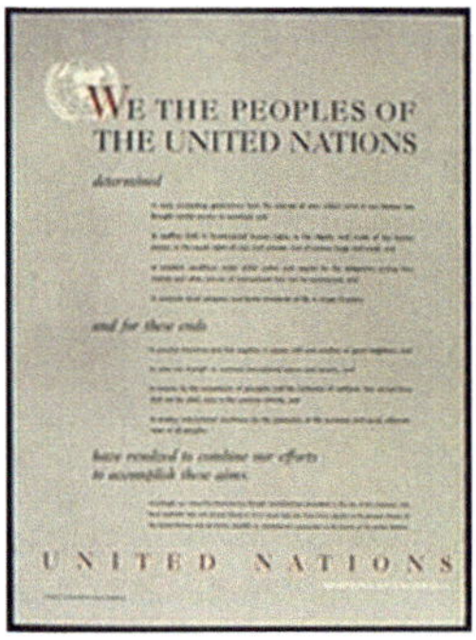

Article 1 [goals]

The United Nations sets itself the following goals:

1. to preserve international peace and security and, to that end, to take effective collective measures to prevent and eliminate threats to peace, to suppress acts of aggression and other breaches of peace, and to settle or settle by peaceful means, in accordance with the principles of justice and international law, international disputes or situations which could lead to a breach of peace;
2. develop friendly relations between nations based on respect for the principle of equality and self-determination of peoples, and take other appropriate measures to consolidate world peace;
3. to establish international cooperation to resolve international economic, social, cultural and humanitarian problems and to promote and consolidate respect for human rights and fundamental freedoms for all without distinction of race, sex, language or religion;
4. to be a centre in which the efforts of nations to achieve these common goals are coordinated.

Article 2 [principles]

The organisation and its members shall act in accordance with the following principles in pursuit of the objectives set out in Article 1:

1. The Organisation shall be based on the principle of the sovereign equality of all its members.
2. All members shall fulfil in good faith the obligations they assume under this Charter in order to secure for them all the rights and benefits of membership.
3. All members shall settle their international disputes by peaceful means in such a way that world peace, international security and justice are not endangered.
4. All Members shall refrain in their international relations from any threat or use of force contrary to the territorial integrity or political independence of any State or otherwise incompatible with the objectives of the United Nations.
5. All Members shall render to the United Nations all assistance in any action taken by the Organisation in accordance with this Charter; they shall not render assistance to any State against which the Organisation takes preventive or coercive measures.
6. The Organisation shall ensure that States which are not members of the United Nations act in accordance with these principles to the extent necessary to preserve international peace and security.
7. No authority of the United Nations to intervene in matters which by their nature fall within the internal jurisdiction of a State, or obligation of Members to submit such matters to regulation under this Charter, may be derived from this Charter; the application of coercive measures under Chapter VII shall not be affected by this principle.

Security Council—Tasks and powers

Article 24

In order to ensure prompt and effective action by the United Nations, its members shall confer on the Security Council's primary responsibility for maintaining international peace and security and recognise that the Security Council shall act on their behalf in the discharge of the duties arising therefrom.

In fulfilling these obligations, the Security Council shall act in accordance with the objectives and principles of the United Nations. The specific powers granted to it for this purpose are listed in Chapters VI, VII, VIII and XII.

The Security Council shall submit annual reports and, if necessary, special reports for consideration by the General Assembly.

Article 39

The Security Council shall determine whether there is a threat or breach of peace or an act of aggression; it shall make recommendations or decide on measures to be taken pursuant to Articles 41 and 42 in order to maintain or restore international peace and security.

Chapter VI—The peaceful settlement of disputes

Article 33

1. The parties to a dispute whose continuation is likely to jeopardise the maintenance of international peace and security shall first seek a settlement by negotiation, inquiry, mediation, settlement, arbitration, judicial decision, use of regional facilities or arrangements, or other peaceful means of their choice.

The Security Council shall, if it deems it necessary, invite the parties to settle their dispute by such means.

Chapter VII[coercive measures]

Article 51 [right of self-defence]

In the event of an armed attack against a member of the United Nations, this Charter shall in no way prejudice the natural right of individual or collective self-defence until such time as the Security Council has taken the necessary measures to preserve international peace and security. Measures taken by a member in the exercise of this right of self-defence shall be notified immediately to the Security Council and shall in no way affect its authority and duty under this Charter to take at any time such measures as it deems necessary to maintain or restore international peace and security.

Article 103 [normative prevalence]

If the obligations of members of the United Nations under this Charter and their obligations under other international instruments are inconsistent, the obligations under this Charter shall prevail.

References

Annan, Kofi. 2006. The address by UN Secretary-General Kofi Annan to the United Nations Association of the United Kingdom. London. https://www.un.org/News/ossg/sg/stories/statments_search_full.asp?statID=49. Accessed 8 Aug 2021.

Bellamy, Alex, Paul Williams, and Stuart Griffin. 2010. *Understanding Peacekeeping*. Cambridge: Polity Press.

Berdefy, Anlina-Camille. 2019. Auftrag und Möglichkeiten der Kommission für Friedenskonsolidierung im System der Vereinten Nationen, Staat, Recht und Politik – Forschungs- und Diskussionspapiere No. 9, University of Potsdam.

Bothe, Michael. 2012. Peace-keeping. In *The Charter of the United Nations*, ed. Bruno Simma, Daniel-Erasmus Khan, Georg Nolte and Andreas Paulus, 3rd ed. Oxford: Oxford University Press.

Curtis, Adebajo. 2012. *Peacebuilding, Power and Politics in Africa*. Athens Ohio University Press: 140–157.

Debiel, Tobias. 2003. *UN Peace Operations in Africa. World Domestic Policy and the Reality of Bruges Wars*. Bonn.

Eitel, Tono. 2008. The UN oligarchs and their privileges, Sucharipa Memorial Lecture, 28 May 2008, Diplomatic Academy Vienna.

Gareis, Sven Bernhard, and Johannes Varwick. 2014. *The United Nations. Tasks, Instruments and Reforms*, 5th ed. Opladen/Toronto: Publisher Barbara Budrich UTB.

Guidelines of the German Federal Government. 2017. *Preventing Crises, Managing Conflicts, Promoting Peace.* https://www.auswaertiges-amt.de/blob/1214246/057f794cd3593763ea556897972574fd/preventing-crises-data.pdf. Accessed 8 Aug 2021.

Haslinger, Birgit. 2017. The framework of International Humanitarian Law. In *Global Peace and Security. International Crisis and Conflict Management*, ed. Ursula Werther-Pietsch, 95–100. Vienna: MANZ.

High-level Panel (HLP) on Threats, Challenges and Change, "A more secure world: our shared responsibility", UN-Dok A/59/565 as of 2 December 2004. http://www.un.org/secureworld/report.pdf. Accessed 8 Aug 2021.

Ipsen, Knut. 2018. *International Law*, 7th ed. Bochum - Munich: C. H. Beck.

Ischinger, Wolfgang. 2018. *World in Danger*. Berlin: Econ Verlag.

Kant Emanuel. 1795. *Preliminary Articles for Perpetual Peace Among States.* https://www.constitution.org/kant/perpeace.htm. Accessed 8 Aug 2021.

Krisch, Nico. 2012. Kommentar zu Article 39. In *The Charter of the United Nations*, ed. Bruno Simma, Daniel-Erasmus Khan, Georg Nolte and Andreas Paulus, 3rd ed. Oxford: Oxford University Press.

Paulus, Andreas L. 2001. *The International Community in International Law*. Munich: C.H. Beck.

Rensmann, Thilo. 2012. Reform. In *The Charter of the United Nations*, ed. Bruno Simma, Daniel-Erasmus Khan, Georg Nolte and Andreas Paulus, 3rd ed. 25–69. Oxford: Oxford University Press.

Santner, Friedarike. 2021. Localisation as a principle. In *Powering Universalism*, ed. Ursula Werther-Pietsch, 270–280. Vienna: Klein Publishing.

Van Oosterom, Karel. 2020. With an Orange Tie. A year on the Security Council, Powerpoint Presentation IPI New York, 23 July 2020.

Chapter 5
How To Do It—Strategies of Intervention

5.1 Coping with Security Dimensions

General Preconditions and Inclusive Scope

The consolidation of power in a state or society from fragility to resilience is usually equated with *struggles for hegemony* (Warrior/Buckel/Fischer-Lescano/Gramsci). The argued importance of domestic reconciliation, elections and institution building for sustaining peace illustrates that the intrinsic motivation for state-building is linked to the holding of centres of gravity, more idealistically meaningful participation in decision-making and an overall aspiration to access to resources. In general, power means the ability to assert one's own interests in competition with others (Nida-Rümelin, Salzburger Festspiele, 26 July 2021). If this is managed over time without recourse to arms, an essential feature of democracy is realised: Society-wide cooperative interaction for the peaceful balance of all legitimate interests, building a self-contained resilient and strategically autonomous entity, which may be defined as the desired end state of external intervention. Each formation of a stable social structure thus has to do with the interface of the involved actors and the formation of order, based on a specific relationship of system-shaping elements.

Security Demands in Fragile Settings

In line with this, the concept of *responsible democratic governance* operationalises domestic responsibility: Legitimate, transparent and accountable governance can best circumscribe this principle of limited exercise of power, which characterises democratic contexts. The added value lies in the combination of inclusion and accountability in order to guarantee legal certainty. Elements of democracy support rules-based and inclusive governance and can lead to sustainable peace solutions (V-DEM Institute 2020). The strict combination of external engagement in fragile situations with sustainability in political life could be a decisive step forward compared to earlier state-building approaches. This encompasses the justice and security sectors which are equally subject to democratic accountability and control.

U. Werther-Pietsch, *Transforming Security*, Global Power Shift,
https://doi.org/10.1007/978-3-030-87097-3_5

The international consensus in the Paris Declaration of 2005 and the broad-based International Dialogue on Peacebuilding and State-building guided by the OECD and the g7 + countries from 2008 onwards reflected the growing political will to lay the foundations for responsible democratic governance in fragile situations (OECD State-building Guidance 2010). As expressed in the ACP-EU 2000 and its respective successor agreement, the EU Consensus on Development of 2005 or the 2015 SDGs, this societal orientation is linked to the insight that

> *[s]tates are not only abstract entities, [but] are also the organization of human beings who have formed a political community to determine their common life.* (Simma 2009)

Of course, security is a sensitive issue for all state cabinets. In this sense, actors of the new cooperative intervention logic do not present themselves as "regime changer" but accompany and reinforce processes with regard to the legitimacy and responsibility of political decision-makers and thus makes social systems more resilient.

5.1.1 The Case of Sovereignty

When it comes to international responsibilities, it should be reiterated that IL in principle does not interfere in the domestic sphere. Developments in various areas of law have, however, contributed to internationalising internal affairs insofar as they

- responded to the *human rights movement,* and—most clearly established by international criminal law—
- addressed *extremely fragile situations* as "*shocking human conscience*",

giving ultimate reason to international interventions.

In general, international law demanding a certain internal behaviour of states in order to comply with human rights relativizing sovereignty by means of "good governance" (Herdegen 2019) remained rare:

- International statutory law
  - *International criminal law*: Since the entry into force of the Rome Statute in 1998, genocide, war crimes and crimes against humanity (from 2017 onwards complemented by the element of "war of aggression") can be individually punished under international criminal law (waiver of immunity, cf. Pinochet case, ICJ 2001[1]; "*widespread or systematic attack directed against any civilian population*", Article 7 ICC; Dubler and Kalyk 2018; ILC Report, 2019, A/74/10 as of 20 August 2019). Application though reveals politically sensitive questions of interpretation with often open outcomes.
  - *Special regimes/law of contract*: Compliance to international rules usually manifests itself internationally in adopting and implementing special

[1] https://www.icj.org/crimes-against-humanity-pinochet-faces-justice/. Accessed 8 August 2021.

regimes like climate protection treaties, disarmament, arms control and others. The rules-based international order, above all for the protection, preservation and sustainable use of natural resources, developed a number of sovereignty-restricting conventions imposing obligations that can significantly damage the international legitimacy of rulers in the event of a breach (Fridays for Future movement and "climate claims" such as 2021 at the ECHR). This was reflected in recent steps of withdrawal that have been announced or realised by countries like the USA in 2019 (Climate Protection Convention; JCPOA), primarily for economic reasons and strategic competition.

- *Soft law*: Concern for internal dimensions of security and human rights led to the establishment of standards of state recognition such as the Copenhagen accession criteria for EU enlargement during the 1990s or in the peace process in South-East Europe (report of the Badinter Commission 1990 to 1993, especially No. 2 1992). This debate disappeared in the following years from public discourse, nevertheless remained on the agenda of bureaucracies to be re-intensified and popped-up again later in the 2020 Work Programme of the European Commission featuring a proactive West Balkan policy, or in the EU Turkey relations.
- *Supranational organisations*: In federal groupings of states such as the EU, an institutional division of labour both in the legislative and executive branches always favours multi-layered solutions, constantly fighting overloaded national interests and aspirations. That is why institutions themselves need a system of checks and balances due to intrinsic dynamics of national lobbying, appointment procedures and procurement.

A more progressive normative consolidation of these traits of relativisation of sovereignty in IL would clearly mean a general limitation in political leeway of states and is therefore met with reluctance by states. This position is also supported by the older position of the ICJ on "judicial self-restraint" addressing non-justifiable dimensions of public life and governance and, formally speaking, Article 103 of the UN Charter.

As for the ICCM, a special regime on international transition law that would contribute to the establishment of responsive interim governance in post-conflict situations does not (yet) exist. The UN Charter only provides the criterion of "peace-loving states" when becoming a member of the International Community. As already mentioned, there is a significant trend that non-state actors, insofar as they operate government-like supply networks or hold local monopolies of violence and exercise quasi-state functions, are increasingly bound by the afore-described criteria. This is, of course, in general to be denied since IL does not oblige non-state actors to commit themselves. A unilateral obligation, however, depends on which intentions the regulatory norm bears and how it is drafted and designed, for instance, child protection in treaty law, UNSC resolutions or UN mission mandates.

OECD is especially focussing on work with social movements in a new "cadre" of post-pandemic engagement, tending to include all relevant actors and entities irrespective of what organic composition they are. Relevance, be it action or concernedness, matters (INCAF series June 2021). So, policy frameworks exist for almost the entire spectrum of actors. Two of the most important layers in ICCM are described below.

5.1.2 Triple Nexus

Today, 90% of humanitarian operations last more than three years, with an average length of up to seven years (UN-OCHA). The serious consequences for affected societies, which last for decades (WDR 2011: 10) are obvious: fragmentation, polarisation, hybridisation (McGinty 2011). They are reflected in prolonged disruption and persistence in unresolved political tension zones, a reduction of the economies by up to a third of their GDP (African Development Bank 2009 in World Bank, and UNDP 2018), but also the constant marginalisation of vulnerable groups and thus a growing propensity to violence. How do external actors deal in practice with hostile environments?

In response to this, mutual dependency of military and civilian components in the ICCM—for example in the OSCE observer mission in Eastern Ukraine—may be recalled: Success in coping with acute basic needs such as the equipment of seasonal camps, electricity supply, schools, mobile health stations or centres equates the management of sound administration in the justice and security sector, information and democratic participation as well as mediation or medical health care in case of war traumas.

This led to a closer connection between "*humanitarian aid, development, and peace-building*", i.e. short and long-term perspectives in external engagement, "HDP thinking" or "Triple Nexus". At the occasion of the UN Humanitarian World Summit in 2016 and its "Agenda for Humanity" first reflections were set in this direction, followed by OECD studies and work at EU Commission and Council level. (Günther 2016: 147–150; Austrian Humanitarian Strategy, forthcoming 2022)[2] Efforts by the International Community to respond adequately to protracted crises should be reflected in the overall picture of a revised ICCM. The DAC Recommendation 2019 became the guiding policy document directed to the UN family in 2021.[3] The planning and design of external interventions must be adapted to meet these challenges. From there on, it is only a step towards improving a comprehensive approach in its conceptual and methodological foundations. In response to these donor policies, the "Sustaining Peace Approach" has been developed by the UN; accession of the UN family to the DAC Recommendation is planned.

[2] Under the Austrian EU Presidency in the second half of 2018, an intensive debate was held on whether, in addition to immediate and long-term aid in the sense of conflict transformation, an interwoven active peace policy should be pursued. However, it is impossible to imagine this early phase of state and social consolidation without the inclusion of the political aspect and it must therefore be included in the commitment while respecting the independence of the mandates. This position is i.a. laid down in the strategy of the Austrian Federal Government for development policy, the Three-Years-Programme for the years 2019–2021 of 19 September 2018.

[3] https://legalinstruments.oecd.org/public/doc/643/643.en.pdf. Accessed 8 August 2021.

According to those insights, the UN introduced a broad integrated methodology of working together by the UNSC in 2016 and incorporated the concept in its UNGA Declaration on Peacekeeping 2018. The core message of the Triple ("HDP") nexus is that several strands of action in ICCM run parallel and must therefore be addressed simultaneously, an understanding which is underway and will be complemented in discussions on practical implementation at the 3C Conferences in Austria (see Part I Sect. 5.3.1) as well as the Interim Report on the HDP nexus:

- Political and economic stabilisation in a tense geopolitical environment
- Reconciliation of the past for those burdened by armed conflicts
- Improving the short-term supply situation and
- Measures against resurgence of violence, (re)development of state structures.

5.1.3 Sustaining Peace Approach

The HDP nexus highlights the holistic approach of a multi-domain concept based on UNSCR 2282/2016 and pre-resolutions:

> *Recognizing that an integrated and coherent approach among relevant political, security and developmental actors, within and outside of the United Nations system, consistent with their respective mandates, and the Charter of the United Nations, is critical to sustaining peace.* (preamble paragraph 13)

To proceed with a bundle of security policy, humanitarian, development and peacebuilding strategies in crises and conflict scenarios, however, requires not only consistent programming according to one's own mandate but also "integrated action", i.e. managing successfully the operational interface with other players on the ground. (Starlinger 2012: 137–148, EU Strategic Compass: Capabilities and New Technologies – issues and ideas, 21 May 2021) Initiator and High Representative of the EU in 2016, Federica Mogherini put it that way: "*[W]e need to deepen the integrated approach*".[4] This view is connecting the ICCM with a holistic development-oriented perspective, the overarching aspect of sustainability (WDR 2011; Werther-Pietsch 2019: 155–166). By its orientation towards long-term and sustainable peace, the "Sustaining Peace Approach" refers directly to resilience; it can, therefore, be regarded as a valid conceptual basis for ICCM in the twenty-first century with the objective of creating more resilience and enabling peace by comprehensive action.

Consequently, the Sustaining Peace Approach takes a clear stand on the HDP debate treated above: Whether peace consolidation is part of the triple nexus package—ranging from humanitarian emergency aid to development cooperation—can become vital for the survival of those affected by crisis and armed conflict. With a view to lasting progress and in-country stability, it seems indispensable that strategies and interventions of external and internal actors used in the field be designed in a joint effort. Or, as Louise Anten of the Clingendael Institute in The Hague puts

[4] https://eeas.europa.eu/topics/eu-global-strategy_en. Accessed 8 August 2021.

it: "*All peace and state-building measures must be taken in such a way that they structurally prevent a relapse into armed conflict.*"

ICCM is, therefore, a cross-actor endeavour in the sense of a comprehensive, multi-domain, integrated engagement, which is today confronted with the following challenges:

- **Interaction of civil actors and military forces**
  In principle, independence of actors should be assumed as a principle (Thaler, Feichtinger and Werther-Pietsch 2015; Werther-Pietsch, Guest Lecture, YouTube "Videos UWP", 5 Oct 2021). In practice, however, collateral damage of military actions on civil society aid programmes, such as the attack on a hospital in Eastern Ukraine, in January 2018, is not uncommon (EJIL 30/2019 No. 2). On the one hand, this underlines necessary delimitations of the different actors "in theatre". Mutual effects require steady attention at the interface. So, humanitarian personnel must be distinguished from other civilian actors in order to enjoy both acceptance and personal safety. On the other hand, the military may and must be able to carry out humanitarian tasks if no other assistance is available, for example, because civilian aid convoys do not have access to the crisis area (Vienna 3C Appeal, Principle 13). The progressive flexibilisation of mandates favours an approach based on principles and adapted to the respective context. In response to the diffuse geopolitical situation, this often appears to be the only viable path.
- **Intertwined roles and simultaneity**
  Findings of a British-Scottish research project with Austrian participation on "political settlements" presented in London, in 2018, confirm the connection between state-building and sustainable peace structures, an insight that underpins concepts of joint action (Bell and Pospisil 2017). The following factors can be quoted for the widely accepted "simultaneousness" of today's ICCM fields of action:

  - Since 2010, state-building doctrine has been characterised by the focus on state service and accountability. Legitimacy at international and (sub-)national level, the so-called "*political settlements*", and informed politisation are processes that have emerged particularly during the upheavals in the Arab countries.
  - In addition, dealing with non-state armed groups has become increasingly important for development actors. Mighty networks typically replace state functions where these are weak or non-existent at all. They benefit from increased mobility, also of ideas, and form adaptable supply structures whose leading elites may act in a fundamentalist and violent manner.
  - Finally, the principle that any intervention is political cannot be ignored: whether diplomatic, economic, military, humanitarian or developmental even changes the framework for intervention which is why, according to Schöndorf (2011), intervention can, to the maximum be impartial, but never neutral. Political leadership by local forces in the sense of self-determined transition is, therefore, of the highest priority.

- **Balancing act between neutrality of aid and sustainable peace**
  Does the argued simultaneity of the HDP approach really blur the principles of independence and impartiality protected under international humanitarian law? Of course, humanitarian activities are clearly to be separated from political purposes. First aid has to be delivered without distincion as to who this person is (Feichtinger, Werther-Pietsch and Barnet 2010). At the same time, synergies are to be created, as shown in the supply of water for people in need regardless of their ethnic origin or religious conviction. Equally, early peace-building contributes to the promotion of tolerance and social cohesion and thus has a conflict-preventive effect. According to ICRC President Peter Maurer after a visit to the Central African Republic in February 2018, emergency aid must also be sustainably oriented towards peace in order to minimise damage (NZZ, 9 Feb 2018). Building on this, Maurer later draws parallels between the COVID-19 crisis and experiences of polio pandemic in Afghanistan, North-Nigeria and Kongo; malaria in Bolivia and Venezuela to demonstrate that health, security and political implications of big external shocks are intrinsically linked together (Press statement on 30 March 2020; *TDHJ podcast*, 19 Feb 2021). The very question is not to become party to the conflict or as a mediator, facilitator or donor in a peace process. This is all the more true when failed states institutions are weak and cooperation with the non-state sphere rises.
- **Localisation: Strengthening local capacities for political freedom**
  "Turn to the local"—local actors as first responders—is one of the most important demands of the ICRC's World Disasters Report 2015 to increase the efficiency of external commitments. In addition, there is the dilemma of "shrinking space" which reveals a certain dependence of first aid on the political nomenclature of a post-conflict situation (Christianaid 2015; Santner in Werther-Pietsch 2021: 270). A classic example is the mass expulsion of NGOs from Rwanda shortly before the outbreak of the genocide in 1994, as well as the emergence of Asian centres of self-revolving autocracy nourished by centralised and decentralised monitoring methods, a fact that think tanks and conference forums repeatedly emphasise (Berlin Peace-building Forum 2015; Basler Peace Talks 2018). The 3C Annual Meeting 2017, in Schlaining, summarises the debate by saying that political space for local actors—as part of modern peace-building—can support humanitarian operations. This understanding has since built an essential part of the debates between 3C stakeholders.
- **Digitalisation, e-Governance, social media**
  An essential aspect to consider in modern ICCM is the phenomenon of digitalisation (Boccone, seminar paper at University of Graz, 2020). In public life, creating progress and stimulating positive effects in the virtual space (e-Governance), as well as emerging disruptive technologies of advanced forces, need rules and protection so that equal access for all is guaranteed and inclusive decision-making is legally protected (UNSG Road Map of June 2020). Equally important is the access for rapporteurs, open discussion, the early sorting out and detection of *fake news* or hate speech (social media). This plays into the ICCM to the extent

that new protection tasks arise, also vis-à-vis big tech "Power Houses" (Wank in Werther-Pietsch 2021: 255–269).

The connections between digitalisation, cyber security and democratisation are evident (Kettemann in Werther-Pietsch 2020: 96–100). As early as 2017, the Global Commission for Stability in Cyberspace proposed to adopt universally applicable standards to protect the stability and integrity of the internet: governmental and non-governmental actors should no longer be allowed to take measures—even laws—to endanger the technical essentials of the internet (IP addresses, routers, internet nodes, submarine cables). In 2018, 64 states and almost 700 non-state actors in the Paris Call declared their support for more trust and security in cyberspace (Report of the German Federal Government's Global Change Advisory Council, 2019). The increasingly stronger protection of the Internet under customary IL, especially the concretisation of the obligations flowing from the cooperation principle and the precautionary principle, intensifies the regulatory endeavours around essential questions and makes it an issue of global reach.

However, the broadband internet can be used as an effective means of democratic inclusion and the strengthening of civil society engagement. At the same time, in addition to protecting individual freedoms, the International Community must also be attentive to help ensure the preconditions for social cohesion which is a major challenge in view of the privatisation of platforms and the destabilisation of shared information resources, communication practices and media portfolios. Free internet communication is as basic for an open society as it is crucial as a prerequisite for a functioning democracy. Cyber security is closely linked to the stability, robustness, resilience and functionality of the internet and other critical infrastructure. Cyber security can be threatened by cybercrime and cyberterrorism, but also by a lack of legal and technical cooperation between states to make the internet work for all and a lack of preventive measures, such as the development of crisis intervention centres and teams and inadequate transnational crisis communication structures for cyber incidents. Boundaries between preventive and reactive cyber-defence still remain unresolved (Schröfl in Werther-Pietsch 2021 238–250).

To summarise the above, lessons of interaction, localisation, the need for neutrality and digitalisation revolutionise and guide novel external action:

- Respect for the sustainability dimension as a guiding principle (lessons learned from the SDGs)
- Stop the misunderstanding that a holistic approach means every actor must be all-inclusive replacing it by a functional "patchwork of interactive tools" (specialisation in an integrated framework), connected with
- Stimulation of an improved technologically experienced and IT-facilitated strategy on the ground and well-coordinated joint learning.

5.2 Fields of Action[5]

5.2.1 Classic Civil-military Components

Article 2 (3) of the UN Charter reads:

> *The members of the UN shall settle their international disputes by peaceful means in such a way that world peace, international security and justice are not endangered.*

Where this is the case, there is a subsequent moral or legal obligation—depending on the interpretative point of view—emanating from the spirit of the Charter, to pursue an active peace policy in the sense of combined civil and military intervention.

The methods of external engagement range from the need to stabilise the security situation in the short term, to peace-building measures in the transition phase, and the long-term vision of a stable, resilient state (DFID 2009; INSCT 2009). Accordingly, areas of application in the field of peace and state-building are all-encompassing from preventive diplomacy, transitional justice, human rights dialogues, inclusion, the role of women in peace processes, mindfulness-based approaches of mediation and supporting new political settlements, security sector reform (SSR), promotion of social entrepreneurs, media work and fair digitalisation as well as disarmament, demobilisation and reintegration (DDR) in the form of community violence reduction (Werther-Pietsch 2014: 232–233). These core areas which basically were compiled in the 2003 UN Handbook on Multidimensional Peace Operations, show both synergies and antagonisms, sometimes leading to heavy tensions in coordination and therefore requiring the clearest possible division of labour.

A vital clarification was contributed by Tobias Debiel and Nils Goede: An important distinction shall be mentioned at the beginning: In contrast to military conflict management, civil conflict management deals with the prevention and non-military containment of violent conflicts as well as the promotion of social, political, economic and cultural conditions that promote the peaceful handling of conflicts within and between societies (Debiel and Goede 2009: 194–207; Weller 2007 : 9–18).

Humanitarian Action

Humanitarian action refers to any action aimed at "*alleviating a population's acute need and clearly distinguishing itself from political, economic or military aid, since it is based on humanitarian motivation and pursues humanitarian objectives only*" (Swamy 2000: 233). In the UN Secretariat, the Office for the Coordination of Humanitarian Affairs (OCHA) is responsible for this field. Together with the *World Food Program* (WFP) based in Rome, food aid and food security have become one of the major objectives of the humanitarian complex. On EU level, DG ECHO performs the coordination of member states and runs its own resources for humanitarian action programmes. Since 2018, there has been intense debate as to whether the link between

[5] The overview given updates the results of the annual symposium of the Austrian National Defence Academy 2013 (AG under the direction of the author) as well as materials of the XXI Austrian General Staff Course 2019.

peace, security and development must be reflected in operational work. This is against the background that humanitarian action must satisfy the principles derived from the IHL such as impartiality and neutrality (Haslinger in Werther-Pietsch 2017: 98). These principles also empower the ICRC to effectively exercise responsibilities like visiting prisons or family reunification.[6] Nevertheless, the HDP nexus has growing backing from doctrine and will change methods of working with a view to coordination.

Peacekeeping

In the last 40 years, the scope of peacekeeping activities has expanded considerably on the basis of Chaps. 6 and 7 of the UN Charter: Cold war and the prohibition of intervention initially necessitated an international presence in crisis and conflict zones reduced to the mere prevention of armed conflict (in detail see Part III Chap. 8). Today, peacekeeping mandates include not only the creation of a secure environment and the protection of civilians, but also peace-building activities. (Gareis and Varwick, 2014) Having said this, the term peacekeeping has a wider application area than originally intended. UN-USG Alain Le Roy summed up this smooth transition in a statement to the UNSC on 12 February 2010: "*Many of our Peacekeeping missions are early Peace-building missions*". This is all the more relevant for transforming PKOs into modern ICCM instruments. The monitoring of cyberspace by "cyber patrolling" to protect freedom of expression on the internet is, for instance, a possible future task for peacekeepers. Given the actual insights in practice and academic discourse, peacekeeping will certainly serve enlarged tasks in near future (Belgian initiative on Peacekeeping and Peace-building; EU-wide Initiative on Strengthening EU multilateral action in the areas of Peace-building and Peacekeeping, 27 April 2021).

Peace-Building

The goal of peace consolidation is to open up a sustainable, non-violent way for the state and society to resolve conflicts. Peace-building, therefore, begins with mediation activities at various levels (Track I-III) and the training of "facilitators" for such predominantly intra-societal processes. This interface combines directly security and development policy approaches, as stated in the Austrian Strategic Guideline on Security and Development 2011.[7] Peace-building is assumed to be most effective to start before the end of armed conflict and formal peace agreements, as Sabine Kurtenbach rightly states in an INEF Policy Brief 5/2009. Shaped by a human rights approach in development policy, peace-building activities turn, in particular, to vulnerable groups and aim at strengthening and empowering the individual and marginalised parts of society (Werther-Pietsch 2009). From these findings and as a result of the teleological dynamic interpretation of the UN Charter, the Sustaining Peace Approach confirms the predominance of peace support as teleological centre over all other policy areas and fields of action.

---

[6] https://www.icrc.org/de/node/7450. Accessed 19 February 2021.

[7] http://www.entwicklung.at. Accessed 30 June 2021.

State-Building

In contrast, the older more economic term "post-conflict reconstruction", still used synonymously with the politically more sensitive state-building, refers primarily to activities of effective political democratisation and the security sector. State-building is driven by continuous, but non-linear, processes to interdependently strengthen state capacity, institutions and legitimacy (Dudouet 2007). State-building processes concern core functions of modern statehood, measured by the satisfaction of society's expectations of the state (OECD State-building Guidance 2010). They create the capacity to fulfil basic functions such as security, the rule of law, income generation transparent and gender-sensitive budget management, establishment of a framework for conditions of economic development ("inclusive job creation") as well as basic services with access for all (PSGs 2011; Putzel 2009). Fair digitalisation is also becoming increasingly important for equal rights. The concept of institution building includes regional and local processes in the sense of subsidiarity and self-government (decentralisation). In this view, the concept of legitimacy in its various manifestations—through elections, performance or inclusiveness—which is central to the understanding of state-building is connected with peace-building.

> *Statebuilding and Peacebuilding [...] emerge as distinct but linked fields. Statebuilding and Peacebuilding both aim to assist societies move in directions that are conducive to sustained development and address over-lapping problems. What may vary is the emphasis: as Sisk and Wyeth put it, "Peace-building emphasizes helping states and societies move from situations of great peril to relatively greater safety. The emphasis within State-building is on helping in the transition from lawlessness or arbitrary authoritarian rule to government based on law to which there is general consent. But described in this way, the potential for synergy between the two enterprises is clear.* (OECD State-building Guidance 2010).

Conflict Prevention

To be comprehensive and effective, conflict prevention, especially in ethno-national areas, was given priority from the first half of the 1990s onwards (Dzihic 2010). Lessons learned from the field indicate a shift towards conflict-sensitive approaches in development cooperation, the strengthening of local civil society organisations active in peace work, and a focus on conflict mediation and transformation. Under UNSG Ban Ki-moon, for instance, a series of ground-breaking reports enabled the International Community to turn towards a "culture of prevention" in preparation of R2P. Here too, the boundaries between peace-building and state-building are fluid. A broad concept of peace-building includes qualitative activities, for example, in the area of confidence-building in public institutions, which can also have a preventive effect. The experience of the perpetuation of violent situations similar to civil war in the second half of the 1990s led to alternative approaches to war economies and the profit interests of local non-state violent actors ("spoilers") (Werther-Pietsch and Roithner, 2010). Overall, the main focus is on opinion-forming elites ("political settlements") as power factors. The above-described options for action form a circulus viciosus ("continuum"), as the figure below shows (Fig. 5.1).

Focus/Situation	Fragile situation in the run-up to an armed conflict	Open violent conflict	Fragile situation after the end of the armed conflict
Stabilisation (short-term)	***Conflict prevention/transformation*** and ***de-escalation***	**conflict management** *Crisis management, conflict transformation* and *stabilisation (peace enforcement)* *Humanitarian action*	***post-conflict rehabilitation*** *peacekeeping* *Peace-building* und *State-building* *Socio-economic development* *Digital Development* => ***conflict prevention***
Human Security (medium term)			
Resilience (long-term)			

Fig. 5.1 Multidimensional crisis management in the context of fragile situations caused by armed conflict (Time/strategy track—fields of action overview). *Source* Pospisil and Werther-Pietsch, Strategic Guideline on Security and Development 2011, adapted

5.2.2 Necessary Innovations Post COVID-19

A range of areas of action did not come to full glare till now, be it because they reflect recent emerging developments in methods of warfare, be it they are cross-cutting and should be better mainstreamed. According to new security-relevant societal challenges like extremism, racism, anti-semitism, xenophobia and radicalisation a regrouping of skills and capabilities is asked for. Organised crime and hybrid threats including cybercrime and vulnerability from outer space are part of the most important tasks to modernise UN peacekeeping. Not least, women peacebuilders, gender sensitivity of peace processes and post-conflict life, as well as pandemic health care dimensions should be pursued more rigorously. Digitalisation and environmental aspects of international presences matter and should also be more attentively taken into focus by mission leaders.

5.3 Comprehensive Approach

5.3.1 Whole-of-Government/Society Approach

The establishment of a common framework for interaction between the instruments and actors of foreign, security and development policy has come to the fore to stay (Bertelsmann, and CEPS 2020: 370ff). The spectrum of international organisations involved is broad and includes national civil and military, governmental and non-governmental, but also international organisations such as UNO, NATO, EU, AU, ECOWAS, World Bank, OECD, International Financial Institutions (IFIs) and others, each with a special "ego". Thus, the interaction of different actors on the ground regularly raises questions of common objectives and coordination mechanisms, as shown in the Afghan case, a probable game-changer in future ICCM (de Weck, forthcoming 2022; *TDHJ Special Edition #05 21*).

The Canadian "3D formula" (diplomacy, development and defence*)* can be seen as the first manifestation of what later built the so-called Whole-of-Government Approach (WGA) bringing together government actors in the wider range of ICCM.

From an institutional point of view, in addition to the now relatively undisputed main WGA axes other policy fields in and after armed conflicts as well as to their prevention became increasingly recognised. This movement was further triggered by the emergence of the Sustainable Development Goals (SDGs) at UNGA, in September 2015.

As demonstrated above, to act fully engaged in fragile situations, and in addition to the military, diverse civil expertise from the police to the health sector including the judiciary branch, the financial administration, education and information, social and economic sectors, sanitary infrastructure, climate and environmental expertise is required (DIMES approach: diplomatic, informational, military, economic/financial, and societal/cultural, Feichtinger, Werther-Pietsch and Barnet 2010: 17–22, 18). This applies both to planning for coherent national or multinational policy formulation and to implementation on the ground. In order for the actors to be able to master these tasks in their different frames of reference, it proved necessary to develop common mechanisms and principles ("Whole-of-Government Approaches"). When the interface to the international level is added, one speaks of a "Whole-of-System Approach" (Bertelsmann, and CEPS 2020: 7–9). Starting from an actor-driven perspective, the international debate focussed on activities and measures to be taken jointly—finally reaching a common understanding of the "comprehensive" or "integrated" multi-domain approach.

The Comprehensive Approach (CA) will—as a lesson learned of the COVID-19 crisis - continue to provide the framework for action for the ICCM. We expect rather to see its further development in the area of capability-driven interdisciplinary action and specialisation. As early as 2006, the UNSC stresses that

> *the need for a comprehensive approach through promoting growth, poverty eradication, sustainable development, national reconciliation, good governance, democracy, the rule of law, and respect for, and protection of, human rights*;

and underlines

> *the importance of a coherent, comprehensive and coordinated approach by the principal organs of the UN.* (UNSCR 1674, 28 April 2006, UN Doc. S/RES/1674, paragraph 2).

The discourse on the CA was conducted in NATO under the term CIMIC, "civil-military cooperation". This includes cooperation and coordination between NATO and civilian actors for the strategic support of NATO missions with the latest development in multi-domain strategy (CIMIC Center of Excellence[8]). Civil society humanitarian organisations have long been sceptical about this approach due to the implicit subordination of civil actors to the military agenda (AGGV 2009). The OECD, on the other hand, has classically stressed the interaction of civilian forces in the WGA and propelled a dominance of intrinsic development thinking. The EU/CMCO—somewhat more sensitive than NATO—called this interface "Civil Military Coordination", the USA named it "Interagency Cooperation". The Capstone Doctrine 2008 offers an overview of related fields of action, respectively, cross-cutting issues. (De Milliano in Gibbons and Heintze 2015: 17–30).[9]

On the part of academic think tanks, and with the research work of the Center for International Peace Operations in December 2020, this approach is aimed at.

> *resources of diplomacy, development cooperation, civilian peace forces and military and police security forces at national, international and local level to coordinate across departments and institutions and - through bundling or division of labour - to optimise their use with the aim of effectively dealing with international (violent) conflicts and thus contributing [...] to peace and security.* (Zentrum für Internationale Friedenseinsätze Berlin[10])

According to Brzoska and Erhard (2008), the civil-military relationship can generally be understood in a broader sense as cooperation of civil and military activities and actors focussed on coherence, based on the concept of comprehensive, integrated security:

- *Comprehensive security*: external and internal as well as civilian and military security aspects are closely linked
- *Integrated security*: division of labour among the state and non-state actors involved and security as an overall package (Österreichische Sicherheitsstrategie 2013[11])

In addition to the provision of physical safety, these security terms also promote the social, economic and democratic development of states and places good governance, the rule of law and sustainable peace-building on an equal footing and at the centre of intervention. From there, it becomes clear how the ever-increasing shift in the security policy mandate of peace missions to human rights protection has changed the original intention. Clarity, of course, needs to prevail as to the implications of this, in particular, with regard to risk management and the balance of geopolitical interests. Separate from this evolvement, the tendency of "mission creep"—a steady overloading of UN peacekeeping operations according to Chaps. VI and VII of the Charter—is to be observed, which suggests a turn to make "protection of civilians" the core task of UN ICCM 2030 (EU-Sahel Comprehensive Approach, Weiszegger UN Management Reform 2020). Lessons from Afghanistan will take the International

[8] http://www.cimic-COE.org/. Accessed 3 March 2021.

[9] https://www.un.org/ruleoflaw/blog/document/united-nations-peacekeeping-operations-principles-and-guidelines-the-capstone-doctrine/. Accessed 3 March 2021.

[10] https://www.zif-berlin.org. Accessed 21 April 2021.

[11] http://www.bka.gv.at/site/3503/default.aspx. Accessed 21 April 2021.

Community a step further (Werther-Pietsch, Guest Lecture, YouTube "Videos UWP", 5 Oct 2021).

The Role of Civil Society

Vienna Conference 2010, the Beginning of the 3C Process[12]

It is obvious that expertise and resources within this framework cannot only come from the state but are to be supplemented by Non-Governmental Organisations (NGOs) and other non-state actors. Local civil society is a unique mirror of the needs of the local population in fragile situations. NGOs working in fragile situations contribute to the process of linking states and their citizens through their access to local civil society and can thus work towards sustaining peace. The element on which the Vienna 3C Conference in the spring of 2010, therefore, concentrated on, following an integrated peace-building and state-building approach, the search for fruitful cooperation between state actors and committed civil society—across different approaches, objectives and working cultures. As a result, the Austrian 3C Initiative ("coordinated, complementary and coherent action in fragile situations") has included precisely these aspects in a jointly negotiated catalogue of principles for cooperation (Vienna 3C Appeal). This Appeal was presented to the EU in Brussels, the OECD in Paris, at the German Federal Academy for Security Policy (BAKS) in Berlin and the Federal Department for Human Security and Swisspeace in Bern, and was further developed in subsequent years. (Bertelsmann, and CEPS 2020: 49) 3C dialogue entered in an annual stakeholder conference and the underlying strategy will be revised during 2022.

Principles of the Vienna 3C Appeal

In the *Vienna 3C Appeal* of 26 October 2011,[13] the impulses of the various policy communities in the fields of diplomacy, development policy, military, financial and economic policy, police and justice, as well as of non-governmental organisations in the fields of development cooperation, humanitarian action, human rights protection and promotion, and peace-building, are brought together. Departing from joint negotiations, recommendations were acceptable to all engaged actors and paved the way in the longer term. The special element of the Vienna 3C Appeal was pioneering in the acknowledgement of non-governmental organisations as equal partners.

5.3.2 New Insights and Developments[14]

Further developments of the CA are based on the impulses set in the 2010s. The starting point is the identified congruence in the overarching objectives, which argue

[12] This contribution was developed together with Dr. Katharina-Anna Roithner, EAD.

[13] http://www.entwicklung.at/uploads/media/Wiener_3C_Appell_01.pdf. Accessed 21 April 2021.

[14] This section follows an essay by the author in *Austrian Military Journal* 02/2019; 155–166.

Players	Superordinate viewpoints / instructions for action
External Engagement / International Actors	
Humanitarian Aid	Emergency aid, lifesaving, neutrality in conflicts
Development cooperation	Long-term perspective, links between security and development
Peace policy work	Peace perspective, non-violence (pacifism), conflict transformation
Military actors	Containment of violence by military means
External engagement in fragile situations overall	Concept of human security
Internal / Actors at national level	
Strategic/political actors (Political parties, government officials, elites, economy, minorities, religious communities, separatists, *spoilers*...)	Power, Influence, Hegemony Striving economic superiority, Use of weapons, legitimation strategies..., Fundamentalisms

Fig. 5.2 Limited cooperation of constructively motivated *stakeholders* in a crisis region (own source)

for an operational management and at the same time also against a mutual interrogation of the different perspectives, which can be summarised in the figure below (Fig. 5.2).

The Overseas Development Institute and the Humanitarian Policy Group at Harvard University have illustrated the existing overlaps in a diagram parallel to John Putzel's work at the London School of Economics on the "Do no harm" principle (De Milliano in Gibbons and Heintze 2015: 17–30) (Fig. 5.3).

Following the analysis of the effects of the Sustaining Peace Approach, fields of action shift even more towards each other than is shown in the figure: The new approach is based on a combination that requires the flexible interaction of mandated tasks, an "instrument mix" or toolset. Action lines in the diagram above would consequentially be more condensed. Resilience is not reached within a certain timeframe, but ultimately depends on the quality of the fulfilment of the tasks themselves: The overarching objective ("endstate") of all sub-areas in the sense of resilience is the return to a state of self-supporting development ("to bounce back"; Werther-Pietsch, Human Security, YouTube "Videos UWP", 13 August 2020): https://youtu.be/gsDs-q4tzHI

> *The best way to prevent societies from descending into crisis, including but not limited to conflict, is to ensure that they are resilient through investment in inclusive and sustainable development.* (Pathways for Peace, Executive Summary, paragraph xviii)

The Triple ("HDP") nexus as described above finally brings together all fields of intervention at the operational level in Biscop's sense of a "full spectrum package" and can thus be regarded as a catalyst for an "Integrated Approach 3.0". The nexus is geared towards sustainable peace and a secure supply of basic needs and creates the basis for socio-political stability. Without conflict prevention and resolution of armed conflicts emergency aid and the effort to support a local perspective

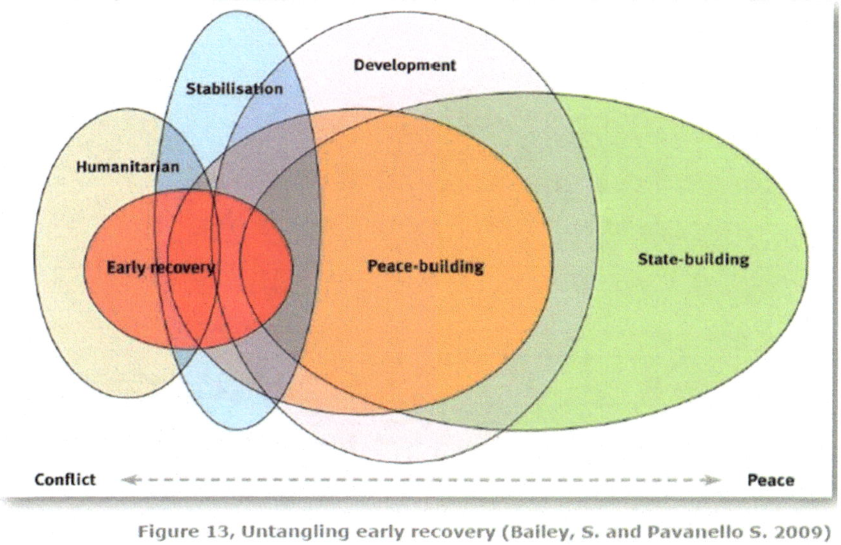

Fig. 5.3 The intrinsic simultaneousness of external action

is doomed to failure. The majority of ICCM actors at first instance responded reluctantly, often operating side by side in "silos", as described by the ECDPM 2014 as *"living apart together"*. In this sense, addition of an "S" for security ("HDPS") would signal even more clarity over the essential part of the security component and thus its co-responsibility for success (ICRC President Maurer and Werther-Pietsch, Humanitarian Space–Triple Nexus, *TDHJ Podcast*, "Videos UWP", 19 Feb 2021, https://youtu.be/zdu4itayH6o) (Fig. 5.4).

The imperative of being meaningful and responsive to each other can also be deduced from a human rights-based approach to development cooperation, which strives for the simultaneous realisation of political-civil and economic-cultural-social human rights for all (d'Hollander, Marx, andWouters 2013; HRBA Evaluation of the Austrian ADC 2021[15]).

Future Expectations

Practical experiences reveal the fact that there are regularly on-site coordination mechanisms versus strategies at headquarters and, as a remaining challenge, struggles for the development of joint assessments. It is equally important not to ignore the relationships between levels in ongoing engagements and missions. Therefore, future engagements will follow a capability-driven approach with a task specific profile. The starting point should be a "joint assessment" by all participants, a strategic analysis of the situation, from which common goals for commitment are derived and defined, a definition of means and a realistic timeline by which these goals are to

[15] https://www.entwicklung.at/en/. Accessed 3 March 2021.

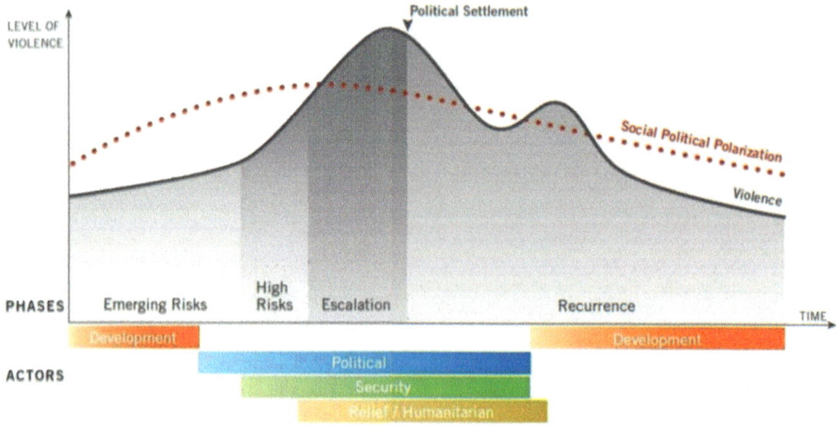

Fig. 5.4 Siloed approach to prevention. *Source* World Bank, and UNDP (2018): Pathways for Peace

be achieved. (Starlinger and Werther-Pietsch, Operationalisation of the Comprehensive Approach, YouTube "Videos UWP", 13 August 2020; https://youtu.be/Tb4tCV0RgPU OECD INCAF Meeting 3 June 2021) Only with such a rational strategy, which encompasses the dimensions of human rights, children in armed conflicts, women in peace processes, and the protection of civilians as aspects of human security that addresses human needs and opportunities (UNSCR 1325, 1612 and 1894), missions and operations in the context of fragile situations will have any chance of success at all. In this endeavour, coordination with the affected population in the sense of meaningful inclusion must not be neglected (Werther-Pietsch 2020).

Experience shows that some military commanders and their civilian counterparts, when equipped with unrealistic, non-integrative mandates and inadequate resources, in the past had to (re-)define common goals on the ground and create ad hoc coordination instruments. From the perspective of the 3C/CA approach, multidimensional operation plans should be guided by common strategic goals along with the established coordination tools and formulated in such a way that they are rightly achievable (UN Peacekeeping Ministerials, New York, 29 March 2019 and Seoul, 7–8 December 2021).

Evolution and Future of the Comprehensive Approach

Holistic approach	**Based on UNSCR 2282/2016, paragraph 11:** "*Emphasizing* the importance of a comprehensive approach to sustaining peace, particularly through the prevention of conflict and addressing its root causes, strengthening the rule of law at the international and national levels, and promoting sustained and sustainable economic growth, poverty eradication, social development, sustainable development, national reconciliation and unity including through inclusive dialogue and mediation, access to justice and transitional justice, accountability, good governance, democracy, accountable institutions, gender equality and respect for, and protection of, human rights and fundamental freedoms." (to be revised in Fall 2021)
"3C" Approach ***("coordinated, complementary and coherent action in fragile situations")***	**"Any successful operationalisation of a Comprehensive Approach in the future will be based on a couple of key elements**: – The sine-qua-non prerequisite is the willingness of all involved individuals, departments, and organizations to implement the approach, which would mean "a real cultural revolution – breaking with conventional thinking, and re-organizing to be able to work together more effectively." (NATO Secretary General Rasmussen, 2010) – The development of a Planning and Operating Mechanism and its tools to cope with the multi-dimensional interdependencies, be it civil security, political governance, economy & infrastructure, or social systems, as well as to carry out concerted actions on the basis of joint strategies. – A functioning interacting triangle of peace-building and state-building, consisting of the three elements transparency, ownership and progress (result-orientation and joint monitoring)" (Starlinger in Werther-Pietsch, 2017: 207f)
"Integrated approach" ***"Multi-domain operations"***	**EU Global Strategy, 2016** (further sources: SDG 16, A4P 2018, NATO Directive 2013, NATO Bratislava Seminar, November 2020) ***"An integrated approach to conflict management***: When violent conflicts erupt, our common vital interests are threatened. The EU will work together on peacebuilding in a practical and principled way and support people's security through an integrated approach. The implementation of a "comprehensive EU approach to conflicts and crises" through a coherent use of all EU policies is essential. But the importance and scope of this "comprehensive approach" will be further extended. The EU will act at all levels of the conflict and act promptly to prevent, respond responsibly and decisively to crises, invest in stabilisation and avoid a premature retreat at the onset of a new crisis. The EU will act at different levels of governance: Conflicts such as those in Syria and Libya have local, national, regional and global dimensions that need to be addressed. After all, none of these conflicts can be resolved by us alone. Lasting peace can only be achieved through comprehensive agreements based on broad, deep and lasting regional and international partnerships promoted and supported by the EU."
Effect-based and Capability-driven comprehensive approach	**Renewed intervention logic and Key CCCM principles**: The future lies in more precise, targeted and specified missions (Part III).

References

Brzoska, Erhard, and Hans-Georg Erhard. 2008. *Policy Briefing on Civil-Military Relations*, ed. Development and Peace Foundation (SEF). http://www.sef-bonn.org/fileadmin/Die_SEF/Veranstaltungen/PB/2008-11_pb_kurzbericht_de.pdf. Accessed 8 August 2021.

Christianaid. 2015. http://www.christianaid.org.uk/Images/ACT-Alliance-World-Humanitarian-Summit-jan-2015.pdf. Accessed 8 August 2021.

Debiel, Tobias, Nils Goede, Holger Niemann, and Robert Schütte. 2009. From new interventionism to R2P. *Die Friedens-Warte* 84 (1): 60–80.

De Milliano, Cecile et al. 2015. Resilience: The Holy Grail or Yet Another Hype? In *The Humanitarian Challenge*, ed. Pat Gibbons and Hans-Joachim Pat/Heintze, European Network on Humanitarian Action (NOHA), 17–30. Berlin: Springer.

D'Hollander, David, Axel Marx and Jan Wouters. 2013. Integrating human rights in development policy: Mapping donor strategies and practices. https://papers.ssrn.com/sol3/papers.cfm?abstract_id=2286204. Accessed 8 August 2021.

Dubler SC, R., and M. Kalyk. 2018. *Crimes against Humanity in the 21st Century—Law, Practice and Threats to International Peace and Security*: Boston/Leiden: Brill.

Dudouet, Veronique. 2007. *Surviving the Peace. Challenges of war-to-peace transitions for civil society organizations*. Berghof Report No. 16. Berlin: Berghof Foundation.

Dzihic, Vedran. 2010. *Ethnopolitics in Bosnia-Herzegovina: state and society in crisis*, Baden-Baden: Nomos.

Feichtinger, Walter, Ursula Werther-Pietsch and Günther Barnet. 2010. *Coordinated, complementary and coherent action in fragile situations—Die Wiener 3C Konferenz, Coordinated, Complementary and Coherent Action in fragile Situations—The Vienna 3C Conference*, Vienna: Schriftenreihe der Landesverteidigungsakademie 12/2010/S.

Gareis, Sven Bernhard, and Johannes Varwick. 2014. *The United Nations. Tasks, instruments and reforms*, 5th ed., Opladen/Toronto: Publisher Barbara Budrich UTB.

Günther, Annett. 2016. The humanitarian world summit—there are no short-term solutions to the challenges of humanitarian aid. *United Nations* 4: 147–150.

Herdegen, Matthias. 2019. *Der Kampf um die Weltordnung*. München: C.H. Beck.

Haslinger, Birgit. 2017. The framework of international humanitarian law. In *Global peace and security. International crisis and conflict management*, ed. Ursula Werther-Pietsch, 95–100. Vienna: MANZ.

Institute for National Security and Counterterrorism (INSCT). 2009. Project on Resilience and Security, Workshop Report: Longstaff Mergel, Ines, Armstrong, Nicholas, Syracuse University Patricia.

Kettemann, Matthias C. 2020. Zum Zusammenhang von Digitalisierung, Cybersecurity und Demokratisierung. In *Kollektive Sicherheit 2030. UNO Friedenssicherung im Wandel*, ed. Ursula Werther-Pietsch, 96–100. Vienna: National Defence Academy. Series Volume 3/2020.

McGinty, Roger. 2011. *International Peacebuilding and Local Resistance: Hybrid Forms of Peace*. London: Palgrave Macmillan.

OECD Statebuilding Guidance. 2010. https://www.oecd-ilibrary.org/development/supporting-statebuilding-in-situations-of-conflict-and-fragility_9789264074989-en. Accessed 8 August 2021.

Putzel, James. 2009. *Statebuilding in fragile situations*. London: Joint Study by the London School of Economics and Pricewaterhouse Coopers.

Santner, Friedarike. 2021. Localisation as a principle. In *Powering Universalism*, ed. Ursula Werther-Pietsch, 270–280. Vienna: Klein Publishing.

Schöndorf, Elisabeth. 2011. From traditional peacekeeping to complex statebuilding operations, status and further development of international peace insets. In *Strategie und Sicherheit*, ed. Johann Pucher and Johann Frank, 323–334. Vienna: böhlau.

Schröfl, Josef. 2021. Cyber power as main trigger of hybrid threats. In *Powering Universalism*, ed. Ursula Werther-Pietsch, 238–250. Vienna: Klein Publishing.

Simma, Bruno. 2009. Universality from the perspective of a practitioner. *EJIL* 20(2): 273ff.

Starlinger, Thomas. 2012. The comprehensive approach. a way to operationalize it in (Post)-conflict scenarios. In *Responsibility to Protect*, ed. U. Mathis-Moser, vol. 11, 137–148. Innsbruck: Canadiana Oenipontana.

Starlinger, Thomas. 2017. Creating a planning and operating mechanism—a stance by a military. In *Global peace and security. International crisis and conflict management*, ed. U. Werther-Pietsch, 176–209. Vienna: MANZ.

Swamy, Gita. 2000. Humanitarian Aid. In *Lexikon der Vereinten Nationen*, ed. Helmut Vogler, 232–239. Munich/Vienna: morawa.

Thaler, Mario, Walter Feichtinger and Ursula Werther-Pietsch. 2015. Together or strictly separated. *Die Furche*, 5 March 2015.

V-DEM Institute. 2020. Autocratisation surges—resistance grows. Democracy Report 2020, https://www.v-dem.net/media/filer_public/de/39/de39af54-0bc5-4421-89ae-fb20dcc53dba/democracy_report.pdf. Accessed 6 March 2021.

Weller, Christoph. 2007. Civil conflict transformation. *INEF Report* 85: 9–18, University of Duisburg.

Werther-Pietsch, Ursula. 2009. *Security and development—two pillars of a system?* Series of the National Defence Academy in collaboration with DCAF Geneva, S/2/2009.

Werther-Pietsch, Ursula, and Anna Katharina Roithner. 2010. Coordinated, complementary and coherent action in fragile states. NGO between Peacebuilding and Statebuilding. INEF Policy Brief 6/2010. Institute for Development and Peace, University of Duisburg. http://inef.uni-due.de/cms/files/policybrief06.pdf. Accessed 8 August 2021.

Werther-Pietsch, Ursula. 2014. Trends and innovations in civil crisis and conflict management—options for Austria, Annual symposium of the national defence academy 2013, Series vol. 1/2014, 71–96.

Werther-Pietsch, Ursula. 2019. Auslandseinsätze: Schluss mit dem Silodenken. *Die Presse*, Commentary, 2019: 32.

Werther-Pietsch, Ursula. 2020. *Women as drivers of inclusive peace*. Blue Helmet Forum Series, National Defence Academy.

World Bank. 2011. *Conflict, security, and development, world development report*. Washington DC: World Bank. http://wdr2011.worldbank.org/. Accessed 8 August 2021.

Part II
Towards a New Balance-of-Power Doctrine

Chapter 6
Changed Geopolitical Framework

6.1 Towards Trilateralism

Interconnectivity of IR and IL is a central perception of modern global affairs. Therefore, and to complete the preconditions for peace and security, changes of the current geopolitical framework is analysed with regard to explore its potential increating new solutions of peaceful collaborative power balance.

In this context, since 1989, circles of political science spoke in unison of an era of **geostrategic multi-polarity in two hemispheres**. Recent developments suggest that models further evolve and the picture gets more differentiated between old and new forms of multi-polarity, peripheries, centres of gravity and future proxies. Overall, observations of movements in geopolitical tectonics suggest that there are now two hemispheres, liberal democracies and more autocratic types of regimes (Freedom House 2021; V-Dem 2020; The Summit for Democracies, US Department of State, White House, 9-10 De 2021.[1] In this sense, the old multi-polarity after the breakdown of the Cold War, i.e. bi-polarism between liberal-democratic Western and communist Eastern concepts, lost ground in favour of a new big rivalry, calling for a triad of global players, acknowledging two opposing gopolitical centres, outweighed by entities of strong degrees of strategic autonomy at regional level, paving everybody's path. Additionally, the emergence of big-tech powerhouses and their interwoven impacts on sovereignty, the new "invisible hand" (Lukas Wank, Roundtable 27 May 2021[2]), will certainly shape future cooperation between the world powers. Approchement movements like a strategic closing of ranks between Europe and the US shall reconfigure China's geopolitical ambitions and leave a lesson to non-EU-friendly Russia.

---

[1] This section follows my article "Global Regionalisation and the Regionalisation of Security", The Hague Yearbook (submitted).

[2] https://youtu.be/7JylX_7LwkU. Accessed 28 May 2021.

U. Werther-Pietsch, *Transforming Security*, Global Power Shift,
https://doi.org/10.1007/978-3-030-87097-3_6

Trade routes by see, air and land, “sanctionism”, “weaponisation” of foreign policy, Western and Russian interests in the post-Soviet sphere, the fragility of the MENA region and nuclear insecurity are interfaces in which the interests of “rising stars” touch directly those of the P-5, and the P-5 among themselves—creating an explosive mixture. (ISS 2018: 9–13). The concept of the 1945 UN System of Collective Security in contrast builds on three major political premises of international cooperation:

- The global political and military dominance of the great powers on any aggressor worldwide (Kissinger thesis)
- The UN as an effective “buffer” for observation, peacekeeping and peace consolidation through peace operations (since 1956, Hammarskjöld’s heritage)
- From the immediate experience of WW II, the equipment with accepted means of coercion (effective multilateralism, responsible sovereignty) (Vitzthum et al. 2007: 627).

However, in normative terms, any intended “protection mechanism for the long peace” (GIDS, 2019) suffers from inapt assumptions in relation to the current challenges:

- With Antonio Cassese, the non-containment of conflict and war by the great powers can be seen as the main obstacle to establishing an ideal functional world legal order (2005: 352, Krause 2007: 17).
- Martti Koskenniemi critically adds that not only the Cold War and decolonisation processes, but also technical progress and particularly the expansion of the tasks of international organisations define the (lacking) functionality of the UN Charter: “Progress often moved from IL to amorphous systems of functionally specialised governance of international problems.” (2005). This ultimately causes gaps between decision-making and effectiveness “on the ground”.
- Equally, Ulrich Schneckener’s 2011 perception of the backlog of reforms—establishment of “club governance”, decline in efforts to achieve international legitimacy and failure to adjust representation in the UNSC—remains valid (inaugural lecture at the University of Osnabrück).
- In the COVID-19 crisis, geostrategic thinking all the more sharpened global constellations, giving rise to a regionalisation of security. Borders became again relevant, mobility reduced and interests turned to one’s own challenges.

The perception of the **fall of effective multilateralism** reflects the long exhaustion of international organisations that has characterised past decades and there is only one step from erosion to decline. Political science analysis and political consulting must, therefore, follow a twofold strategy: dealing primarily with the various “pairings” of the great powers, China–Russia, Russia–USA, USA–China on the one hand, and the untangling thereof through regionalisation, (re)emphasising, for instance, the role of the EU, as the preferable room for manoeuvre, on the other. (Gu, *TDHJ Special Edition #03 21*).

How are these premises impacting the operational framework of the ICCM?

After all, it is evident that large powerful states in a UN mission no longer start from ideas of idealistic "Weltinnenpolitik" (Czempiel) or "global governance" (Nuscheler), but from particular driving forces:

- *National interests*: protection necessities, critical infrastructure, vulnerable groups, resource management and capabilities, domestic and international legitimacy, strategic autonomy;
- *Geopolitical considerations*: contraction into regionalised security concepts, exacerbated by COVID-19, the perceived "vicinity" of hybrid threats and terrorism; rivalry of big players with so far no real "imperial appetite";
- *Intervention logic*: limited willingness to take risks, cautious calculation regarding the nature and scope of missions (Santos Cruz and Alberto report 2017), broad reluctance to meet the challenge of protection of civilians, resistance to long duration of missions, while perception of unsatisfactorily low regional influence.

Thus, efficiency considerations, risk-sharing and the degree of solidarity, maybe in a trilateral world, are played off against each other. A short profile to illustrate the "security mind-sets" of world players shall be undertaken below in a nutshell.

6.2 Current Power Puzzle

6.2.1 Chinese Dragon 2049

While China was the most active veto power during the Cold War (70% for reasons of non-intervention and stability), it is now the second-largest UN troop-providing state and contributor to UN peacekeeping. China currently (ISS News 1-2018) provides more than 20,000 people in 30 missions worldwide. The Chinese People's Army is also one of China's instruments which, in view of the 100th anniversary of the Communist Party in 2049, will stand ready to demonstrate the superiority of the "Chinese way".

Given these high figures, one has to compare them to China's reluctance in earlier intervention policy. It, therefore, seems unlikely that it will abandon its previous restraint in the near future. Despite a series of fairly aggressive steps like threatening gestures against the island state of Taiwan ("Formosa") and the "war" against people of the Republic of Hong Kong, high international tension zone of the South China Sea, the new Cold War scenario, and the Straits of Malacca, illegal isles in the South-Chinese Sea, a huge "debt trap" along "pearl"-habours and airports (e.g. Piraeus or Entebbe) increased economic engagement in Africa and the Middle East or the hot trade war with the USA, especially in 2019 and 2020, could of course quickly turn to social unrest and instability when a large-scale failure of state-citizen-relations, false labour market policies, etc. occur and turn into national unrest. What is certain is that a rising economic and technological giant (tunnel construction, high-speed trains, Mars conquest, Arctic run) with economic projects of global scale such as the "Belt and Road Initiative" (New Silk Road) should internationally be countered with more attention, sensitivity and "strategic intuition" than just erratic deals and rhetoric.

The "Wuhan crisis" has nevertheless made clear that China, as everybody in the world, is vulnerable. Handling the pandemic from the beginning lacked systemic - collaborative - protection of world population.

Beijing Consensus, hot war—cold war—or something other

Economic charisma, even when growth rates were reduced to one third during the COVID-19 crisis according to OECD reporting (Statement of 8 April 2020), rather than military expansion could indeed replace the Washington model for development. The latter is for the moment looking more stranded than the Chinese approach: China's economy has been growing disproportionately for 40 years and presents itself as one of the greatest "development successes" in history. Seven of the world's top-ten container harbours are operated by China. Observers say that China is not looking for a direct military confrontation with other great powers; but one day it could well ask itself with a view to the USA: "Can two tigers live on one mountaintop?" (Fitzthum 2018: 47–65) Trade relations between these two largest economies count for the most important in the world. Competition and aggression, even "rivalry" (Beeson and Li 2015: 93–100) such as sanctions under WTO violation have so far tended to emanate from the USA, as became clear during the World Economic Forum in Davos in 2019. One year later, the world watched when China built its hospitals in one-week time and was able to export millions of masks in the COVID-19 crisis when the first wave of the pandemic started in Europe and the USA.

China's self-image

To sum up, the former "spokesman of developing countries" is now on the threshold of becoming a global player with the largest army in the world (Reiterer, n.d.) The "Chinese Dragon" has thus developed from the "Five Principles of Peaceful Coexistence" of Indian President Jawaharlal Nehru (founder of the NAM 1961) and Party Leader Zhou Enlai, continued by the long-standing doctrine of President Deng Xiaoping (1979–1997), turning to the more progressive "New Asian Concept" 2014 and, finally, risky "actions on the high seas" of President Xi Jinping. These findings ascribe China a strategic leading role in the coming world, softly but steadily translated through Confucian Institutes spread all over the world. This changed self-image is also reflected in the June 2019 White Papers and Doctrine on Chinese National Defence. Peace in the region remains at high risk where manifest political system rivalry with the "West" occurs, such as in Taiwan and Hongkong. The main conclusions lie in the role of China as a rising star, attracting much attention (Winter 2021: 298–328) when viewing the US stumbling in the crisis like Jens Stoltenberg, SG of NATO put it on 14 April 2020, not to oversee its own problems on a big continent such as overcoming COVID-19 in early 2020, amid wide public resistance as to how the crisis was managed (e.g. "Dr Li movement").

6.2.2 American Bison Post-2020

Again in pole-position

In comparison to China's long breath, the USA seemed to be isolating itself more and more. Moreover, despite rich sources of production and enormous capacities in research and innovations, the US leader does not follow any strategic coordination model of thinking. Presidential elections in fall 2020 were decisive for further developments.

Repeated unilateral action of the Trump-led US administration, the only military "hyper" power in the post-Cold War Bush era (former French Foreign Minister Védrine, Le Monde Diplomatique, August 2008[3]), has also complicated manoeuvres in the UNSC. Clear signs of a gradual withdrawal from the current international order in favour of an interest-driven American "directness" are the abandonment of its membership in climate and medium-range weapons treaties which immediately caused massive reactions. In North Syria after the surprising announcement of the reduction of the US forces in December 2018, stark irritations on the ground were spreading like witnessing direct confrontation of major powers and alliances behind their "proxies" on the Strait of Hormuz in August 2019. The same goes for the window of 11.000 US troops from European Headquarters Stuttgart/Germany to Belgium. What remains decisive for the near future is the still existing military dominance of the USA.

A world player at a turning point?

Concerning the hot spots of Syria and Iran or recent develoments in Afghanistan, it is questionable whether the USA will stick to its geopolitically predetermined and calculable stance. From 2017, zones of external influence in Syria solidified, especially around military bases. Russia began the modernisation and expansion of its naval base in Tartus, commanded risky air strikes and a Russian-Kurdish training camp was set up in Afrin together with YPG. Russia negotiating for a cease fire in the region is therefore considered—much to Washington's annoyance—to be a "winner" in the Syrian conflict alongside Iran, and this despite recent complications with its "ally" Turkey. The USA supported by its "victory against the IS" remains present in parts of the Kurdish region rather due to Iran's influence, that has further been curbed by the killing of an influential Iranian general in February 2020.

We saw the USA increasingly neglecting international places of high fragility where it has always been present and a factor of stability as demonstrated in the Afghan case. With Biden administration, the commitment to multilateralism is back, e.g. the appointment of former Foreign Minister John Kerry as Special Presidential Envoy for Climate Change. "Trumpism", of course, can re-emerge in a few years so that the lesson learned for Europe unequivocally sounds cautiousness. The EU as the traditional ally in the "Western configuration", cannot shoulder robust international engagement in core conflict zones alone. China as a rival stands near. Recession in

[3] http://www.hubertvedrine.net/index.php?id_article=337. Accessed 21 April 2021.

the aftermath of COVID-19 will further sharpen the strengths and weaknesses of transatlantic relations.

Dealing with partners

Harsh confrontations of US President Trump with EU/NATO partners at international summit meetings from 2017 to 2020 were relatively rigorous. The USA, however indispensable part in the framework of NATO, had thus to a certain extent played itself off against its European partners.

The 2017 National Security Strategy aims to build on the strong political and military global presence of the USA under President George W. Bush (2000–2008) which raised criticism as being nationalist, neo-mercantilist and neo-colonialist. (ISS 2018: 21) The assessment of high volatility in the behaviour of the US under President Trump is therefore only partly correct: The withdrawal from the Middle East and the engagement with the North Korean leadership as well as the sanctions policy towards China and the cautious position regarding the establishment of an "Army of the Europeans" are steps relevant to foreign policy in a strategic puzzle that differs less from the other world powers by its internal messaging than in the twittered version of the muscle play of an "angry bison" as it was the case from 2017 to 2020. To this adds the lasting nuclear threat scenario following uncertainty about the future of the JCPOA and the sanctions regime on Iran. The Biden administration will probably have to stick to this line in principle. But "election lies" transported to the world's audience, repeated boiling up of President Trump in press conferences during the COVID-19 crisis contributed to the remaining open question of whether the US is ready to uphold its liberal "hyper" power status at the global stage. Against the retarded response to COVID-19 pandemic and rivalry between republicans and democrats in both legislative chambers, the brilliant vision of "America first" will have to turn into a constructive struggle to survive in a differentiated more alliance-like cooperation with partners. A successful fight against the pandemic and internal appeasement after the assault on the Capitol on 6 January 2021 will keep "democratic ally no. 1" busy.

6.2.3 Russian Bear 2036

Idiosyncratic interpretation of international law

The Russian doctrine of IL has always been concerned with constructing legality for its own behaviour and action. Against its ideological communist background, it is not surprising that this perspective on legal figures of peaceful coexistence, self-determination and sovereignty separated Russia from the rest of Europe, though originating from the same continent. With the new "sandwich effect" for EU and Russia between the US and China, relations probably have the chance to improve.

Bearing in mind that Russia has been "enemy no. 1" in times of Cold War, political relations and strategic alliance between Russia and the US, in particular, were totally opposed and lacked warmth even after the collapse of the Soviet empire (The Russian Federation's National Security Strategy 2015[4]). This, under President Vladimir Putin, to be possibly re-elected until 2036, sometimes worsened in recent cases of large espionage abroad (Galeotti 2019: 52) but was again reduced in COVID-19 friendly cooperation when the Russian President helped the USA with masks and medical equipment. A further provocation that is meant more against the USA but equally hits Europe's energy security is the pipeline project North Stream 2.

"Glasnost" and "perestroika" did not detach Russian foreign policy from the independent positioning it always sought in international affairs, for instance regarding its constant role in "the near abroad": the Chechen war in 2008, self-determination cases in Georgia and other "frozen conflicts" in the Caucasian neighbourhood (Fawn 2008; Halbach 2009 or, most recently, Nagorno-Karabakh (Steiner 2021, *TDHJ Special Edition #01 21*). The brutal elimination of regime critics like Litvinenko or Politkovskaya in the 2015s, the treatment of his opponent Navalny in 2021, a pro-Serbian course in South-East Europe and corridor and pipeline projects with China fall under this Munich category of "westlessness".[5]

In this sense, the pro-Assad position of Russia in Syria, its attitude to the nuclear power struggle with Iran, the alleged illegitimacy of Israeli attacks on Lebanon and Gaza including the shooting down of war fighter-jets by Russian technology from Syrian soil show the Russian diplomatic and strategic strength, which is traditionally nurtured by the narrative of constant discrimination and division of Russia and Russian citizens. Just as the West "exaggerates" human rights, Russia, the "third Rome", can be said of pursuing messianic ideas and possessive thinking in its vicinity assuming special rights as representative of the Orthodox church, interests of Russian-speaking populations and the right to use violence to protect "Russian citizens living in the neighbourhood".

Role in the UN

Russia's abstention from granting the R2P mandate for the no-fly-zone in Libya and its repeated refusal to do so in Syria with the exception of the use of chemical weapons reflects the Russian balancing act between non-intervention, self-interest and real assessment of the situation. Direct confrontation with the USA is avoided strictly. On the contrary, friendship and assistance, well disseminated in social media during COVID-19, prevail. Occupation of the Crimea and support for East-Ukrainian pro-Russia forces is rather a case against the EU "rule of law" empire to demonstrate the EU's inability of reaction when a massive breach of IL occurs (University of Bremen 2018).

Russia's overall attitude towards the UN can be characterised as follows:

- Partners among the G-20; rivalry but not militarily with the USA
- Friends among the BRICS, especially Brazil and India

---

[4] http://www.ieee.es/Galerias/fichero/OtrasPublicaciones/Internacional/2016/Russian-National-Security-Strategy-31Dec2015.pdf. Accessed 8 August 2021.

[5] Munich Security Conference on 14–16 February 2020, https://securityconference.org/en/. Accessed 8 August 2021.

- Support for the Assad regime in Syria
- Under the top-10 strongest troop contributor to UN peacekeeping
- Focus on IT based defence
- Nuclear power

Readiness for UN reform is only slightly pronounced. Above all, the *status quo* option of the veto right is maintained combined with a relative openness regarding the composition of the UNSC. (Sergunin 2019: 362).

As part of foreign policy instruments, military means do not appear to be the only or dominant of the "Russian Bear". Restructuring and containment of military influence under President Putin, Foreign Ministers Medvedev and Lavrov albeit in favour of the presidential power also contributed to this and makes Russia a difficult to grasp but a potential strategic partner of the EU. The media-effective cyberspace playground including intrusive tactics in cases of Eastern Ukraine or the COVID-19 pandemic as well as nuclear threat and China collaboration in the Arctic trade corridor will stay attractive for Russia. To complete the limbo, China and Russia opened a new cooperation format in 2016 with a joint declaration to strengthen the principles of IL, with a focus on territorial sovereignty and non-intervention—a bluntly anti-Western pact.

6.2.4 The Europeans 2050

The "E3" format

Daily telephone calls between Berlin, Paris and London could not hide nor prevent post-Brexit developments in the COVID-19 crisis and beyond: Less money for defence, less external engagement, a strategic reorientation of NATO-EU - members. France and the United Kingdom (in the following UK) as major European powers had before been neutralised by the close association of EU foreign policy since 1 December 2009 (Lisbon Treaty). In the face of growing Anglo-American friendship to be expected as a corollary to Brexit and the (formerly more) volatile Franco-German axis, different views are now brought into play. Squeezed between them, and all the more since the "enemy states" clause in the UN Charter was abolished, mediating Germany has been a country dedicated to multilateralism in a Kantian sense and a "hub of unselfishness". However, lately confronted with large-scale migration, German foreign policy partly turned away from unconditional solidarity commitment and offers cooperation preferably to "high performers" (e.g. Africa Policy Guidelines 2019[6]).

---

[6] https://www.auswaertiges-amt.de/blob/2203542/6274c1b95ddfe1126f9d466a8d9e10c5/190327-afrika-ll-volltext-data.pdf. Accessed 7 March 2021.

World power or *mini mundus*?

As an international player, the EU is one of the few remaining representatives dedicated to the UN as guarantor of a transparent, universal rules-based order. A fact that is clearly responded to in the European Commission work programme of January 2020: "The EC goes geostrategic", at least until 2050, and, not only in climate protection matters, will be more visible in the multilateral scene. However, although the 2016 EU Global Strategy focuses on one out of five pillars on reforming the UN, it does not contain any substantial proposals. The special future role of the EU may lie in the foundation of a European Security Council as a model for successful regionalisation of security (Werther-Pietsch 2022; Werther-Pietsch, 2021). The best option for Europe could be a trilateralism where the EU tips the scales between the great powers (Gu, *TDHJ Special Edition #03 21*).

Permanent Structured Cooperation—the European way

In particular, since Brexit, the EU is in a very interesting albeit delicate phase of its development in terms of defence policy. Incentives in the EU Global Strategy 2016 provided for in Article 42(6) and 46 of the Lisbon Treaty, as well as Protocol No. 10 to the EU Treaty, have deepened into a model of "forerunner of a common defence and security policy". Overall, and facing French resistance, the Permanent Structured Cooperation ("PESCO") aims at the following (Austrian Ministry of Defence 2019):

- Increasing defence spending in EU member states
- Medium-term increase of the share of the respective defence expenditure to 20 per cent of the defence budget
- Increase in defence research expenditure to 2 per cent of defence expenditure
- Implementation of joint projects, supported by European Defence Fund (EDF)
- Coordinated cooperation in the field of cyber defence
- Troops and logistics for EU battle groups and crisis management operations
- Joint budgeting of missions
- Strengthened competition in defence markets.

The establishment of the EDF in 2018 also contributed to the realisation of a long-cherished vision of European military circles in the spirit of a multi-domain capability-driven comprehensive approach. Positions regarding the deepness of integration in Defence and Security Policy, PESCO, CARD and EDF, Emerging Disruptive Technologies (EDT) and military mobility like Early Entry Forces (FAC 6 May 2021) and the Battle Group Roster are constantly debated at EU Defence Council in Brussels.

6.2.5 *The Newcomers of Today*

Developing and emerging new powers such as the BRICS or Turkey are grouped in this category. Ethiopia, India, Pakistan, Bangladesh, Egypt, Indonesia, Ghana,

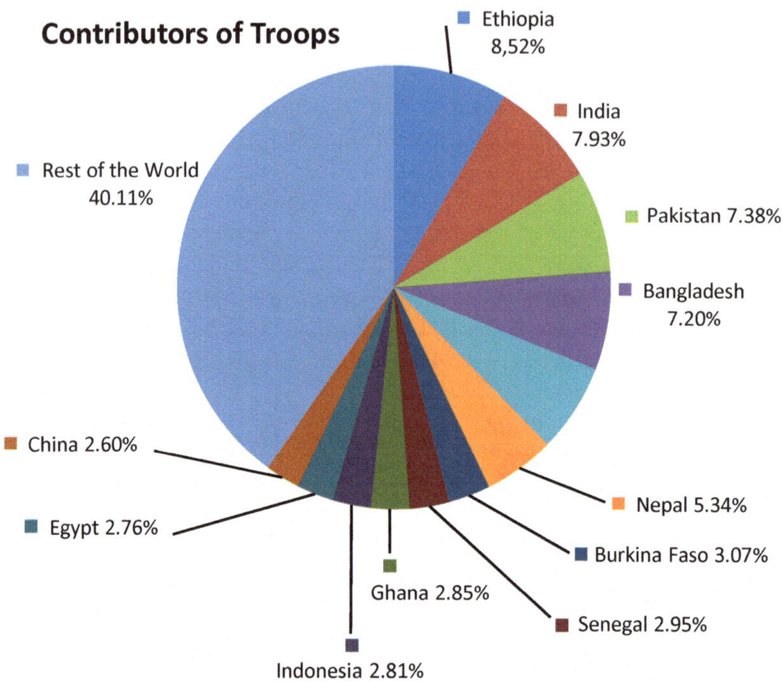

Fig. 6.1 Walter Feichtinger in Ursula Werther-Pietsch 2017: 87 (Illustration M. Eibensteiner)

Senegal, Burkina Faso, Nepal, Rwanda are among the most important TCCs in the UN context, by the way, most of them already have drone powers. Taken together, this is about 60% or more than half of UN peacekeeping personnel. Comprising upcoming stars and strategically important countries, they range from 2 to 8% (see Fig. 6.1 below).

6.3 Future Proxies and New Centres of Gravity

During the post-bipolar era, the game of the great powers has become more vulnerable. The growing weight of the middle powers, the courted "second world" (Parag Khanna, Lecture at International Security Conference of the Austrian Institute for International Affairs, Vienna Diplomatic Academy, 14 October 2009), dynamics of regional integration and IT-supported Facebook and Twitter and COVID-19 have altogether minimised political predictability and strategic room for manoeuvre (US Interim National Security Strategic Guidance, March 2021).

In sharp contrast to the early phase after the East–West conflict, now regional organisations themselves have to cope with intrinsic effects. One example is NATO's development into an offensive military alliance: the strategic change in NATO's course decided in Wales in 2014 as a result of the covert Russian Crimea intervention and aggression in Ukraine has been successfully implemented since then and underlines the flexibility of the 29 alliance members. However, in addition to overall US pressure, an increasingly authoritarian and less trustable Turkey (US F-35 vs Russian S-400a). NATO's cohesion is threatened by a severe internal erosion problem. Another case would be the deepening of AU–IGAD–UN cooperation, as declared in the Joint AU, IGAD and UN Statement of 12 April 2019, worth being examined more closely.[7]

Fragile zones such as the Middle East (Syria) or Latin America (Venezuela) emerge as "proxies" of Russia against the US, engaged in Colombia or Guatemala with tough peace and mediation processes. The euphoria about becoming a state in the decolonisation period has subsided and largely given way to clubs around multiple "empires" to finally find themselves faced with the new categorisation of the "alliance of democracies",[8] led by the US, versus China and the rest. Regional blocks gained influence on world affairs but have not been sufficiently granted representation in decision-making bodies of the UN like the UNSC. On top, large parts of the world population such as the Arab, Latin American, Asian or African group were generally marginalised disproportionately (Makinda and Okumu 2008: 86).

In summing up, the changes in the political framework, compared to the old strategic backyards managed from 1945 to 1989, are today shaped to a large extent by:

- Systemic rivalry between democracies and autocratic regimes
- Necessary reinvention of Europe and the West
- Chinese and Indian rising in the volatile Indo-Pacific region
- US to readjust its hitherto role of "global stabilisator"
- Russia's future after 2036
- Sunni-Shiite polarity and regional rivalry in the MENA region
- New hubs for progress and development especially in Africa
- To this adds the Pandemic with its subsidiarity and resilience impact.

Is there a "common denominator" in an adapted framework for peace and security system that works? The System of Collective Security of the UN, which is decisive for the post-war order after 1945 and which strengths and weaknesses have become clear in the confrontation with the changed conditions for at least two decades, must take account of these politico-developmental impulses. The fundamental compatibility of the concept of human security with the system as theoretically and practically established still remains a good entry point for doing this. Orientation towards "human-centrism" as political leitmotiv of the new intervention logic, while strengthening regional conflict resolution mechanisms and responsibilities is one of the most important takeaways from the analysis.

---

[7] https://www.peaceau.org/uploads/joint-statement-12-april-2019-au-igad-un-statement.pdf. Accessed 14 March 2021.

[8] https://www.allianceofdemocracies.org/. Accessed 7 March 2021.

References

Austrian Ministry of Defence. 2019. Sicher. Und morgen? Sicherheitspolitische Jahresvorschau 2020. https://www.bundesheer.at/wissen-forschung/publikationen/publikation.php?id=991. Accessed 8 Aug 2021.

Beeson, Mark, and Fujian Li. 2015. Geopolitics and paradigms in China and the United States. *International Affairs* 91 (1): 93–100.

Cassese, Antonio. 2005. *International law*, 2nd ed. Oxford: Oxford University Press.

Cruz, Dos Santos, and Carlos Alberto. 2017. *Improving security of United Nations peacekeepers (Santos Cruz Report)*. New York: United Nations.

Fawn, Rick. 2008. The Kosovo—and Montenegro—Effect. *International Affairs* 84 (2): 269–294.

Fitzthum, Robert. 2018. *Understanding China. From the rise to economic power and the containment policy of the USA*. Vienna: ProMedia

Galeotti, Mark. 2019. *We need to talk about Putin. How the West gets him wrong*. London/New York: Penguin.

Gu, Xuewu. Eine G3-Weltordnung. *TDHJ Special Edition #03 21*: 22–26, https://www.thedefencehorizon.org/special-editions?lang=dett. Accessed 8 Aug 2021.

Halbach, Uwe. 2009. "Georgia Crisis" and "Caucasus Conflict": The regional dimension of the recent war in the South Caucasus. *European Journal for Minority Issues* 1: 4–19.

Freedom House. 2021. Freedom in the World 2021: Democracy under siege. https://freedomhouse.org/report/freedom-world/2021/democracy-under-siege. Accessed 6 Mar 2021. Accessed 8 Aug 2021.

V-DEM Institute. 2020. Autocratisation surges—Resistance grows. Democracy Report 2020. https://www.v-dem.net/media/filer_public/de/39/de39af54-0bc5-4421-89ae-fb20dcc53dba/democracy_report.pdf. Accessed 6 Mar 2021.

ISS News 1. 2018. Vienna: National Defence Academy.

Koskenniemi, Martti. 2005. *From apology to Utopia*. Cambridge: Cambridge University Press.

Krause, Joachim. 2007. The international order in crisis. *International Politics* No 7/8: 8–20.

Makinda, Samuel M., and Wafula F. Okumu. 2008. *The African Union—Challenges of globalisation, security and governance*. Abingdon/Oxon/New York: Routledge.

Sergunin, Alexander. 2019. *The United Nations*. London: Routledge.

Steiner, Anna. 2021. Nagorno-Karabakh and Eastern partnership—Is there a role for the EU? *TDHJ Special Edition #01 21*: 22–25. https://ca9d3787-8643-4d85-9af7-d052377ac9b8.filesusr.com/ugd/0d3ede_730a5ba77e0c40fb9637da417752d0eb.pdf. Accessed 14 Mar 2021.

University of Bremen, Russia analyses no 362 of 16 November 2018

Vitzthum, Wolfgang Graf, Michael Bothe, et al. 2007. *International law*, 4th ed. Berlin: De Gruyter.

Winter, Martin. 2021. Chinas Aufstieg - Europas Ohnmacht. München. Langen Müller Verlag.

Werther-Pietsch, Ursula. 2021. EU key for strategic autonomy—A proposal. In *AIES yearbook 2021*, ed. Clemens Fischer. Berlin: Springer, 127-151.

Werther-Pietsch, Ursula. 2022. Global pandemic and the regionalisation of security. In *The Hague yearbook of international law*. The Hague.

Chapter 7
Dynamics and UN Reform from 1990 to 2030

7.1 "Milestones"

After its foundation in 1945, the UN peace and security architecture experienced many years of geopolitical dominance by the allies of WW II and later bloc-leading powers, additionally overshadowed by deep-rooted ideological patterns of the East–West confrontation. At the same time building and expanding the modern world of states, especially on the African continent, took place. Leaders at the beginning of the independence waves in the 1960s, 1980s and recent cases on the African continent embedded themselves reluctantly but smoothly into the global normative system with only limited waivers or were brought to accept the overall picture of the Washington consensus. Today the UN faces new extra-systemic challenges not least the COVID-19 pandemic, big tech governance as well as Emerging Disruptive Technologies (EDT; see Part I Sect. 2.2). Besides considerable risks of escalation, this evolution, of course, also offers opportunities for change.

In the following, important steps in the development of ICCM within the United Nations are carved out. This is an evaluative approach considering multi-layered overlapping events that can be interpreted in various ways. The purpose of this chapter, which is based on the analysis before, is, therefore, to provide an overview of historical and strategic changes with reference to the UN framework that explains the traits of the current System of Collective Security.

Those "milestones"[1] are:

1. Agenda for Peace1992
2. "The Age of Human Security"
3. Reform Summit 2005
4. Agenda for Humanity 2016
5. Agenda 2030 and Sustaining Peace

[1] The "milestones" analysis is based on Ursula Werther-Pietsch. 2020. *Kollektive Sicherheit 2030. Globale Friedenssicherung im Wandel.* Vienna: National Defence Academy, Series Volume 3/2020, complemented and updated.

U. Werther-Pietsch, *Transforming Security*, Global Power Shift,
https://doi.org/10.1007/978-3-030-87097-3_7

Fig. 7.1 Circular cognitive arrow

6. "The Age of Human-centrism"—ABPD

Milestones identified are broken down along a set of criteria in order to gain comparability and make it easier to understand trends and draw conclusions for sequenced developments. These criteria are:

- Integration into the geopolitical framework
- Trigger/cause
- Goals/objectives/characteristics/new elements
- Derived trends/intervention logic
- Operationalisation/balance of the range of instruments
- Global political commitment and willingness to reform ("mood"/motivation)
- Acting UNSG: Relevant for the "history of ideas"

Along the subtitles of the sections to follow, central messages and characteristics of a given period were collected. Considerations are based on a constantly evolving cycle of knowledge acquisition in response to political and factual events (cognitive spiral). Unlike decisions of full intention, however, progress in knowledge is neither reversible nor wrong. This may stimulate positive thinking in the sense of circular learning reaching ever higher operational capacity, as captured in the figure below (Fig. 7.1).

7.2 Agenda for Peace 1992

Situational overview

The end of the bipolar post-war order frames the genesis of the Agenda for Peace. Human-centrism is on the rise. This was triggered by a climate of openness and a preference for multilateral solutions with new institutions. New impetus came from human rights and the extension of the peacekeeping tasks to post-conflict situations. Regarding the intervention logic, a start-up of networked thinking is predominant. The focus of operationalisation lies in preventive diplomacy and peace-building. All actions are carried out in a "new beginning" mood under the visionary acting UNSG Boutros Boutros-Ghali.

- **Integration into the geopolitical framework**

7.2.1 *End of the East–West Conflict: Dag Hammarskjöld's Heritage*

The collapse of the Soviet Union (Union of Soviet Socialist Republics, USSR) in 1989 brought more personal and economic freedom and a considerable breakdown of stereotype dichotomisation of politics to the populations concerned, but also entered an era of growing oligarchy, opacity and corruption. "Glasnost" and "perestroika" (Russian: гласность: openness, transparency, publicity)—Gorbachev's reform programme—induced the end of the East–West conflict that had split the global political climate for decades. This move had been associated with the successive dissolution of the rigid "proxy" division into two hemispheres, the liberal-democratic West and the communist East. The then UNSG Boutros Boutros-Ghali was able to make visionary use of emerging pluralism and newly prevailing diversity for the UN.

- **Goals, characteristics, new elements**

7.2.2 *Peace-Making and Peacekeeping Are Moving Closer Together*

In January 1992, the Heads of State and Government met for the first time in the formation of the UNSC. The UNSG was commissioned with a study "*on ways of strengthening and making more efficient within the framework and provisions of the Charter the capacity of the UN for preventive diplomacy, for peace-making and for peacekeeping*". The latter then submitted the "Agenda for Peace", a far-sighted concept for institutional and operational instruments and structures to preserve the UN's peacekeeping task in the new setting of post-bipolarism. He added the concept of "post-conflict peace-building" to the mandate of the UNSC as an essential part of peace-making and peacekeeping for sustainability. The document is based on confidence-building measures, fact-finding and early warning mechanisms—an operationalisation and substantial extension of the good offices of the UNSG.

7.2.3 *Early Step for Coercive Action Failed*

The "standing forces" according to Article 43 of the UN Charter remained an unrealized point of discussion that reflects the idea of the UN as a "world police" and anticipates the responsibility to protect under IL. "*Consent of all parties*" as a criterion for mandating UN missions under Chaps. VII and VIII officially remained to be applied in all cases, although this had not yet been achieved in this phase. These at the time were controversial proposals which were dealt with in a supplement to the Agenda. In parallel and intensified from 1997 onwards ("Razzali Plan"), the debate on the reform of the UNSC unfolded slowly, which after its first failure was only resumed in the preparation of the 2005 World Summit.

7.2.4 *Concept of "Post-conflict Peace-Building"*

The "Agenda for Peace: Preventive Diplomacy, Peace-making and Peace-Keeping" of 17 June 1992 (UN Doc A/47/277-S/2411, § 21 i.) is the basis for the expansion of competences and the assumption of the UN far-reaching role in the stabilisation and post-conflict area, in connection with "Supplement to an Agenda for Peace" of 3 January 1995, UN Doc A/50/60-S/1995/1; Renewing the United Nations: A Programme for Reform, 14 July 1997, UN Doc A/51/950, § 66). The visionary concept valid until the Sustaining Peace Approach of 2016 closes a gap in the UN peace and security architecture by initiating a UN presence with the aim of progressive elimination of the causes of conflicts and long-term engagement, "*that entails the action to identify and support structures which will tend to strengthen and solidify peace in order to avoid a relapse into conflict*".

7.3 "The Age of Human Security"

Situational overview

Efforts to establish an ICCM framework and the huge process to set up the Millennium Development Goals frame the age of human security. This is based on progress in individualisation of security as well as development-sensitive action for vulnerable groups. A new Common Understanding on Human Security changes the hit-her-to intervention logic: UNSCR 1325, 1612, 1894 and the 2008 Capstone Doctrine translate this approach. Regarding operationalisation, the Brahimi Report (2000) leads the reform process of peacekeeping. All action seems to be carried out in the mood of "constructive openness". Progressive multilateralism is aptly guided by the then UNSG Kofi Annan.

- **Integration into the geopolitical framework**

The rise of the human security approach took place in the final phase of the classic North–South antagonism, the severe setback of UN peacekeeping in Sierra Leone, Mogadishu/Somalia, the genocide in Rwanda in 1994 and the massacre in Srebrenica/Bosnia in 1995. Developing countries were increasingly positioning themselves in the multilateral arena, such as the strong *Non-aligned Movement* led by founder personalities like Presidents Tito (Former Yugoslavia), Nasser (Egypt),

Nehru (India) and Sukarno (Indonesia). Beyond this, the waves of democratisation in Africa and independence movements in the 1960–1980s cleared the later path to the adoption of MDGs and SDGs.

This lasting human condition of pockets of extreme poverty, inequality and powerlessness—also under the advocacy of world public, media and a strong human rights-driven civil society—has perpetuated the dominant strategic axiom for reform in Africa: Although political and economic progress was partially present, human security remained largely absent. International mobility, global networking of people as well as values and digitalisation also affected only parts of the continent. At the same time, forms of violence and threats, and thus the strategic concept of security, were changing from territorial security to the individual.

7.3.1 Antagonism and Competition Within the UN System

Since the end of the Cold War, there was a certain concern that the strengthening of peacekeeping tasks could push back the UN's development agenda. (Rensmann in Simma et al. 2012: 55).

In this period, indeed, it became common knowledge that security and development are interrelated and that one cannot be achieved without the other (Kofi Annan). Good governance as a conceptual approach in development cooperations was established as conditional for the transparent and accountable use of donor funds. Debates such as about global public goods, in order to lead old-fashioned development cooperation out of its post-colonial theory of change, were based on the work and findings of important think tanks like the Club of Rome, *primus inter pares* committed to an ecological way of thinking. Development cooperation, however, remained to play defensive in comparison to the burning peace and security problems that the world powers were dealing with at that time.

Against this background, the Secretariat of UNSG Boutrous-Ghali was restructured to consolidate ECOSOC agendas, followed by the publication of the "Agenda for Development" in May 1994. The report presented an early multidimensional, comprehensive approach to development. The UN reform process gained momentum with UNSG Kofi Annan, who later established the highly respected Senior Management Group around him. Funds and programmes were divided into four sectors, each headed by an Executive Committee. The driving requirements of strengthening the leadership (introduction of the position of a deputy UNSG) and "*acting as one*" on the ground as well as increasing effectiveness and efficiency by stimulating the private sector ("Global Compact Initiative" 2000) and civil society were recognised and promoted as decisive.

- **Goals, characteristics, new elements**

7.3.2 *Human Security as a Driving Force*

The concept of human security, with its focus on the individual, presents the spearhead of scholars who identified a deep erosion of the state when non-state capacity and interdependence ("*interconnectedness*") increased. In some cases, the need for adaptation and far-reaching changes of IL principles were argued (Parlett 2011: 336f; Peters 2009). It was precisely this opening that caused strong resistance to scholars of human security on the part of small, weak and underdeveloped states, but also from Russia and China, who saw and still see their best defence in their sovereignty.

While UNDP tried in vain to introduce the term in 1995 as the organising concept of the 1996 Copenhagen World Social Summit, human security at least succeeded in turning upside down the policies of the World Bank and the IMF, which had previously focussed exclusively on economic development, and established the more comprehensive parameters of "human development" in the Human Development Index. Seven prismatic elements of human security ("*food, health, environment, personal, community, politics, and economy*"; Mahbub ul-Haq (1995) were published in the Human Development Report in 1994[2]. It is easy to grasp that too many perspectives were subsumed in the broad spectrum of human security and thus hindered, if not destroyed, the effectiveness of the concept.

Nobel laureate Amartya Sen's perception of development as the promotion of individual opportunities ("Capabilities Approach") contributed to sharpening human security, combining it with a human rights approach. The initiatives of the *Human Security Network*, of which Austria was one of the founding members in 1999, gradually gained greater acceptance. In 2005, human security in its original form—"*freedom from fear and freedom from want*" (Human Security Commission 2003: 4)—officially found its way into the UN (Reform summit, paragraph 140). But the political rejection of "relative sovereignty", which would have been the consequence, gained the upper hand.

Therefore, and much to the detriment of the suffering people, the UN forged a very conservative contribution to clarify the term on 25 October 2012. In UNGA Resolution 66/290, after protracted negotiations, the International Community agreed on a "Common Understanding of Human Security", which, however, lagged far behind the substantial reform potential. On the contrary, essential elements of this declaration still strengthened the old system: The connection between security, development and human rights was recognised ("*human security is people-centred, comprehensive, context-specific and prevention-oriented*"), but mutual reinforcement of human security and the responsibility to protect as well as the prohibition of the use of force denied ("*does not entail the threat/use of force or coercive measures*"). Difficulties in implementing the concept lasted for the entire decade, especially in the area of peacekeeping.

[2] http://hdr.undp.org/en/content/human-development-report-1994. Accessed 8 August 2021.

7.3.3 *Millennium Summit 2000 ("MDGs")*

In September 2000, the Millennium Summit adopted by consensus the so-called "Millennium Declaration", which became in the following the basis for all UN development and poverty reduction activities (World Development Goals, MDGs). The MDGs—even without naming human rights explicitly—can thus be counted among the UN's strongest strategy documents for human security-influenced thinking. Its eight objectives comprise: Poverty reduction, education, gender equality, reducing child mortality, improving maternal health and combating HIV/AIDS and other communicable diseases, global partnerships and a sustainable environment.

7.3.4 *Revitalising Collective Security*

Following the failures in Sierra Leone, Rwanda, Somalia and the former Yugoslavia, the UNSG convened a High-Level Panel of Experts to review the UN's peace and security activities. In the upstream of human security and as an outcome of the end of the East–West confrontation, UN Special Representative and former Algerian Foreign Minister Lakhdar Brahimi, upon commission by the UNSG, presented a ground-breaking report on UN peacekeeping missions. Issued in 2000, this report became the most important basis for reform of UN peacekeeping. Recommendations, i.e. argued for "*clear, credible and achievable mandates*", which was seen as the main cause of the failure of operations in the 1990s. The US, upon this, returned to the Peacekeeper Forum as a potent payer (1 billion US Dollar p.a.).

7.4 Reform Summit 2005

Situational overview

"9–11" (2001) terrorist attacks in New York trigger persistent inequality, poverty, new hotspots of violence. Counter-terrorism triggers a new "constitutionalisation" of multilateralism with instruments of R2P, POC and extended peacekeeping. Intervention logic turns from forum to actor, revitalising universalist thinking. In the operationalisation of missions, implementation of lessons learned from previous engagement prevails. Mechanisms of multilateralism are in their "zenith", but the international community is finally failing to build a supranational order. UNSG Kofi Annan is still navigating the UN through agitated water.

- **Integration into the geopolitical framework**

This period is a troublesome back and forth, heavily overshadowed by the "9–11" terrorist attack in New York in 2001. However, after the UN's legitimacy crisis in the 1990s, a phase of reform begins between 2005–2015. The range of peacekeeping instruments was expanded and put to test. First, a consolidation of the multilateral capacity to act can be observed. Whether the 2005 reform summit was about utopia or real progress, remains heavily disputed at that time. Equally, the rapprochement of security and development turned out to be an extremely challenging task for the UN system, not only politically but also in terms of implementation. The continued "overstretching" by the expanded concept of UN peacekeeping ("mission creep") at the end of the twentieth century finally heralded the solo efforts of the USA and its allies or NATO in Afghanistan, Iraq and South-East Europe. After the terrorist attack in New York in 2001, a fierce and protracted debate on the right way to fight terrorism—definitions, treatment under national criminal law or at international level—occupied diplomats and state chancelleries alike.

- **Trigger/cause**

The *weaknesses of legitimacy and effectiveness* of the period is diametrically opposed to the intervention culture of collective security. In narrower terms, the genocide in Rwanda in 1994, which could not be prevented by the UN, the interventions of NATO in Kosovo in 1999 and the US-led invasion in Iraq in 2003, became the direct triggers of the will to reform for a "San Francisco II". Finally, it was about to find a response to massive human rights violations and the "*universally recognized imperative of effectively halting gross and systematic violations of human rights*"—the core of *ius cogens* yet still in flux—to complement advances of the international individual criminal law for genocide, ethnic cleansing, war crimes and crimes against humanity. In 2008, the positions of a Special Adviser on the Responsibility to Protect and a homologue for Prevention of Genocide with a joint office were installed (Dubler and Kalyk 2018). The then UNSG Kofi Annan timely recognised the danger of lacking subordination of security powers under the multilateral umbrella and thus of a turning away from UN's universalism. Political trust had to be restored.

7.4.1 "A Fork in the Road" (Kofi Annan)

With this in mind, the UNSG set up a 16-member expert commission headed by Thailand's Prime Minister Anand Panyarachun to deal with collective security in the twenty-first century (HLP on Threats, Challenges and Change; report "A More Secure World: Our Shared Responsibility). More than 100 recommendations were elaborated and presented at the 2005 World Summit. At the same time, an independent advisory group led by the US economist Jeffrey Sachs worked on an implementation plan for the MDGs up to 2015 ("Millennium Project"): Decisive reforms in the field of security, human rights and operability throughout the UN system were to be balanced by a clear focus on development and with the interests of the G77 states. Finally, the results of the HLP and the Millennium Project were brought together in a comprehensive approach in the UN strategy "In Larger Freedom—Towards development, security and human rights for all", the final document of the Heads of State and Government of the 2005 UN Reform Summit (UN Doc. A/59/2005 of 21 March 2005).

- **Goals, characteristics, new elements**

7.4.2 "No Development Without Security"

The outcome of the 2005 Reform Summit recognised the connection between the three pillars, peace and security, development and human rights, on which the system rests ever since (paragraph 9). This emanates above all from the preparatory process and the genesis of the summit.

International peace and security at its zenith

The final document confirms the UNSC's primary responsibility for international peace and security. Progress in working methods, involvement of non-UNSC member states, transparency and accountability were consensual. Cautiously, however, the concept of a "responsibility to protect" (R2P) came about in response to the humanitarian challenges and the terrorist threats that had reached a new dimension of immediacy since 9–11, whereby the new instrument was explicitly to be implemented only by the UN (peak of multilateralism 2005). Criteria for legitimising the collective use of force could again not be agreed upon. This, however, propelled attempts of arguing self-defence outside the Charter or at least in its broadest possible interpretation (Article 51), as stated in the 2002 US National Defence Strategy relying on preventive self-defence ("Bush Doctrine").

The establishment of the *Peace-building Commission* in 2006 covered a long-standing deficit in the field of post-conflict rehabilitation. Nevertheless, here too, full responsibility for "*preventive action in countries which are under stress and risk sliding towards state collapse*" could not be established. Initially, it only seemed possible to consolidate UN-wide coordination for sustainable peace in post-conflict situations. Neither a definition nor a treaty on international terrorism and on the non-proliferation of weapons of mass destruction and respective disarmament could be negotiated successfully.

"In larger Freedom"

The final document reflects the commitment of the Millennium Summit, the 2003 International Conference on Financing for Development in Monterrrey and the 1992 World Summit on Sustainable Development in Rio. A "revitalisation" of ECOSOC as "*a principal body for coordination, policy review, policy dialogue and recommendations on issues of economic and social development*" took place, and the establishment of the biennial Development Cooperation Forum as a development dialogue in a broad multi-stakeholder format with an annual "Ministerial Review" (paragraph 155 b and c) also sent positive signals.

UN Human Rights Council

The universality and indivisibility of the human rights regime (CPESC rights) established at the 1993 Vienna World Conference were endorsed at the reform summit. Their particular importance was underlined by the establishment of the UN Human Rights Council, the negotiation process of which was completed in 2006. Although the Human Rights Council has not been accorded the status of a main organ of the UN, the term "Council" indicates the important meaning which emphasises its construction as a subsidiary organ of the UNGA (and not of ECOSOC). With 47 members, the Human Rights Council is working with the UNGA and can suspend a party's membership to the body in case of serious and systematic human rights violations, which raises the legitimacy far beyond the UN Human Rights Commission as its forerunner. Lately, the HRC came under fire for inefficiency and blockage of resolutions.

- **Trends for intervention**

7.4.3 Human Rights and Development Are Interdependent

As a result of the great basic documents, the various "communities" of the ICCM can celebrate an interim success: The human rights approach in development cooperation boomed, the military began to direct their perspective beyond the events "in theatre" to "the day after" and draw conclusions for their own presence and design of operations. The development track, in turn, became "politicised", but to the realistic extent that all actors should work together and make joint efforts towards the same goals of peacebuilding and state-building. The "Comprehensive Approach" was thus approaching a climax in this phase.

- **Operationalisation in the mandate**

7.4.4 New Instruments "R2P" and "POC"

What was created in the ICCM on the civilian side by the PBC and the Human Rights Council is reflected in the "responsibility to protect" (R2P) as a multilaterally driven crisis response mechanism for the "protection of civilians" (POC) on the military side. With these new instruments, an experimental phase was launched in 2005, concretised in 2015, and essentially continues to this day—a retrospective appraisal.

Bruno Simma's ground-breaking treatise on the lack of legitimacy of the NATO military strike, which nevertheless contributed to the stabilisation of South-East Europe in 1999 (Simma 1999, as opposed by Habermas 1999) has raised the much-discussed question of the emergence of new customary IL with regard to humanitarian intervention, not mandated by the UNSC. Simma attributed this to the observation that the relationship between the UN and NATO had temporarily changed from mutual reinforcement to fundamental competition—a picture that is further blurred today. The dominant position of the challenger was indeed transferred from NATO to the USA at the beginning of the first decade of the twenty-first century, as could be seen from the division of EU partners in the assessment of *Operation Iraqi Freedom* into an "old and a new Europe" (US Secretary of State Powell before the UNSC on 5 February 2003) on the one hand and, a decade later, the lines of the Trump administration as from 2017 on the other. Developments in the Arab world like Iran and in other places suggested that the two actors were complementing each other in an increasingly delicate way, overlaid by Russian President Putin's solo actions.

At the beginning of the 2000s, intervention not taking place in the exercise of the right of self-defence and acting without UN mandate was still approved by the High-Level Panel as *ultima ratio*. In contrast, former UNSG Kofi Annan in his 2005 reform paper assumed a mandatory devolution to the UN in accordance with the Charter, if the state concerned is unwilling or incapable of exercising its protective function at the national level. The responsibility of the UNSC, if it does not act in the sense of the later paragraph 139 of the outcome document of 2005, rested unresolved in Annan's position. Even the path taken with UNSCR 1894/2009 did not answer the question, but clearly focussed on national obligations and international assistance in the run-up to military intervention. The aforementioned robust "pillar 3" was presented in the consecutive reports by UNSG Ban Ki-moon under the leadership of SRSG Ed Luck 2009 as already in the framework of the existing international legal order, which derives from the broad-based "campaigning" that was intended to create a corresponding legal conviction. (Luck 2008; UNSG Report on Implementing R2P, 2009).

This changed in 2005. The view that the repeated situation of military intervention without a multilateral mandate should mark the beginning of a development in customary IL was finally outdated with reference to paragraph 139 of the outcome document of the 2005 Reform Summit (Luck, Edward, The R2P, Lecture, 39th IPI Vienna Seminar, Vienna Diplomatic Academy, 14–16 June 2009) and can, in view of the subsequent practice, be denied from today's perspective. (as opposed by Richmond 2003) Matthias Herdegen already draws the same argument from the case-related fact that the NATO procedure in Kosovo had only been supported partly by international lawyers, and therefore, produced a significant but not consensus-based evidence. (Herdegen 2004: 580) The analysis shows that a UN mandate must be assumed, regardless of whether R2P were to be falsified.

Important for an effective ICCM is its operational capability to counter all risks of human security, whether these emanate from states or non-state actors (Tadic case, ICTY). The final document of the 2005 UN Reform Summit in paragraph 138–140 reaffirms the adherence to the multilateral approach to R2P, as a systematic interpretation of the UN Charter shows, only against states. (Dorband 2006: 4, 7f) Similarly, in its 2004 opinion on the construction of the Wall, the ICJ stated very briefly that the right to self-defence can only be exercised against states. (Construction of the wall, Advisory Opinion 2004, ICJ Reports 136) Again, this changed in the further development regarding the analysis of resolutions in the field of terrorism (UNSCR 2249/2017) without explicit reference in the text, however, this orientation did not appear to halt. Whereas there is no reference to non-state actors in the operative part of UNSCR 1368 and 1373/2001 as well as 1973/2011, the UNSC itself does not confirm the opening of Article 51 of the UN Charter for defence strikes against non-state actors, but pursues the attribution of "complicity".

A further challenge for R2P and POC missions arises in the nature of capturing attacks in cyberspace: Pre-emptive actions extending the Webster formula from the famous "Caroline incident" are still not covered by this (see opposing US position). However, the immanence link is particularly difficult to be established in cyberspace attacks due to ultra-short time-slots of location, evaluation and response. The orientation towards a multilateral conflict prevention imperative that broadens the reactive spectrum does not change this. The criterion of proportionality of the reaction in the case of intervention includes the assessment of the source, magnitude and success of a possible mission vis-à-vis the expected consequences of non-intervention.

In order to safeguard human security as an interest of the International Community, the question must, therefore, be answered as to against whom a (state) intervention may be carried out, i.e. from whom the threat can emanate, and whether non-state entities in this sense are at all capable of a systematic, organised armed attack in the sense of UNGA resolution 3314/1974. The point is that if there is a massive imminent threat to individuals, it follows from the human security approach that all these cases can be affirmed from a teleological point of view (Werther-Pietsch 2013): Both the averting of danger against non-state actors and the qualification of a terrorist act as an "armed attack" are recommended in this sense, even if terrorists, in turn, appear to be privileged. Conversely, an expanding interpretation or analogous application of Article 51 of the UN Charter for the execution of unilateral action must fail because of the lack of systemic identity between Article 39 and Article 51 with regard to their intended regulatory content ("*any threat*"). With regard to a conflict prevention imperative, it can, therefore, be questioned if these reform approaches to revitalising, functionality and effectiveness of the UNSC with a view to increase operability of the world security system were sufficient.

- **Balance sheet and further developments**

Nevertheless, R2P must today be regarded as a stalled project (Dubler and Kalyk 2018: 597). The first timid applications did not bring the hoped-for progress. The concept remains on paper, for the majority of practitioners, it is already totally falsified as lacking strategic power. By R2P, UNSG Annan and UNSC Luck pushed for zero-tolerance of most serious human rights violations as a common entry point, which led to the spectacular merge of China's and Russia's position when rebellion ousted Col. Gaddafi's regime in Libya, 2011, both overcoming their long-standing non-intervention stance. However, the evacuation of Chinese citizens from Libya and the solidity of positions between China and Russia against the US and allies may also have been decisive for this. However, the "dual use" in public debate and literature of this very first application case of R2P in UNSCR 1973 as a "regime change" more than "rescue action for peace" has again enormously reduced the momentum. Further, inconclusive cases emerged in Syria from 2011 onwards and in Myanmar 2021.

Critical success factors in other areas of peacekeeping addressed at the UN Summit can be outlined as follows:

- "*Peacekeeping needs to be understood as one tool on a continuum of options in the existing global peace and security architecture*". (HIPPO Report 2015) Realistic mandates and political will, reflected in resources, diplomatic support and proactive implementation, have been identified as key conditions for success at the strategic level.
- "Rapid deployment mechanisms", effective coordination and positive, reciprocal relations with local communities are among the most important prerequisites for sustainable peacekeeping. The struggle for setting respective structures continued. Reform of the UNSC, an important fact in the background, could not be advanced because of the resistance of the P-5, but also due to diverging ideas of the member states (fragmentation into 5 groups). This contributed to the stagnation of the instruments.

Active work on a window of opportunity for the proposal of the "Group of Four" on the representation in the UNSC (Germany, Brazil, India and Japan together with other 23 members) was probably the most promising approach in a 75 years period. This suggestion would force a model of six new permanent states (two African, two Asian, one Latin American and one Western European) and four new non-permanent ones (one each from Africa, Asia, Eastern Europe and Latin America). The permanent members should have the same rights as the P-5 but should be allowed to exercise their right of veto only after a review after 15 years. In May 2012, the "Small Five"—Costa Rica, Jordan, Liechtenstein, Switzerland and Singapore—attempted to submit a draft resolution demanding that the right of veto be exercised and that it not be applied in the case of genocide, war crimes and crimes against humanity. However, the P-5 were in no way impressed by this, and the S-5 eventually withdrew their draft resolution. With regard to countless other proposals and years of tug-of-war about the different interests to be respected, this seems fair and can be deduced from the new geopolitical constellation and the idea of universality.

7.4.5 *System-Wide Coherence—Remedy or "Overstretching" the System?*

Meanwhile, system-wide coherence became the buzzword for structural reform projects as a result of the 2005 summit. The HLP on UN System-wide Coherence in the fields of development, humanitarian aid and environment prepared a report "*Deliver as one*" on the ground by November 2006. Regional teams were brought together under the leadership of the UN Resident Coordinator (UNDP). At the same time, UN Women was founded. However, human rights remained the "*pillar of glass*" of the UN (Darrow and Arbour AJIL 2009)—more fragile than visible.

7.5 Agenda for Humanity 2016

Situational overview

One could call this period the "peace-building and state-building era", developing on societal human-centrism. This may be triggered by migration, a focus on North-Africa ("Arab Spring") and the Middle East (Hotspot Syria). What is new is the cumulative use of joint ICCM instruments, peacekeeping as human rights protection and an intervention logic that stagnates while progress in concrete terms seems possible. In this time, 3C/CA, HDP Nexus and the Sustaining Peace Approach come up and dominate international action. The mood under a less progressive UNSG Ban Ki-moon is "tense, but capable of progress."

- **Integration into the geopolitical framework**

Complex conflicts such as the Near and Middle East around Syria, mixed with negative experiences of operations in Afghanistan, Iraq and on the African continent, the Crimean and Ukrainian crises as the "crisis of IL" showed an incipient erosion of values and the rules-based world order. During this time, the focus continued to lie in individual identity, belonging, protection abilities, needs and future perspectives of the populations concerned (Werther-Pietsch in Giner-Reichl 2017) and the renewal of human security as the only remaining (not falsified) theory of global security. One can speak of a prolonged implementation era of human security.

- **Trigger/cause**

The UN is confronted with an unprecedented number of hot spots and internal armed conflicts: Worldwide more than 400 conflicts, at least 45 of them highly violent and most of them "protracted", i.e. long-lasting (Heidelberg Conflict Barometer, 2014)[3]. This development led to the largest refugee and migration movements in the world since WW II which accumulated in 2015 (approx. 60–80 million refugees, 85% of whom are IDPs; UNHCR, 2021; Webinger in Werther-Pietsch 2017: 117ff) Ebola as a challenge to the international response mechanisms in the disaster relief and health sector stimulated willingness for coordinated international action bolstered by civil society engagement.

- **Goals, characteristics, new elements**

7.5.1 Endorsement of the Comprehensive Approach

Along the three big 2015 reform strands—the HIPPO Report on Peacekeeping, the PBC Review and the Global Study on the Implementation of UNSCR 1325—it was becoming more and more apparent that the UN can only meet expectations of providing effective assistance if it succeeded in intervening in essential situations in a more coordinated manner and with appropriate capacities. One response was the formation of clusters in the humanitarian field and the longer-term orientation towards development. In this way, "silo thinking" was avoided and synergies could be exploited.

The basic document of this period, the "Agenda for Humanity", was prepared by the World Humanitarian Summit in Istanbul on 23 and 24 May and finally adopted on 23 August 2016 in New York by the UNGA with its five core responsibilities: (1) Protection of the civilian population, (2) "leave no one behind"—the human rights approach to human security for vulnerable groups and individuals, (3) a "new way of working"—meaning national and local *leadership* and *ownership*, increased reliance on automated risk analyses and databases, involvement of non-state actors, (4) a focus on natural disasters and climate change and (5) more resources for emergency aid and increased efficiency.

- **Trends for intervention**

7.5.2 Humanitarian, Development and Peace-Building Action Interfere

Shaped by the concept of resilience, the 2016 Humanitarian World Summit in Istanbul established a broad *nexus* understanding: The individual components of humanitarian aid, development cooperation and peace-building ("HDP") converged logistically and in the strategic perspective. The prerequisite for this is coordination and exchange. In this debate, the peace component appeared particularly controversial contributing to a "politisation" of aid (OECD, USAID, later EU; Werther-Pietsch

[3] https://hiik.de/konfliktbarometer/. Accessed 12 October 2021.

2009). However, the counterargument per se refers to the political task of intervention which takes place in crisis and conflict areas (OECD DAC Recommendation on the HDP nexus 2019, to be adhered by UN, ongoing; see Schreiber and Abendroth, *TDHJ Special Edition #02* 13).

- **Operationalisation in the mandate**

The central criticism is that the so-called cross-cutting issues and protection of civilians overextended the capabilities of UN missions. The reform process launched in 2019 following the Action for Peacekeeping Declaration in response to the 2017 Santos Cruz Report reflected this when engaging in "bettering mandates" and the protection of own troops.

7.5.3 Thematic Lead Resolutions of the UNSC

To foster and make visible multilateral system thinking on nexus applications, the consecutive lead resolutions of the UNSC in Fig. 7.2 below have been put together:

- **Balance sheet and further developments**

With the consolidation of all components in the ICCM and the Comprehensive Approach, parallel to regional organisations like NATO or the EU, the International Community is in the prime of technically-informed missions that have been equipped with the expertise of many missions over 80 years. Nevertheless, the structures remained rigid and often the necessary reform steps were not implemented for geopolitical or other reasons. Forthcoming challenges put the prospects of success into question. Nevertheless, a tool of interoperable instruments has become ripe for immediate use.

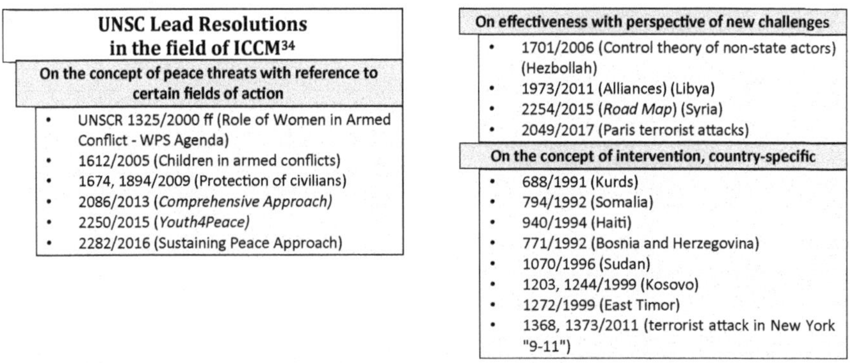

Fig. 7.2 Own source

7.6 Agenda 2030 and Sustaining Peace

Situational overview

The framework has now changed. Power competition and rivalry, weaponization, and a global arms race cannot be denied. The "triad of presidents" (US Trump, Russia Putin and China Xi) mark a turning point in history. We now face an era of hybrid threats, struggle with digitalisation and the IT-age. New warfare methods and settings come up. As intervention logic reformulation of "Key principles of Cooperative Crisis and Conflict Management (CCCM)" is recommended. Operationalisation includes scenarios on AI, space and nuclear components, as well as multi-domain operations. All this in the mood of "deep erosion of international consensus", alienation and the awareness of risk of escalation. Acting UNSG Antonio Guterres nevertheless starts initiatives such as the global appeal for ceasefires after the outbreak of the COVID-19 pandemic.

- **Integration into the geopolitical framework**

7.6.1 "Five Breaches of Trust" (Ischinger)

While the security architecture is subject to a new realism, the human rights and development world continue on their idealistic path. But also premises such as new partnerships, new trade cooperation as well as new collaborations in security policy emerge. The change in the development paradigm is most strongly demonstrated by China. The OECD states are challenged to redefine their location. Wolfgang Ischinger of the Munich Security Conference 2019 spoke of an epochal move which was even more heralded by the COVID-19 crisis. According to him (2018), five "loss" phenomena are decisive for this:

1. *"Epoch break" in political power*, established power structures lose influence; questioning of NATO by the USA, detachment from the transatlantic track and the weakness of the EU as a peace project through Brexit
2. *No "common truth*": Facts go lost in a multifaceted media and social network's dust, further loss of trust in dealing with each other. No corrections of facts on new media, explosive proliferation without verification mechanism
3. *The formal monopoly on the use of force* (states, UN) is abrogated and *the capacity to inflict damage* fall apart; terrorism as well as other non-state armed groups act with a large reach at low cost (cyberspace)
4. *"Era of digitalisation":* Besides blessing effects, hybrid threats and new methods of warfare changed fundamentally, with ostensibly no national territorial interests but concealment tactics ("proxy wars", e.g. Russia is officially

not a conflict party in the incident in the Sea of Azov): Prevention, management and termination by the UN is, therefore, difficult because coming from a different geopolitical context. Resultantly, general compliance with IL largely undermined

5. *Conflict resolution methods*: Formerly kinetic, today "weaponisation" of information, energy, cyberspace, the financial sector (economic sanctions) as preferred means. The EU is lagging behind but presents itself as the only player that strives for global solidarity. Still, majority decisions in foreign affairs are currently not in sight.

As a mega-trend in response to complex local involvement, a *regionalisation of security* is underway, manifesting itself in partly deliberate encapsulation, partly driven by the search for more effectiveness upon lessons from the COVID-19 pandemic.

- **Trigger/cause**

7.6.2 Internal and External Security Become Blurred

The "triad of presidents" of the great powers USA, China and Russia reveal an already fragmented world situation. Different approaches to the challenges of the time—economic growth, development strategy, supply of raw materials and sustainable use of resources, attitudes to IL and ethical considerations—significantly coin international relations. Partnership, or at least coexistence, changes into "power competition", in the new rhetoric, rather "turn to rivalry", whereas none of the actors is seriously interested in an armed conflict due to the high risk of global destabilisation. Atomic energy and upgrading in the high-tech segment of artificial intelligence in the civil sphere could become decisive for future issues such as resource scarcity due to climate change. The "personalisation" of politics (US-China trade wars, Chinese–Russian information policy regarding COVID-19 help) and weaknesses of the established "headquarters" in Brussels coincide. Military readiness for action is certainly given after years of pure "exercise reality", and the strategic relativisation of IL causes pressure on democratic states. Concern about the high risk of escalation prevails.

- **Goals, characteristics, new elements**

7.6.3 "Leave no One Behind" and A4P Declaration

On the other hand, the Agenda for Sustainable Development is an exemplary, albeit challenging, summary of the good efforts to "save the world"—a necessary, lively, but somewhat abstract crown jewel in the history of the UN. The implementation of the 17 Sustainable Development Goals (SDGs) within a horizon until 2030 is ambitious and involves all levels from the local to the international. If there is a new global consensus, then it lies in this approach of investing in people.

This ground-breaking orientation is also contained in Principles 1–8 of the Action for Peacekeeping Declaration of September 2018. The Sustaining Peace Approach as a generic method for the ICCM and on the basis of teleological interpretation of the UN Charter shows an understanding of deep inclusion of developmental issues in peacekeeping that is thus completed and irreversibly merged in a Kantian sense.

- **Trends for intervention**

Although instruments now seem readily available, the ICCM is declining overall, on the one hand, there are hot interfaces where big powers meet, but on the other hand, the unclear conflict between regional and local power struggles make the International Community shy away from intervention. In view of the increased use of "smart power" and low threshold but efficient deterrence through "information wars", the ICCM must renew itself (Key CCCM Principles and Road Maps to Peace, see Part III Sect. 9).

- Operationalisation in the mandate

Therefore, increasing demand for the inclusion of IT-supported components in UN peace support operations and the construction of capacities in the new sectors, including for self-protection, is underway.

- **Balance sheet and further developments**

Adherence to the common goal of human security and CCCM instruments for "Road Maps to Peace" seems crucial for a positive balance. It remains to be seen to what extent the system will be undermined by a neo-bipolarism, power projection and reform, interests and provocative solo attempts, and if the Sustaining Peace Approach based on experience can prevail in international engagement.

A further fundamental shift by "climate conflicts" (Rwanda, Seychelles, Maldives, etc.) became apparent regarding global environmental problems: resources, economic activity and wars will be more closely linked than before. This development has already started with water resources in the Middle East, in Sub-Saharan Africa with the consequences of the El Nino phenomenon, the exploitation of rare earth in the Congo or the discovery of further oil resources in the Arctic. The yet false promise of the "digital dividend" will probably turn to-date prospering development sectors upside down: rising unemployment, increasing dependence on (metallic) raw materials and on IT groups due to growing concentration in global production chains will occupy development cooperation in the future, according to Sven Hilbig (2019: 57–64). Whether the COVID-19 crisis will further deepen the divide, remains to be seen.

7.7 "The Age of Human-Centrism"

Situational overview

Overall, the COVID-19 polycrisis, technological neo-bipolarism, and a trilateral constellation of power make up the new picture. At the same token, the Afghanistan experience end of August 2021 may turn out as a gamechanger in ICCM. Autocratic versus democratic ways of life keep human rights defenders and political scientists busy. Shifting forms of sovereignty, new actors such as geotechnical clusters, alliances of democracies, and a trend to regionalisation reflect the revitalised principles of subsidiarity and resilience. Intervention logic lies in modernisation, new technologies, specification of tasks, and smaller more specialised missions. Actions occur against the background of "cold" confrontation of political, economic and values concepts, forging alliances, and an alert UNSG Antonio Guterres.

- **Integration into the geopolitical framework**

7.7.1 "Five Answers"

The "five breaches" require five responses. They sharpened over time and, especially after the withdrawal of the USA and its allies from Afghanistan. Regarding technological progress, steered by non-state power houses behind world players, there is a need for a new "language" to grasp change in its entirety and to translate the "dark sides" of new technologies into human-centred applications. Geopolitically, what is certain is that China is there to stay, at the same time the US is not to leave. There is a new role to be filled in between them, the role of a door opener in an interactive dialogue or, perhaps, peace broker from a regional strategic autonomy perspective. This is the given "third" to make up a forthcoming model of geopolitical trilateralism.

- **Trigger/cause**

All powers seek for new positions:

- The Russian mode of uncomfortable "enfant terrible" with historical ties to Europe; a common line of positions in multilateral fora like the UNSC with China ("the Dragonbear"), is successful, but erratic.
- The "bright" Chinese path of silent take-over and "unintended" expansion will erode in as much as human dignity and freedoms will challenge ambitions of the Belt-and-Road-Initiative (BRI), signs to be detected in Indonesia, Myanmar or Greece (Cernusca 2021).

- The US finally woke up after blind "Trumpism" to reinvigorate multilateral cooperation and its own strengths. It could of course be hamstrung by internal struggles. The total withdrawal of troops in Afghanistan by the Biden-Administration in 2021 is partly due to such considerations.
- Europe has the choice.

- **Goals, characteristics, new elements**

7.7.2 Foundational elements of a new balance-of-power doctrine

A new paradigm of world politics may come up, equidistance and human-centrism. Global goals would be reduced to its lowest common denominator to remain manageable and close gaps of regulation in essential domains such as G5, energy security, climate change, cyber sovereignty, space. At the same time regions may be strengthened in the area of peace & security, conflict prevention and solution by new responsibilities. Only a combined approach is feasible resembling a "*do ut des*" situation between world leaders.

- **Trends for intervention**

A two-pronged way is suggested: The new intervention logic follows a common roof of global treaty law in the areas suggested including a new common *ius cogens*-formula where peace is at stake ("widespread or systematic attacks"). Regional peace and security structures equipped with new responsibility are obliged to implement that formula in their respective area of action.

- **Operationalisation in the mandate**

Global and regional, peace and security structures would have to apply the same lessons learned post-COVID-19 and post-Afghanistan, summarised in consensual future "Key Principles of CCCM" (see Part III).

- **Balance sheet and further developments**

The new balance-of-power doctrine, comprising a geopolitical trilateralism with two antagonists and one mediator is a visionary approach.

It will however not very easily be brought to life. But with a view (1) to prevent global conflict in a very large scale, (2) to deter "accidental" mistakes by irrational actors and (3) to find one's way as European community of EU member states, a credible future global peace mechanism on two pillars, the universal and the regional, should at least be useful to prepare for "peaceful strategic autonomy".

References

Cernusca, Sabrina. 2021. Aspekte der Wirtschaftspolitik Chinas am Weg zu Weltwirtschaftsmacht, Vorwissenschaftliche Arbeit, Innsbruck, 3 Mar 2021.
Darrow, M., and Louise, Arbour. 2009. The pillar of glass: Human rights in development operations of the united nations. *AJIL* 103: 446–501.
Dorband, Jana. 2006. Perspectives on American foreign policy beyond Iraq. *SWP Magazine review* 2 stiftung wissenschaft und politik, German Institute for International and Security Affairs.
Dubler, SC, R., and M. Kalyk. 2018. *Crimes against Humanity in the 21st Century—Law. Practice and Threats to International Peace and Security*: Boston/Leiden: Brill.
Herdegen, Matthias. 2004. Asymmetries in the world of states and the challenges of "constructive international law." *Zaörv* 64: 571–582.
Hilbig, Sven. 2019. Development policy 2.0? The global South and the false promise of the "digital dividend." *Papers for German and International Politics* I: 57–64.
HIPPO-Report. 2015. UN report of the high-level panel on peace operations, New York, 17 June 2015. http://www.un.org/en/ga/search/view_doc.asp?symbol=A/70/95. Accessed 8 Aug 2021.
Human Security Commission. 2003. Human Security now: protecting and empowering people. https://relief.int/report/world/human-security-now-protecting-and-empowering-people. Accessed 12 October 2021.
Ischinger, Wolfgang. 2018. *World in danger*. Berlin: Econ Verlag.
Luck, Edward C. 2008. The responsible sovereign and the responsibility to protect. *United Nations* 2: 51–58.
Ul-Haq, Mahbub. 1995. *Reflections on human development*. New York/Oxford: Oxford University Press.
Parlett, Kate. 2011. *The individual in the international legal system: continuity and change in international law*, Cambridge Studies in International and Comparative Law No. 75. Cambridge: Cambridge University Press.
Rensmann, Thilo. 2012. Reform. In *The charter of the united nations*, ed. Bruno Simma, Daniel-Erasmus Khan, Georg Nolte and Andreas Paulus, 3rd ed. 25–69. Oxford: Oxford University Press.
Schreiber, Dan and Kulani Abendroth-Dias. 2021. Unpacking the black box of fragility. *TDHJ Special Edition #02 21*: 13–22. https://ca9d3787-8643-4d85-9af7-d052377ac9b8.filesusr.com/ugd/0d3ede_e7c96c4fd93945a9bfe58c6c564427c2.pdf. Accessed 8 Aug 2021.
Simma, Bruno. 1999. NATO, the UN and the Use of Force. *EJIL* 10: 1–22, https://www.ejil.org/journal/Vol10/No1/ab1-4.html. Accessed 8 Aug 2021.
Webinger, Peter. 2017. Migration Policies. In *Global Peace and Security*. International Crisis and Conflict Management, ed. Ursula Werther-Pietsch, 117–133. Vienna: MANZ
Werther-Pietsch, Ursula. 2009. *Security and Development—Two Pillars of a System?* Series of the National Defence Academy in collaboration with DCAF Geneva, 2 Sep 2009.
Werther-Pietsch, Ursula. 2013. *Selbstbestimmung, Gewaltverbot und Friedenssicherung heute*. Habilitation. Vienna/Graz: Neuer Wissenschaftlicher Verlag.
Werther-Pietsch, Ursula. 2017. The Rise, Fall and Power of Reform of the Human Security Council. In *Entwicklungspolitik 2030*, ed. Kurt Bayer and Irene Giner-Reichl, 95 - 106. Vienna: MANZ

Part III
Collaborative Regional Security

Chapter 8
Learning from History

8.1 Vision—Potential to Be Activated for Peace

An inadequately decentralised world order, as detected 2001 by Andreas Paulus, supported evolvements of global peace and security for the last decades. Much lip-service to regionalisation of action has been paid, also around the foundation of the PBC, but is to be readdressed again under changed circumstances (former OSCE-SG Thomas Greminger, bilateral meeting on 12 September 2019).

One way of remedying this weakness is be to substantially regionalise the global system of collective security along the lines of "geotechnical ensembles" (Criekemans, ISPA, 15 July 2021, Brussels). This is why the current authorisation model is overcome and neighbourhood might be a new way to be considered. Enhancing regional conflict resolution capacity, based on proximity of players willing to live in peace and capable of working on the causes of conflict, would reverse the responsibility for the initial assessment of a peace threat. This "relocation" however can be perceived as a major entry point for regulation of hot spots by regional powers, decoupled from the major P-5 logic or other global players' geostrategic interests, with the argument of probably spreading more arms and terror. On the contrary, one can argue that regional powers should shy away from hasty military strikes due to their direct involvement. At the same token, regionalisation of security structures could clearly push back the continuing oversize of power exploitation by the great powers. In such a scenario, an alternative theory of change is to be identified: The prevailing dominant global interconnectivity, including extraterritorial military bases, should be replaced and satisfied by shifting influence to respective regional configurations. Expeditionary interventions such as NATO air strikes in Kosovo in 1999, the deployment of Russian air force in Syria in Spring 2018 or the US engagement in post-Hussein Iraq from 2006 to 2020 could be diminished.

These preliminary thoughts are already partly reflected in practice. An interesting comparative study on IGAD and ASEAN, for example, reveals tensions that govern security structures at the regional level. Different speeds of integration guide for instance the AU with its affinity for mutual intervention in "brother states" (Article

U. Werther-Pietsch, *Transforming Security*, Global Power Shift,
https://doi.org/10.1007/978-3-030-87097-3_8

4h AU-Charter, 2000) and the founding ethos of the ASEAN states, which has in the meantime been subject to competition by the SCO. The ASEAN group explicitly excludes intervention in the case of serious human rights violations and moves on to a contradictory stance to the Charter (ascertained inconsistency with the UN canon of values; Acharya 2001: 58). It increasingly relies on non-transparent informal diplomacy and institutional minimalism (Kefale and LSE 2015: 25) and is under heavy pressure of growing Chinese influence (case of mediation in internal matters of Myanmar in 2021). These organisations are therefore closely monitoring NATO in terms of adherence of its mandate under the auspices of the UN. Regional trouble spots such as along the Chinese Belt and Road Initiative (see Part I Sect. 6.2.1), the competitive role of Japan and other ASEAN members undermine the autonomy of the regional formation. For these reasons and forming globally communicating vessels, the US is increasing its influence vis-à-vis the rise of perceived "partners/rivals". The tug-of-war between the Arab League and IGAD around Ethiopia and Chinese "aid industry" in many African countries shows similar movements. A clearing of the regional level of interests between big powers would be a tremendous step forward.

8.2 The A and Ω of Peacekeeping Will Change

In any case, regional security governance remains the hot topic, whether in the South Chinese Sea or the Middle East. Solutions at regional level appear especially sustainable, conflict-preventive and are certainly part of future UN action.

To assess this assumption in practice, examples of activating Chapter VIII through UN mechanisms of global peace and security have to be reviewed. The most prominent case of a US-led operation that was not mandated and steered by the UNSG is given by the Gulf War in 1990/91. On behalf of the UN, an alliance under the command of the USA carried out the liberation of Kuwait, the annexation of which Iraqi President Saddam Hussein had attempted in violation of IL. In the mid-1990s, the International Community used to entrust NATO with such "liberation" missions, further examples are Afghanistan or Bosnia-Herzegovina. The EU and OSCE, already "real" neighbours to the conflict, conducted civilian missions in the former Yugoslavia. Concentration of such operations based on regional organisations under Chapter VIII took place each time when the UN needed powerful TCCs; and this has always been successful when own interests of the TCCs were involved. The UN thereby upheld a kind of "residual competence" for forgotten crises, which it tried to cover with political missions.

The "monopoly" for robust missions today, not least due to military strength, lies clearly with NATO, USA and UK with a high upstream potential of China. Russia largely disposes of the most developed IT capabilities in hybrid warfare, for the good or the bad, and doesn't shy away from external engagement as proved in several theatres. The EU follows with highly qualified Battle Groups and specialised Early Entry Forces. An important fact from the COVID-19 pandemic will be whether ad hoc-partnerships between the big powers entangling their regional clientele will continue or not. What do we learn from successes and failures of peace operations so far in this context and what potential role regional settings can play?

8.3 Strengths and Weaknesses, Paving the Way

As follows from the cognitive cycle described in Part II, critical thinking and innovations are closely interrelated. Against this background of geopolitical deliberations time is finally ripe to revisit step-by-step how the UN delivered on global peace and security on the ground.

Maintaining or restoring peace by military means was present in the conceptualisation of the UN from the very outset. A military approach based on consensus and cooperation mindful of the integration of big power projection for the common good had already been cultivated in the League of Nations. This mindset served finally as basis for UN peacekeeping in the 1956 Suez crisis and prevailed till UNSCR 2538/2020. When the then UNSG Hammarskjöld and Canadian Foreign Minister Pearson established a "buffer zone" between Israel and Egypt, the basic principles of classical peacekeeping were born and may be reiterated here as follows:

- Intervention only with the consensus of all parties to the conflict,
- Operations under the auspices of the UN and impartiality of the mission, and
- Use of force restricted to the purpose of self-defence (UNRIC 2008).

Building blocks of reform

Many stages of reform based on field experience and against the background of geopolitical developments followed (Thiemann 2019). In 2005, UNDPKO (now UNDPO) launched a "comprehensive programme for reform". In 2008, the administration developed the Capstone Doctrine in response to a series of UNSC guidelines, which largely implemented the concept of human security in peacekeeping. The "New Horizons 2010" initiative took a fresh approach to PKO planning, management, and leadership. The reform efforts, culminating in the reform year 2015, finally resulted in the "Action for Peacekeeping (A4P)" Declaration 2018. Administratively, the Department of Field Support (DFS), which was set up in 2007, was reintegrated into UNDPPO and UNDPO in the course of the subsequent restructuring in 2018.

Embedded in the outlines of the general ICCM, UN reform stages so far can be replicated as follows:

- 1992 Agenda for Peace
- 2000 Brahimi report and 2001 ICISS report
- 2003 UN Handbook on Multidimensional Peace Operations
- 2005 "Compressive Programme for Reform" to implement the reform summit
- 2008 Capstone Doctrine ("integrated missions")
- 2010 "New Horizons" reform project (French/British project)

- 2011 "Civilian Capacities (CivCap) Initiative" (based on World Bank Report 2011)
- 2011 Socio economic footprint of PKOs (Austrian initiative in the C-34 Committee)
- 2015 HIPPO Report
- 2016 Agenda for Humanity
- 2017 Santos Cruz Report
- 2018 A4P Declaration (Sustaining Peace Approach, Triple ("HDP") nexus)
- 2020 Renewal of the "Women, Peace and Security" (WPS) agenda
- 2021 Overall management reform (ongoing).

Stuck half-way?

However, there is a new theory of change. In the wake of the "new wars"—"weaponisation", EDT, and other new forms of warfare including AI, the above-mentioned peacekeeping principles like the consensus criterion has already altered but remained decisive in practice. Is this outdated? As far as the use of force is concerned, it became clear that the International Community, based on the intervention logic of R2P, continues to pursue no other global security approach than that of human security in its second-generation version (Mary Kaldor, ÖFSE, Vienna, 11 December 2018). The potential of human-centrism as a renewed universal conceptualisation of human security against a regionalised body of actors, to the contrary, has not yet been experienced respectively: A clear line on the tight conditions under which a peace operation must take place could not be agreed upon. Despite all progress made, the UN remained trapped in geostrategic considerations.

This *strategic weakness of multilateralism* in a decisive phase is similarly reflected in the "principled pragmatism" of the 2016 EU Global Strategy, with which the EU figures possibly as the only "true friend and advocate of effective multilateralism", while the need for reform in the UN system is basically acknowledged. What lacks is the own positioning, not only in reaction to others. This factum becomes clear when looking at intra-European tensions concerning the vision of a defence union, which were reduced by Brexit but still exist (Biscop 2018: 191–195; Gu, *TDHJ Special Edition #03 21*; Werther-Pietsch 2021: 143). But only sufficiently institutionalised and clearly innovative positioning will enable multilateralists, the supposed "third", to balance geopolitically poerful entities and calculations.

What ist more, across the interests of the major armed forces and UNSC members, *protection of civilians* as the central peacekeeping task becomes apparent—for some the human rights-based, for others the more concise concept compared to the responsibility to protect. The theory of multilateral system thinking shows that a precision by the definition of crimes against humanity is possible. As will be argued, human-centrism classifies to figure as common denominator for future ICCM.

8.3.1 From Observer to Stabiliser

Basement 1948–1960

When the UN was founded in 1945, significance of peacekeeping was not fully grasped. Although the UN was mandated with the core objective of "preserving world peace and international security and taking effective collective action to that end" (Article 1 of the UN Charter), peacekeeping in this form was not provided for in the Charter. The legitimacy of peace missions was therefore based on a link between Chapters VI and VII of the Charter (the latter "Chapter VI ½"): While Chapter VI contains the "peaceful" means for maintaining peace and security, such as mediation and preventive diplomacy, Chapter VII describes "robust" measures which also include the use of military force, for example, to enforce a ceasefire.

On the basis of this interpretation, the UN deployed its first peacekeeping mission just three years after its foundation. The deployment in the Middle East which is still active today reflects the typical pattern of deployment in the early phase of peacekeeping. The mission consisted essentially of lightly or completely unarmed troops and was set up as a "buffer zone" to monitor a ceasefire between belligerent states. In connection with this original objective, the term "traditional" peacekeeping or peacekeeping of the first generation is used today (UNRIC 2008).

Expansion 1960–1980

In the following years, more robust missions under Chapter VII were increasingly equipped with more complex mandates. Due to the veto right of the P-5, however, the UN was marked by a political stalemate during the years of the Cold War, whereby only 13 missions were authorised until 1987 (Werther-Pietsch and Ritzer 2012, 2013). Towards the end of the Cold War a gradual rapprochement between the USA and the Soviet Union occurred.[1] In the course of "glasnost" and "perestroika, a more cooperative atmosphere developed in the UNSC, which resulted in a rapid growth of peace operations. Between 1988 and 1994 alone, the UNSC approved 22 new missions—more than before in its entire history.

Not only did the number of missions increase during this period, their ambitious goals also reached their first peak. In addition to the new, almost euphoric mood with regard to the possibilities of peacekeeping, this was a consequence of the changed structure of armed conflicts: while during the Cold War these were mainly carried out between rival states, since the end of the bipolar era they have mostly been of a domestic nature (Human Security Research Group 2010, as described in Part I). For the first time, the framework conditions for peacekeeping changed substantially.

[1] I would like to thank my students of the summer course 2019 at the University of Graz for the preparation of facts.

Pragmatic progress 1980–1990

Instead of monitoring international peace agreements, from the end of the 1980s blue helmets were mainly engaged to stabilise national conflict situations. Characterised by weak or collapsed public institutions, a disturbed social and political relationship between state and society, ethnic rivalries, fragile peace treaties, a typically high number of conflict parties and the frequent occurrence of "spoilers", domestic conflicts posed new challenges for peacekeeping. These fragile environments manifest themselves to this day in the following aspects, among others:

1. A *complex conflict context* makes it difficult to conclude a stable and comprehensive peace or ceasefire agreement. However, solid contracts are an essential prerequisite for successful peacekeeping. If this condition is not fulfilled and the danger of a renewed outbreak of violence thus increases, peace operations are often confronted with the almost impossible task of "*maintaining an inherently untenable peace*" (Doyle 2007).
2. The higher *number of conflict parties* makes it more difficult for all major factions to agree to the deployment of a peace mission. Frequently, individual parties would prefer to settle the conflict themselves, partly in order to play off their own military advantage (Guéhenno 2010). If the first principle of peacekeeping was lacking with the agreement of the parties to the conflict, then compliance with the other two basic principles of peacekeeping—impartiality and the use of force only for self-defence—seemed also more difficult (Weber 2007: 3ff).

8.3.2 The Brahimi Report: Answers to Past Failures

Enhanced tasks 1990–2000

In the period following the end of the Cold War, there was not only an unprecedented expansion of peace operations in terms of numbers and complexity. The UN also experienced some of the most spectacular failures in its history in the first half of the 1990s: its mission in Somalia failed miserably, and even peacekeeping in Rwanda and Bosnia's Srebrenica, too weakly equipped, were unable to prevent genocide. Although the "blue helmets" (see Part I Sect. 4.4.5) have been successful in the same period in Mozambique or El Salvador, the tragic failures have left a lasting impression (Gareis and Varwick 2014).

The changed character of armed conflicts since 1989 meant that military tasks were no longer the sole focus of missions. The international discourse in the field of conflict and peace research supported this trend. Whereas previously it had traditionally been assumed that international stabilisation measures would be sequenced according to which peacekeeping would first provide security in fragile situations and then be replaced by peace-building ("post-conflict peace-building"), there was now increasing awareness of a simultaneous, integrated challenge, and coordinated structure for both tasks. Thus, peacekeepers, like UN-USG Alain Le Roy expressed, acted as early peace builders.

From the mid-1990s, the first major peacekeeping boom came to an end and entered a phase of consolidation. At the same time, peace operations were being seen more and more critically (Autesserre 2019: 108). The innovative rethinking, which had led to a stronger focus on the improved integration of traditional peacekeeping with peace consolidation tasks, could not really live up to the high expectations of embedding it in broad political processes. The holistic concept for international support in the transition phase from conflict to peace had to be optimised. In this sense, peace operations must not be seen as an isolated function but can only be one component of international engagement (see A4P 2018 in the following).

Culmination point in 2000

Characterised by multidimensionality and ambitious integrated mandates, peacekeeping was thus entering its second phase ("second generation peacekeeping", Kühne 2005). Since then, the most important tasks in the post-conflict area have included securing humanitarian aid, reforming the security sector, rebuilding public institutions, building infrastructure, and promoting local reconciliation (Ban 2010: 12ff; Starlinger 2017: 176-209). In view of these tasks, however, more and more civilian and police forces were needed to implement the mandates, as a result of which peacekeeping has changed radically and key positions have gone to civilian experts. This comprehensive approach culminated at the end of the last century in Kosovo (UNSCR 1244/1999) and East Timor (UNSCR 1272/1999) in the most complex missions to date. In both cases, classic peacekeeping activities clearly receded into the background: under the leadership of the UN Secretariat, the UN established a political transitional administration that took on state-building agendas far beyond core military tasks.

In order to provide a systemic response to the growing challenges and to overcome the setbacks of the 1990s, towards the end of the decade UNSG Annan convened a commission of experts led by the Algerian diplomat Lakhdar Brahimi. The aim was to analyse the role of UN peacekeeping missions in armed conflicts and to develop recommendations for action. The Brahimi Report, presented in 2000, concluded that in many cases there was a lack of political will on the part of the member states—and consequently of material support—and of an effective structure within the UN.

Among the many recommendations of the Brahimi Report were a refocusing of missions on realistic mandates while observing the basic principles of peacekeeping, improved cooperation between relevant stakeholders within the UN, and an increase in human resources (Brahimi et al. 2000).

8.4 Challenges Revisited

8.4.1 Strategic Trends Post-Brahimi

Developments 2000–2010

Although by no means all recommendations of the Brahimi Report were implemented, a new wave of peacekeeping missions began at the turn of the millennium, strengthened by the overall reform process and the relative successes in Kosovo and East Timor. In Africa in particular, a number of multidimensional missions have been established since then. These include, for example, the missions in Burundi and Sierra Leone, which have now been successfully completed, as well as the missions that are still active in Liberia and Côte d'Ivoire. What was remarkable about this expansion was not only the number of new missions, but also their size and thus the formal explosion in capital and personnel employed: the annual budget grew from less than 1 billion in 1999 to over 7 billion US Dollar in less than ten years; in the same period, the number of uniformed employees worldwide skyrocketed from around 17,000 to over 100,000.[2]

This period of growth, which lasted almost ten years, brought the UN to the limits of its capacity, resulting in a decline in peacekeeping activities from around 2008. Since then, peacekeeping missions have only been sent to Sudan and South Sudan and an observer mission to Syria. The missions in the Central African Republic and Chad as well as between Ethiopia and Eritrea, however, were terminated and other missions partially reduced (Guéhenno 2010), a fact that has lately been reversed in the Ethiopian Province Tigray in Spring 2021 (Leitner, *TDHJ Special Edition #01 21*). The renewed consolidation phase is also reflected in a slight decline in the budget and the number of employees, who are no longer reaching the level of 2008 and 2009 (Ritzer in Werther-Pietsch 2017).

All in all, an extremely broad spectrum of international crisis management, military protection of aid supplies, military enforcement of sanctions, guarding of selective no-fly zones, administration of security cordons, execution of air strikes, extensive occupations and basically entire invasions, but legitimately not regime change, can be assumed at this point in time (UN Handbook on UN Multidimensional PKOs 2003). At the same time, missions encompassed components such as mediation, early warning, security sector (system) reform, and scenario-based PKOs (Haery, CIC 2010).

New tasks entail new risks

The package of 57 Brahimi recommendations met with a previously unknown intensity of internal conflicts with their specific challenges for the UN. Surrounded by weak peace agreements and disintegrating state structures, peacekeeping missions must be robust in order to have a deterrent effect on combatants—also thanks to at the beginning typically superior armament—and to enable the cessation of armed

[2] https://peacekeeping.un.org/en. Accessed 8 August 2021.

activities. In many missions, blue helmets were attacked or victims of acts of sabotage, restricted in their actions by their own rules and international regulations. In the last 15 years, mission mandates have therefore mostly been issued under Chapter VII of the UN Charter, which gives missions the opportunity to carry out their tasks with military force. How and under what circumstances armed force may be used is defined separately for each mission in the so-called "Rules of Engagement" (Santos Cruz Report 2017).

Many considerations were made to ensure an adequate response to the risk increases associated with the enlarged tasks. One possibility was the reactivation of a "world police force", as already provided for in Article 42 of the UN Charter. However, the establishment of "stand-by forces", as proposed in the report, could only be partially fulfilled and complied. UN Standby Arrangements System (UNSAS) for rapid operational readiness within 30 days was implemented in the Standby High Readiness Brigade (SHIRBRIG). The core staff consisted of 15 nations (including Austria), operations in Ethiopia/Eritrea and Liberia took place in 2001 and 2003. Beyond that, however, "Rapid Reaction Forces" could not record any international peace operations. Another consequence of the implementation of the report was the creation of 184 new peacekeeping posts in the UN Secretariat. All in all, two strategic long-term trends can be observed in response to the changed situation:

1. On the one hand, *the UN in this period makes greater use of the possibilities offered by Chapter VIII of the UN Charter and seeks cooperation with regional and sub-regional organisations* such as the AU, ECOWAS, the Arab League, and the OSCE. Although long underestimated, the importance of cooperation for the UN is obvious: Strategic partnerships not only allow the costs of peace operations to be shared, they also enable a better understanding of the local context and can thus contribute to greater legitimacy in the perception of the local population (UNDPKO and DFS 2010: 34ff).
2. On the other hand, *attempts have been made to improve cooperation between the relevant units within the UN*. After a recent restructuring in the UN Secretariat, the main decision-makers in the field of peacekeeping should cooperate more closely, jointly develop realistic strategies and conduct a constructive dialogue (UNDPKO and DFS 2009: 9ff; A4P Declaration 2018).

8.4.2 Influence of Development Thinking

Integration 2010–2015

The tendency towards internal conflicts not only triggered a rethinking of the operational and strategic concept of peacekeeping, but also inevitably changed the normative reference system which serves the International Community as a basis for interventions in third countries. Compared with traditional peacekeeping, such as an observer mission in the buffer zone between two states, a peacekeeping operation in intra-state conflicts is politically significantly more delicate politically and must be seen in a balance with the principle of non-interference in the "internal" affairs of a sovereign state. The Brahimi Report contributed to the fact that peace missions in the last twenty years have increasingly relied not only on the UN Charter but also on aspects of the international human rights regime and humanitarian law as well as dimensions of development policy dimensions of engagement (UNDPKO and DFS 2008: 14f).

Human security plays an important role in the legitimacy of peace missions, and not only from a security policy perspective. Conversely, in recent years a view has also established itself in development policy that sees security as a central prerequisite for sustainable development. Development is therefore inextricably linked with peace (Annan 2006: "*No development without security, and no security without development*"). Peacekeeping can play an important role in establishing a minimum level of security necessary for development. This resulted in common strategies at the interfaces between the policy fields (Austrian Strategic Guideline Security and Development, 2011, WDR, 2011, States of Fragility Reports of the OECD, World Bank, and UNDP 2018). In the course of the debate, POC in particular gained significant importance as a legal justification for missions. The controversial R2P was replaced in subsequent years by a standstill. After the ambivalent experiences in Libya and Syria, this path proved to be the only viable compromise formula. First mentioned in 1999 in UNAMSIL's mandate as the task of a peace mission, the protection of the civilian population has now become the core task of almost all UN peacekeeping missions.

Today the missions are measured by the world public against the successful protection of the civilian population. Although most mandates today include POC and provide for more and more robust execution ("*use all necessary means up to and including the use of deadly force to protect civilians from physical violence*", UNSG Report on R2P, 2009), these expectations are rarely met. The divergence between expectations and de facto implementation is partly due to unrealistic claims. On-site conditions and scarcity of resources make it impossible for blue helmets to protect everyone, anywhere, anytime. *This brings peacekeeping into a phase of near "hypocrisy".*

8.4.3 Unrealistic Goals and Weak Capacities[3]

In contrast to the legitimate development policy dimension, the exaggerated expectations of peacekeeping instruments that arose in the phase following the founding of the UN unfolded a loss of legitimacy in the long term. Conflict calming was successfully carried out by the UN, but, unlike fighting the causes of conflict, it could not lead to genuine "pacification" for the populations (e.g. Palestine, Lebanon, etc.).

[3] I thank my colleague Thomas Ritzer, UNDP, for his valuable contribution; first published in: Werther-Pietsch, Ursula. 2017. *Global Peace and Security*. Vienna: MANZ, 101–110.

The task definition for modern peacekeeping operations reflects this essential problem of peacekeeping: How can short-term goals such as the establishment of a minimum level of security be reconciled with medium- and long-term goals like sustainable economic development and institution-building? Peacekeeping is constantly moving in the direction of tension and must constantly check which goals can realistically be achieved. Integrated "Road Maps to Peace" (e.g. UNSCR 2254/2015 on Syria) try to solve this problem. However, both the public and the International Community wrongly see peacekeeping as a solution to almost all conflicts. Crises in fragile states are regularly followed by calls for the deployment of a peace mission, without sufficiently validating the existence of the necessary preconditions (especially with regard to the basic principles of peacekeeping) and thus the probability of a successful deployment (Gareis and Varwick 2014). Reasons for that lie in "mission creep" (creeping expansion of mandates), the suppression of problems, via a small share of conflict resolution competence, to missions such as Haiti or East Timor that have been declared successful prematurely.

In addition to the complex tasks, areas of operation also present the UN with major challenges: They are spread across the globe, often in difficult terrain or landlocked regions and are often difficult to reach due to the lack of infrastructure. In combination with the tight budget and the lack of equipment and troops, these circumstances mean that the UN is moving along the limits of its capacities (zif 2009: 42).

8.4.4 *Financing, Equipment, and Training*

Although with around 100,000 soldiers one of the largest "mobilised armies" in the world to date, the member states of the UN have not yet been able to persuade themselves to provide the blue helmets with an appropriate budget (Ritzer in Werther-Pietsch 2017: 101–110). And this already lasts for a while: So represented the 2011 budget of around 7 billion US Dollar just over 1 percent of the budget of the largest military apparatus, the USA (based on figures from UNDPKO 2011).

Similar to the budget, material and training reflect the lacking political will of the member states. Although the UNSC determines the troop strength and equipment for each deployment in the mandate, these requirements are rarely actually met. In most cases, the UN Secretariat must act as a petitioner to the member states to request technically sophisticated equipment (in particular vehicles, helicopters and night vision equipment, drones) and the provision of soldiers. A situation has arisen in which the industrial nations of North America, Europe, and Japan bear most of the financial and material burden, while states from the global South (above all Bangladesh, India, and Pakistan) provide the bulk of the troops (Feichtinger in Werther-Pietsch 2017: 87f). A core problem of this constellation is the often inadequate level of pre-deployment preparation of soldiers, who are often poorly trained and unprepared for their difficult task.

A new task is to secure freedom and the free use of cyberspace together with national authorities, as far as this is reflected in the peacekeeping mandate. The vulnerability of the troops in this respect has, on the other hand, increased immensely, in particular due to the possibilities of non-state actors (see Santos Cruz Report, XXII General Staff Training with Integrated Master's Course at the National Defence Academy, role play 2020).

8.4.5 Management of Integrated Missions

Fulfilling the various aspects of a complex mandate has proved difficult in practice because of the divergent objectives (EPON 2019). Although peace missions do not assume sole responsibility for development policy and humanitarian agendas in addition to security policy tasks, their size and nationwide presence mean that they typically play a leading role among the various UN agencies and thus exercise a certain coordinating function.

All agendas and fields of activity in modern peacekeeping must therefore be integrated into the management of peace missions. The comprehensive approach is important as it provides an opportunity to ensure a consistent approach and to improve cooperation and complementarity between the different components. But it also burdens the steering apparatus of the UNDPO and the individual missions in the field with an almost infinite spectrum of tasks, which can lead to slowness and a lack of flexibility in the management of operations. Although this "predominance" is not intended in this form in the concept of coherence, in practice such a tendency cannot be denied (Santos Cruz Report 2017).

Cooperation between civilian and military forces in a mission has proved to be a permanent challenge despite all efforts. Too often the traditional strategies, communication, hierarchy and control mechanisms of the various contingents are too different. CIMIC (*civil-military cooperation*) units were therefore created in most missions to improve the coordination and cooperation of these components (Bertelsmann, and CEPS 2020: 376).

8.4.6 Performance Measurement and Phasing Out

Countries in which a peacekeeping mission is stationed are less likely to fall back into conflict than others. Nevertheless, it is difficult to determine the impact of a mission in a country. The effectiveness of peacekeeping in the pursuit of global peace and security is controversial in academic and practical circles. Historically, there have been both successes and failures from which no final judgment can be derived (Doyle and Sambanis 2000; Bellamy and Williams 2005; EPON 2019). Extensive empirical studies also come to different conclusions, whereby the interpretation of the results is complicated by the assessment of how the chances of lasting peace with or without peacekeeping would stand in a given situation (Page 2004: 269).

Measuring the success of a mission fails primarily because of the lack of clear criteria as to when a particular mission can be considered successful. The difficulty is that each situation is unique and therefore, there can be no single recipe or threshold beyond which countries are considered to be stable in the long term and operations successful. Although the mandates imposed by the UNSC set certain goals, they usually leave room for interpretation and even their fulfilment does not necessarily guarantee long-term peace (Druckman and Stern 1999).

The definition of concrete criteria for success at the level of individual missions is particularly important because it determines when a mission ends (Wolfgang Petritsch, presentation on the occasion of the visit of George Marshall Center, National Defence Academy, 13 May 2019). Peacekeeping missions are, after all, transitional solutions and can ideally only remain in a country as long as it gives its consent and until it has the appropriate capacity and stability to take on the peacekeeping task itself. The challenge here is to find a balance between an early withdrawal, which leads to renewed fighting for lack of stability, and a delayed withdrawal, which can both evoke a feeling of "occupation" among the local population and delay state-building (Le Roy 2010). For example, benchmarking from the start of operations in Liberia and Cote d'Ivoire in 2017 has led to good execution of "exit strategies".

8.5 Lessons Learned

8.5.1 *Santos Cruz Report: Security of UN Personnel*

New challenges 2015–2018

In addition to the complex situations of intra-state conflicts with high fragmentation of the parties to the conflict, and in some cases also the reversal of state authorities into institutions that most disregard the rights of their own citizens, there were non-traditional threats such as violent extremism and international crime, which were associated with *regionalisation, globalisation, but also massive internationalisation of conflict situations.* The combination of these trends was also evident in increasingly "protracted conflicts", which required new forms of conflict resolution and transformation (e.g. operations in Mali or the Central African Republic).

In practice, the response to these challenges was mainly through the Capstone Doctrine and ad hoc initiatives by senior UN officials (e.g. Michael von der Schulenburg, Civcap Initiative, 2013). The HIPPO Report 2015 thus provided a second major push for reform, which also increased the risk of the missions.[4] This clearly shows that the needs of modern peacekeeping in terms of equipment and capabilities

[4] http://www.un.org/en/peacekeeping/fatalities/documents/stats_5feb.pdf. Accessed 1 August 2021.

cannot be met and that effective mandate implementation must remain the exception. Despite financial motives, questions of reputation and international standing, or concealed national interests, peacekeeping is a task that, in addition to privileges, is also linked to obligations and responsibility. The strict insistence of the member states on their own jurisdiction over the primarily military personnel provided has disadvantages in terms of responsibility and loyalty to the UN (German Bundestag 2008).

An increasingly robust exercise of the mandate correlates with the UNSC's correct tendency to set up peacekeeping missions at ever earlier points in the conflict cycle, assuming approval and reducing the expectation that only an established peace should be safeguarded by UN presence. These developments in peacekeeping represent a flexibility and innovation test for the UN administration. Even if a mood is created against a mission, for example, by inciting the population against the UN (Haiti, when Nepalese peacekeepers were to spread cholera in the country with about 8000 deaths), cutting off supplies and violating international legal agreements concerning the mission (especially the SOFAs), the necessity of cooperation is almost impossible. This also undermines the effectiveness of the operation as a peace broker.

8.5.2 HIPPO Report: Capability Development for Rapid Deployment

The UN needs an average of six months to set up a peacekeeping mission and set it up on the ground. This gives "spoilers" of the peace process and armed groups the opportunity to create new conditions and continue committing human rights violations. In addition, the circumstances in which a PKO is conducted today require "special forces". The *traditional infantries that still make up the lion's share* of the Blue Helmets are not equipped to carry out mass surveillance or forensic analysis to investigate criminal networks. UN peacekeeping must therefore adapt to the new methods of warfare.

To some extent, training can compensate for these deficits. The impact, however, is small in view of the immense number of over 100,000 uniformed troops who need training and further education. In addition, there is the *6–12-month rotation of military personnel.* A delegation to private security companies must be ruled out as a matter of principle due to the sovereign function of peacekeeping. This would require consideration of strict liability and a limited *pouvoir* at the operational level.

8.5.3 Coordination Requirement—A Critical Factor

The "primacy of politics" (OECD-DAC Chairman Erik Solheim, New York, 2014, Stockholm, 2016) cannot be emphasised enough. Each mission must implement the policy objectives set by the UNSC and develop a strategy for all activities. Coordination is essential for this. PKOs do not work in a vacuum, effective coordination even with external actors is a must. These include the host country government, local authorities, other UN agencies, international, and national civil society, including religious groups. Of great importance, although still under-represented, are the links with the population and local representatives, which can play a role, for example, in the context of early warning. A return to the Sustaining Peace Approach (UNSCR 2282/2016) seems the logical way at this point.

8.5.4 A4P Declaration 2018

On 25 September 2019, the UNGA adopted a declaration on peacekeeping, which will probably delay a new edition of the Capstone Doctrine 2008 a little longer. In view of the tense situation between the P-5, but also the currents described in Part I that affect the UN, the way forward that was chosen was certainly a cautiously positive one (UN Secretariat, interviews by the author in New York, March 2019). The declaration contains seven guiding principles: (1) Peacekeeping is seen as support for the political process. (2) In addition, protection of civilians is one of the main tasks, followed by—in response to the Santos Cruz report—(3) the security of UN personnel, (4) accountability and accountability. The orientation towards "sustaining peace" (5) and partnerships (6), which are important for the situation in the country, are just as important points as *zero tolerance* against sexual abuse and, in general, the code of conduct of the troops (7).

How does the current implementation of these guiding principles look like? In the recent report on the Effectiveness of Peace Operations Network (EPON) 2019 on the UN Mission in South Sudan (UNMISS), some of the points discussed are partly confirmed, partly further developed. It thus turned out that in the South Sudanese context protection zones function better than joint patrolling for the protection of the civilian population. It is politically sensitive when such zones lead to the "*homogenisation*" of the population. Local involvement with a constructive role of the UN Special Representative at the regional level (IGAD, AU), however, combined with a decentralisation of *pouvoir* to the field presence was successful and has contributed to flexibility and responsiveness. An effects and capability-based approach appears important, in which local involvement must always be geared to the priorities of the mission. Nevertheless, with a splitting of 207 tasks in the mandate, this remains unclear in terms of implementation. On the other hand, the Rule of Law section, one of the few capacity-building roles that UNMISS has maintained in the process of reducing state-building in view of the government's behaviour blocking the peace process, has led to good acceptance through "behind-the-scenes" work. The Regional Protection Forces (RPF) are highlighted as particularly positive for "regional buy-in" to the peace process, although they still leave much to be desired in operational terms (Werther-Pietsch, Strategy Conference Vienna, National Defence Academy, 27 June 2019).

At a global level, and looking far beyond the example of UNMISS, the International Peace Institute (IPI) in New York in 2020/2021 presents a comprehensive discussion series to accompany UN management reform at an academic level, a process that is ongoing for the moment.[5]

8.6 Possible Innovations

In this context, many efforts have been made to make peacekeeping fit for the future: Under UNSG Antonio Guterres' leadership, a review was launched in 2016, including the peacekeeping summit chaired by US President Obama in 2015, which led to increased troop contingents and greater independence of the UN from a few large troop-providing states. This trend was confirmed and continued by the pledges of UN members at the peacekeeping summit in March 2019. It also promoted the creation of a "Peacekeeping Capability Readiness System" (Early Entry Forces, FAC 2021) in order to be able to go into action more quickly. Modern technology is to be used for information collection, observation, and reconnaissance. Legal framework conditions for the responsibility of military peacekeepers are also being brought forward.

8.6.1 Bettering Mandates—More Specialised Missions

There is no more appetite for multidimensional intervention at large. Comprehensive approach is capability-driven and specified in tasks operated by cooperating actors. Therefore, implementable mandates, equipment, and political support in implementation are among the most important prerequisites for a successful mission of whatever configuration. In January 2017, UNSG Guterres described the task of peacekeeping before the UNSC in a concise manner: "*To save lives. To prevent mass atrocities. To set the stage for stability and sustainable peace*" (UNSG, UNSC Thematic Debate on Peacekeeping Operations Review, 2017) this seems to be better communicable than the protection of each individual in a country or the utopian formula of a "new Switzerland". The mode how mandates can be streamlined and clear tasks be articulated is being developed in the UN Secretariat on the basis of the 2019 Summit.

8.6.2 Technology Challenge—More Targeted Action

The tailor-made capability-driven comprehensive approach developed on the basis of the Sustaining Peace Approach paves the way for future intervention logic. To

[5] https://www.ipinst.org/. Accessed 8 August 2021.

underline the necessity to act in an interdisciplinary mode, multi-domain operations could come into being, building on a relatively exact foresight of tools and capabilities and development planning to be used for probable deployment scenarios. With this, the 2018 A4P Declaration could become operative.

Capability components, geopolitical scenario assessments, and technological innovations of responding to non-kinetic low-threshold confrontations such as spreading "fake news" are asked for. Specialisation to fight new versions of old "propaganda" war, cyber warfare using deep data learning and artificial intelligence, drones as well as reconnaissance and increasingly autonomous weapons will complement infantry-based classic UN peace operations. However, beyond social media, the virtual space and the wider universe, securing peace will also remain a task of presence of human beings, of intervening and of visibly protecting civilians.

References

Autesserre, Séverine. 2019. The crisis of peacekeeping. Why the UN can't end wars. *Foreign Affairs* 2019: 101–116.

Ban, Ki-Moon. 2010. Progress report of the Secretary-General on Peacebuilding in the immediate aftermath of conflict.

Bellamy, Alex, and Paul Williams. 2005. Who's keeping the peace? Regionalization and contemporary peace operations. *International Security* 29.

Bertelsmann Stiftung, and Centre for European Policy Studies (CEPS). 2020. *Europe's coherence gap in external crisis and conflict management: Political rhetoric and institutional practice in the EU and its member states*. Brussels: Bertelsmann Stiftung.

Biscop, Sven. 2018. PESCO, strategic autonomy, and ambition. *Security and Peace* 4 (2018): 191–195.

Brahimi, Lakhdar et al. 2000. Comprehensive review of the whole question of Peacekeeping operations in all their aspects. *Vereinte Nationen* A/55/305-S/2000/809. https://www.unic.or.jp/security_co/pdf/a_55_305_e.pdf. Accessed 8 Aug 2021.

Center for International Peace Operations (zif). http://www.zif-berlin.org/de/schwerpunkte/vernetztes-handeln-comprehensive-approach.html. Accessed 8 Aug 2021.

Dos Santos Cruz, Carlos Alberto. 2017. *Improving security of United Nations peacekeepers (Santos Cruz Report)*. New York: United Nations.

Doyle, Michael. 2007. *The John W. Holmes lecture: Building peace*. Academic Council on the United Nations System. https://findarticles.com/p/articles/mi_7055/is_1_13/ai_n28411764/?tag=content;col1. Accessed 8 Aug 2021.

Doyle, Michael, and Nicholas Sambanis. 2000. Making war and building peace. United Nations peace operations. *The Review of Internationale Organizations* 1.

Druckman, Daniel, and Paul Stern. 1999. Perspectives on evaluating peacekeeping missions. *The International Journal of Peace Studies* 4.

EPON (Effectiveness of Peace Operations Network). 2019.*Assessing the effectiveness of the United Nations mission in South Sudan/UNMISS*. Norwegian Institute of International Affairs.

Feichtinger, Walter. 2017. International crisis management revisited. In *Global peace and security. International crisis and conflict management*, ed. Ursula Werther-Pietsch, 87. Vienna: MANZ.

Page, Fortna Virginia. 2004. Does peacekeeping keep peace? *International Studies Quarterly* 48.

Gareis, Sven Bernhard, and Johannes Varwick. 2014. *The United Nations. Tasks, instruments and reforms*, 5th ed. Opladen/Toronto: Publisher Barbara Budrich UTB.

German Bundestag, Wissenschaftliche Dienste. 2008. Attributability under international law of human rights violations during the deployment of German soldiers in peacekeeping forces, SD 2 3000—106/08.
Gu, Xuewu. Eine G3-Weltordnung. *TDHJ Special Edition #03 21*: 22–26. https://www.thedefencehorizon.org/special-editions?lang=dett. Accessed 8 Aug 2021.
Guéhenno, Jean-Marie. 2010. *Lecture on peace operations*. United Nations: Columbia University, New York.
Kefale, Asnake. 2015. *Regional organizations and security governance: A comparative assessment of IGAD and ASEAN*. London: LSE Global South Unit: Working Paper Series No. 1/2015.
Kühne, Winrich. 2005. *The UN peace missions*. Federal Centre for Political Education. http://www.bpb.de/apuz/29023/die-friedenseinsaetze-der-vn?p=all. Accessed 8 August 2021.
Leitner, Matthias. 2021. *Konflikt in Nordäthiopien - Wege zur Konfliktbeilegung*. TDHJ #01 21: 26–28.
Starlinger, Thomas. 2017. Creating a Planning and Operating Mechnaism - a Stance by a Military. In *Global Peace and Security*. 99 Lessons on International Crisis and Conflict Management, ed. Ursula Werther-Pietsch. Vienna: MANZ, 176–209.
UN Handbook on United Nations Multidimensional Peacekeeping Operations. 2003. New York United Nations.
UNDPKO und United Nations Department of Field Support. 2009. *A new partnership agenda: Charting a new horizon for UN peacekeeping*. https://www.un.org/en/Peacekeeping/documents/newhorizon.pdf. Accessed 8 August 2021.
UNDPKO, and United Nations Department of Field Support. 2010. *Peacekeeping and peacebuilding. clarifying the Nexus*. https://www.securitycouncilreport.org/atf/cf/%7B65BFCF9B-6D27-4E9C-8CD3-CF6E4FF96FF9%7D/PKO%20Peacebuilding%20Peacekeeping%20Nexus.pdf. Accessed 8 Aug 2021.
United Nations Regional Information Center. 2008. *60 years of United Nations Peacekeeping (background information)*. https://www.unric.org/html/german/pdf/2008/UNRIC_Hintergrund_Peacekeeping.pdf. Accessed 8 Aug 2021.
Weber, Thomas. 2007. *Cooperation between the United Nations and Regional Organizations in Peacekeeping Operations*. ETH Zurich. http://www.isn.ethz.ch/isn/Digital-Library/Publications/Detail/?ots591=0c54e3b3-1e9c-be1e-2c24-a6a8c7060233ng=end=35888. Accessed 8 Aug 2021.
Werther-Pietsch, Ursula, and Thomas Ritzer. 2012. *Failed states—Statebuilding as conflict prevention*. Vienna/Graz: NWV–Berliner Wissenschaftsverlag.
World Bank, and UNDP. 2018. *Pathways for peace. Inclusive approaches to preventing conflict*. Washington DC: World Bank. https://openknowledge.worldbank.org/handle/10986/28337. Accessed 8 Aug 2021.

Chapter 9
Modelling the Future

9.1 Common Ground and Twin-Track Approach

As a lesson from the COVID-19 pandemic, conceptualisations of resilience, the principle of subsidiarity and localisation, echoing the results of the entire peacekeeping reform, were reinforced. To underpin its strategic relevance in a changed global environment, the UN System of Collective Security must react to these stringent impulses by a much more focussed approach for global peace and security. It is therefore worth re-examining whether a common denominator can serve as a key between collaborative regional orders. That's why efforts in focusing on,

- *a joint orientation towards "fight for humanity" as political leitmotiv;* while
- *strengthening regional conflict resolution mechanisms,*

could be one of the most important conclusions from this analysis and headline goal for the future.

Globalisation has undoubtedly increased prosperity in absolute terms, but it has also widened the gap between the rich and the poor and squeezed the use of resources, since redistribution of wealth and green economy have not been balanced to the same extent. One of the reasons for this is that globalisation, in the course of the expansion of worldwide interconnectivity, caused a weakening of the nation state responsible for satisfying the basic needs of the individual citizen. National structures have increasingly been embedded in a network of restrictive obligations and mutual dependencies, which in turn weakened democracy, and stimulated deep feelings of extra-legal and organic sovereignty (Paris 2002: 6–7). In addition, states were to handle an ever more complex world, increased simultaneity, manage huge orientation tasks and substantial change of communication attitudes. Resulting misunderstandings have contributed to political populism. From this analysis follows that regions come in as actors.

As it stands, two deficits of the UN System of Collective Security (Chapter VII) and system of peaceful conflict resolution (Chapter VI), still central mechanisms of

U. Werther-Pietsch, *Transforming Security*, Global Power Shift,
https://doi.org/10.1007/978-3-030-87097-3_9

peace and security at the beginning of the twenty-first century, have arisen and shall be addressed at this stage:

- There has not been sufficient commitment to *conflict prevention as a collective regional responsibility* of equal rank to the quasi-established responsibility to protect (see in the following). In regard to the COVID-19 crisis this is a clear gap. Reasons can be depicted in
  - Short-term horizon of the UN Charter's Security Chapters
  - Original dominance of security over development
  - Initial human rights "undersupply" of the system
  - Political constellation of the victorious powers in 1945 and long-standing global loyalty pattern of the East–West conflict
  - Continuing prevalence of military weight and potential in a multipolar geopolitical setting
  - Media and political coverage only after the outbreak of conflict or disaster.
- On an equal footing, a general directive for *regional conflict resolution* derived from the concept of human security as a result of combining the three principles of the prohibition of the use of force, sovereignty and the monopoly of the UNSC for military operations could not be established and rests exploitable. This fact is due above all to the veto right of the P-5, which makes the prevailing System of Collective Security only a limited mechanism for peace and security from an equality and justice point of view.

This has been the ultimate response of the UN to encounter the new challenges so far.

The reform processes on peacekeeping of the years 2000, 2008 to 2012 and 2019, flanked by the revision of the new mandate for the UN Human Rights Council in 2011 and, later, the foundation of the Peace-building Commission in 2015, therefore, constitute a *bon moment* in history: It shows that failures and weaknesses of the past advanced important incentives to remedy deficits of the international system in a time when effective reaction gets more and more pressing. The emergence of changed rules of the game in a new era, especially from 2017 onwards, is anew an opportunity to readjust the system (Martin Selmayr, EC Ambassador in Vienna, 29 Jan 2020 at UNA-Austria Vienna) and undertake steps in order to consolidate a non-G1 or G2, though P-5 sensitive link between collaborative regional orders.

From developments above, especially with a view to uphold multi-polarity and diversity under the umbrella of universal values, the "Sustaining Peace Approach" in line with capability-driven comprehensive components of ICCM emanated. Indeed, as progressive global interconnectedness requires, ICCM concepts do not longer reflect the narrow concept of the UN founding era only. Instead, the new principles complement origins and are based today on UNSCR 2282/2016 and the 2018 A4P Declaration. Knut Ipsen's UN as a "conflict resolution order" was thereby, on the basis of progressive landmark agendas (1992, 2005, 2015, 2016; Werther-Pietsch 2020) definitely expanded to a full-fledged sustained global peace and security order, put to test in real life.

Whether this will end in an overstretching of forces cannot be forecast rigorously, it depends on how future challenges will unfold pressure to do so. However, this comes with a consequence from the COVID-crisis, containment and cooperation between the P-5 could become more important, and the UN again made stronger; the organisation should streamline its mandate, proving capable of reform. This may be done through precising criteria for obligatory intervention on the basis of a renewed protection mechanism in cases of "crimes against humanity" and activating regional configurations in the run-up to the involvement of UNSC and thereafter.

9.2 Track One: "Peace and Security Councils"

At the core of the proposal to better respond to the growing role of regional arrangements, Peace & Security Councils (PSCs) could be established under the chairmanship of a rotating regional presidency, a P-5 member and the UNSG. The UNSC would have to designate permanent regional bodies including circles of multilateral institutions active in the region. Former foreign ministers, mediators, "eminent persons" should be involved on a consensual ad hoc basis if required. As a mapping of existing "Chapter VIII houses" and for tactical reasons, PSCs, according to deliberations on military strengths, should not exceed five worldwide.

The discussion as such is not new. In fact, this question was already addressed in the years following WW II: "*The choice between regionalism and universalism weighted heavily on the planning of the post-war collective security system.*" (United Nations, UN-Doc A/CN.4/L.682 as of 13 April 2008, para 196). With recourse to the formula, Winston Churchill's future-oriented appeal to think about "*a Council of Europe and a Council of Africa under the common roof of the world organization*" (1945) culminates in the anyhow regretful objection of Johan Galtung made at the conference "Making the Difference" in Brussels in June 2009, "*the Security Council is not a Peace Council*". Galtung adds that the UNSC focussing on all hot spots of armed conflict worldwide does not dispose of a more comprehensive mandate to include the before and after—prevention and transition, elements that were stressed in the subsequent ICCM debate. The leadership of the PSCs in line with the UNSC could balance this unresolved gap.

9.2.1 The Growing Role of Regional Arrangements

As a model following the composition of the UN Peace-building Commission and equipped with the purposes of the UN Human Rights Council, the PSCs *de lege ferenda* would have to implement universal principles and established rules of the prohibition of the use of force under the guidelines of the UNSC and according to ICC ruling. The 2009 UNSG Report on Peace-building in the aftermath of conflict contains a list of tasks in paragraph 45a, which reads like a start-up set of PSCs performance ("*conflict-sensitive development analysis, [indigenous] mediation capacity, consensus and dialogue, local dispute resolution capacity*"). This list would have to be extended to fields of action in the realms of peace-building and state-building which places the idea close to an integrated "Cooperative- ICCM (C-ICCM)".

In the event of a manifest crisis or conflict, i.e. to invoke a binding reaction in cases of a serious violation of *ius cogens* (see in track 2):

- The decision by the PSC would have to be made *immediately* on the basis of objectified criteria without the express consent of the involved parties to the dispute, legally attributed to the UNSC as primarily responsible that would without exception have to take a final decision on the matter within a fixed period of time (24 h, 48 h, three days, 1 month).
- The PSCs would thus be *empowered* with temporarily limited highest decision-making authority for starting the protective mechanism in the case of a manifest crime against humanity. In a peace policy lens, the possibility of a sharp warning sign to conflict parties, reinforced through the potential confirmation by the UNSC, could generally favour a "cooling off" period like already foreseen in the League of Nations. The Arab League practised a similar role in Libya 2011, even without executing a normative mandate.
- The PSCs would also serve to deal with fragile situations from a *holistic perspective*—a roof under which modern ICCM could be unified and lead to an effect-based comprehensive approach at regional level.

9.2.2 Responsibilities of the International Community

For ready-made operationalisation, renowned independent institutes could be commissioned with an observer function ("*Centres of Excellence for Peace*"; P-COEs). These would have to be placed under the aegis of the UN in order to operate regular reporting and provide input to the respective PSC members. Once or twice a year a direct reporting to the UNSC by each PSC should be foreseen. Furthermore, P-COEs would have to be consulted obligatorily before a protection mechanism operation is released. Often unclear and disputed facts, for instance on armed quarrels at local level due to fake news, could thus be countered by building common understanding, professional oversight and mutual trust over the years. Taylor Owen, as early as 2004 and followed by many, for instance prepared the ground for objectively measuring fragility for early warning with a multivariate bundle of human security parameters (2004: 373–387).

Accordingly, and with a view to increasingly simultaneous conflict phases and scenarios, the responsibility of the PSCs in their respective regional competences is to be interpreted and mandated holistically. Essentials for implementing the interwoven triad of conflict prevention, a regrouping of existent and slight enlargement of tasks to be accepted by the International Community on the whole, the human security and human rights-based "doing good" imperative in status of fragility and transition, consists in:

- "*Responsibility to prevent*": On basis of regular and ad hoc consultations with Peace Centres of Excellence on all issues relevant to peace and security;
- "*Responsibility to mediate*": Expansion and provision of stand-by mediation teams at regional level with special skills that are administratively attributed to the PSCs;
- "*Responsibility to react*": Protection against an imminent crisis or conflict in the event of an acute threat to the lives of a large number of people in the forefront of UNSC action;
- "*Responsibility to rebuild*": Targeted support for the development of democratic regimes and inclusive economic programmes in the phase of reconstruction and reconciliation.

This approach realises a shared responsibility that puts sovereignty in a developing country-friendly light (Von Arnauld 2009: 27–32) but at the same token safeguards the interests of the P-5 through inclusion and leadership.

The EU as a "champion of multilateralism" has a special role to play in this theatre and could take the lead by setting-up an EU Security Council (Whineray 2020). Under the often-emphasised rule of law position of EU partners, member states led by France and partly Germany are in principle ready to build a European defence identity by 2025—a willingness that provokes competitiveness and opposition. It is precisely for this reason that the state of affairs in UN law as centralised while enforcement being left decentralised must be reformed (Werther-Pietsch 2019: 155–166).

To sum up, in the field of peacekeeping the answer to new challenges and constellations lies in an initial push for a two-tiered collective security approach under the roof of "fight for humanity", to be suggested in the following track two.

9.2.3 Visualisation of Argumentation Track 1

In order to make the proposed instrument operational, a trend towards regionalisation that is already under way shall be systematised (Fig. 9.1).

Historical momentum

In combination with the proposed binary structure with arguable advantages for better peacekeeping in the service of "Sustained Peace", a second historical step in IL seems to be ripe and operable these days: The logical conclusion of a two-tiered model, albeit associated with a high degree of diplomatic effort, is that the P-5 would have to agree to a restriction of their veto right in return for augmented stability and the strengthening of their regional autonomy. The following innovative approach to sharpen cases in which the veto would be banned combined with the two-tiered peace alert system shows how the legal figure of *ius cogens* could succeed.

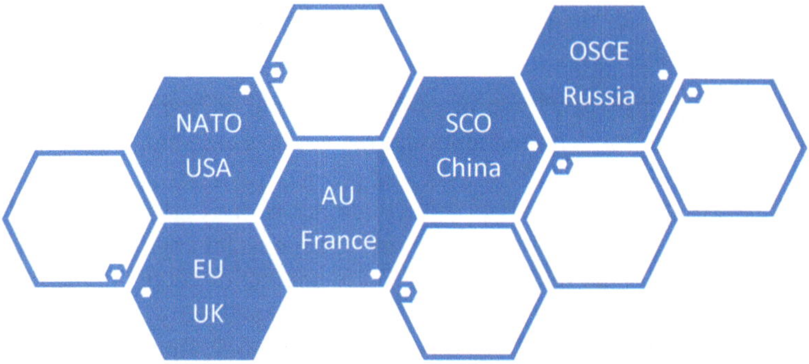

Fig. 9.1 Model of "regional backyards" of UNSC and rough allocation of P-5 to possible PSCs (own source)

9.3 Track Two: "Fight for Humanity "Approach

The fundamental principles of the Charter—prohibition of the use of force, sovereign equality and non-intervention, Articles 1, 2 (4) and 2 (7)—are understood as a concrete operationalisation of the UN's overall objectives of "peace and security, human rights, and development" as expressed in paragraph 9 of 2005 UN Reform Summit Outcome Document. They have therefore also been referred to as fundamental or functional norms (Bernhardt in Mosler FS 1983). However, based on key findings of the 2004 High-Level-Panel on Threats, Challenges and Change,[1] ascertain under-equipment with regard to the required range of effective peace engagement in the sense of human security was to be asserted.

This insight has guided action for the last 15 years confirms what political scientists Mary Kaldor and Gottfried Münkler in line with development policy pioneers such as Franz Nuscheler and Ulrich Preuß in unison distilled from many scholarly and practice sources: Namely that human security has so far crystallised to be the only foundation of peace and security at global level that has not yet been falsified. A stark signal for a revival of human security could be evoked by the COVID-19 global action in 2020.

9.3.1 From Human Security to Human-Centrism

Indeed, human security has been a driving force of the international order in the twenty-first century and has gained the status of "meta principle". How did this interfere with the System of Collective Security? An ambiguous narrative. Early in

[1] https://www.un.org/ruleoflaw/blog/document/the-secretary-generals-high-level-panel-report-on-threats-challenges-and-change-a-more-secure-world-our-shared-responsibility/. Accessed 8 August 2021.

history of thoughts, the Rousseau-like "return to the individual" (Rioux 2001: 41) introduced the now contemporary focus on human beings and vulnerabilities as an axiom for action of the International Community. In the face of realpolitik, autocratic message-control, newly emerging nationalisms as well as international crime and terrorism as roots and causes of irregular violence, human security has proven to be a counterpart to national security thinking and definitely expanded international instruments for peace-building and development. This argumentation is linked to a thrust towards an "effective and strategic multilateralism", which would demand

- a comprehensive understanding and engagement—building a capability-based comprehensive approach on the basis of the "Sustained Peace" model,
- a legally binding veto ban in the case of the most serious human rights violations—revision of Article 27 (3) of the UN Charter—and
- responsible sovereignty as associated element to the acceptance of the prevalence of the Charter—Article 103 thereof.

Essentially, the axiomatic assumption is that the individual, as the subject of the principle of self-determination in IL, is given central importance (Werther-Pietsch 2009: 167–234).

- ***"Responsible sovereignty"***

By establishing human security inspired "responsible sovereignty" (Deng et al. 2005; In Larger Freedom, UN Doc A/59/2005 as of 21 March 2005) as the telos, IL began to look closely at the internal sphere of governance. Finding itself on a "moving scale" (PCIJ, 1923), the question what is to be understood as domestic affairs has changed substantially. This is especially true since the founding of the ICC 1998 (Dubler and Kalyk 2018). The prohibition of genocide, war crimes, crimes against humanity and ethnic cleansing, but also piracy, trafficking in human beings, organs and drugs, violation of the ban on slavery or torture, or systematic exclusion from public life—part of them acknowledged as *ius cogens*—are all linked to human security thinking. In these cases, it would border on cynicism to argue that human rights/human security is striving for hegemony when it comes to intervention. It is the qualified density of protection situations that is guiding in such circumstances. The UNSC's mandate for peacekeeping operations and the PBC's integrated country strategies support this interpretation (Thalhammer 2018; Hänggi and Scherrer 2007; Osuga Takeshi, PBC chair, Lecture at the INCAF Meeting, Paris, 4 December 2008). Under the condition of a UN mandate, these severe cases have therefore increasingly not been judged as a politisation of the domestic sphere but as a concrete engagement for global peace and security—waging fight for humanity as the new *common denominator* of intervention.

Realiter it is to be objected that this approach is pursued predominantly by the IL doctrine more than in politics, as can easily be observed by contradictory positions regarding the Turkish invasion against the Kurdish population in North Syria in October 2019. This is further reflected in UN work streams such as the Commission on the Status of Women or the C 34-Committee. No consensus has been reached on the final reports for their annual meetings. Even "agreed language" must be fought for and actively uphold. This evolution currently gives the upper hand to those forces that speak out against a more open understanding of sovereignty.

- ***"All necessary means/measures"***

From these ups and downs in the multilateral arena it becomes clear that the admission of a legal figure of UNSC mandated military intervention for the purpose of human rights has partly been interpreted as restricting sovereignty. At the same time, cases of particularly qualified human rights violations under certain aggravating conditions ("crimes against humanity") promoted the creation of an instrument beyond traditional peacekeeping that seem to widen the potential of reaction in ICCM, the "responsibility to protect" (R2P) with a robust pillar III to take "all necessary means/measures" if need be (paragraph 139 of 2005 UN Summit final document). The 2009 UNSG report on R2P assists by interpreting the conditions for robust intervention as "narrow but deep" (paragraph 10 lit. c) referring to Article 7 of the ICC Statute. In parallel, attention is drawn to the non-military scope of the common response (pillars I and II).

In real terms, a second simultaneously emerging concept, "protection of civilians" (POC) may remain the politically more acceptable and more broadly supported concept. And indeed, in the first two decades of our century, POC became increasingly relevant, not only for the NATO Civil-military Cooperation Center for Excellence (C-COE) but also for nearly all UN-led missions. Built up for about a decade in the UN system from UNSCR 1674/2006 to 1894/2009, POC is partly seen as synonym or predecessor of R2P. In modern IL doctrine POC justifies the use of military means as "last resort", even—and to the contrary of UN peacekeeping principles—against the will of the parties to the conflict. When massive war crimes are committed against (large parts of) the population, it serves as the perfect *surrogate for R2P* (Werther-Pietsch 2020: 216–219) resuming both the evolution of peacekeeping necessities and a fortified *ius cogens* in IL. The POC regime as applied in UNSCR 1973/2011 (Libya) will further stimulate action under the "Sustaining Peace Approach" and can generally serve as a suitable starting point for renewed intervention logic.

- ***"Widespread or systematic attack directed against any civilian population"***

According to the 1945 Atlantic Charter (Verdross and Simma 1984, Isensee 1995, Hobe and Kimminich 2004) and later coined by Galtung, Senghaas and Habermas, peace can be understood as a status without human rights violations. Positive human rights peace as a global public good (Inge Kaul) is taken up by the UN in its "Sustained Peace Approach". In order to implement this broad vision, which is intrinsically linked with individual human security and human rights, the mandate of any military operation of the International Community in support of peace and security must focus on a "vital core of IL" the application of which is not open to individual interpretation and to which compliance is obligatory for all partners in all circumstances (Commission on Human Security 2003; Debiel and Franke 2008; ILC 2019). Of highest relevance in fragile and conflict contexts, Article 7 of the Rome Statute shows clear roots in human rights and substantial individualisation of the regime on the whole. The common feature in the sense of Article 53 VCLT is its partial codification in IL, partly in the human rights system, the IHL and international criminal law, all of them operationalising a responsibility to fight for humanity, thus triggering customary elements.

Respect for this "core of *ius cogens*" is a prerequisite for democratic and self-determined development (Cassese 1995). Self-determination, the political term for increasing realisation of human rights for all and counterpart of the philosophical concept of freedom, however, is a dazzling concept. Of course, there is much ("splendid") isolation in world politics. Assistance for the good cause emanates only from the obligatory status against "*systematic, flagrant and widespread violations of human rights*" (UNSCR, 1894/2009) that has been reached. That is why it is suggested that *ius cogens* "as a matter of last resort" has to be activated: "*Widespread or systematic attack directed against any civilian population*" specified in Article 7 ICC Statute may be included in a dynamic application of Article 39 of the UN Charter.

9.3.2 Fight for Humanity as Political Leitmotif

Three projects have so far been identified in search for an answer to the UN system's challenges:

- Overall reform project of the UNSC for a binary competence in peace and security matters;
- Identification of a nucleus of the human rights regime with respect to conflict and crisis;
- The "Sustaining Peace Approach" to manage complexity of intervention.

For a renewed ICCM, an attempt has been made to generate a model of "protective peace mechanism" according to incentives from reality and the formulas at hand which can be viewed as the overall objective, common denominator and political leitmotif of an international intervention obligation in armed conflict. The argumentation can be resumed as follows:

- **Conception of violent conflict as a potential human rights violation**

The field of POC is essentially defined in UNSCR 1265/1999, 1296/2000, 1325/2000, 1612/2005, 1674/2006, 1738/2006, 1820/2008, 1882/2009, 1888/2009, and 1889/2009 as well as 1894/2009. In these resolutions, the criterion for intervention is regularly a question of massive effects on the human rights of civilian population either on physical safety, health, environment or property necessary for survival as a collective which corresponds to the concept of "positive human rights peace" (first mentioned in UNSC Presidential Declaration of 31 January 1992, S/23500, UN, 1992, 66) and reflects the human security definition by freedom from fear and freedom from want (UN, 2016: 6–10). This brings together human rights and human security argumentation chains. Here too, the following applies: Not the entire spectrum of the regime qualifies for collective violation of human rights; it is the core of *ius cogens* relevant for peacekeeping that is at issue. Core human rights provisions such as the prohibition of mass atrocities, caused directly or indirectly, are regarded as fundamental principles of international humanitarian law ("*intransgressible principles of international customary law*", ICJ Legal Opinion on Weapons of mass destruction, Recueil 1996: 226). This synopsis may result in a narrow, objectively manageable intervention regime.

- **A progressive logical step beyond the R2P model—UNSC veto right**

Human security adds to the sharpening of protection of civilians in IHL. In the view pursued here, interventions serve to prevent or end serious violations of human rights ("crimes against humanity") without the consent of the state perpetrator (Finnemore 2003; NGO Coalition for an ICJ advisory opinion 2021). In these cases only, a mandatory ban of the use of the veto right by the P-5 would be the legal consequence of the principles of non-discrimination and equality of all human beings—comprising a major humanitarian advance and gesture to humanity. This concession certainly would have to be outweighed by acknowledging a strengthened position of the P-5 in the PSCs as regional settings in which they are attributed respective dominant influence. According to Antonio Cassese, the avenue of intervention lies with:

> "*gross and egregious breaches of human rights, anarchy in a sovereign state or consistent obstructive behaviour of the regime [..] exclusively for the limited purpose of stopping the atrocities and restoring respect for human rights*" (Cassese 2005).

- **Vital core of international law**

With its focus on massive, systematic human rights violations as a reason for intervention, Cassese's argumentation is largely compatible with the pillars of the concept of human security. However, Cassese does not from the outset restrict the idea to the concrete four crimes of international criminal law quoted in paragraph 139 of the 2005 Summit final document. This human rights background of *ius cogens* in conflict—genocide, ethnic cleansing, war crimes, and crimes against humanity—and the suggested protective peace mechanism is definitely a value added on the way to a modern ICCM.

On the relationship between crimes against humanity and the obligation to intervene the following precising changes are to be taken into consideration: Since the Rome Statute came into force in 1998, international crimes against humanity—including from 2017 onwards wars of aggression (ILC Report 2019)—can be individually prosecuted, regardless of the function in which the crime was committed (Pinochet case, ICJ 2001). What is to be understood by these offences as "highly qualified human rights violations" is subject to ICC jurisdiction, which equally refers to international treaty law such as the 1948 Genocide Convention. In the course of the negotiations on the ICC Statute from 1991 to 1998, the formula on the intensity of the infringement as such, namely "*widespread or systematic attack directed against any civilian population*", was identified and emerged as contractual IL (Article 7 ICC; similar to Nowak "*gross and egregious violation of human rights*", conference at the University of Innsbruck, 16 December 2011). Progress towards an agreement grounded in the work of Dubler and Kalyk (2018) which has been painstakingly clustered since 2008 has a unique selling point for a realistic consensus. It should therefore be regarded as the spearhead of progress in IL at the beginning of our century to be made public, implemented and defended.

- **Peace mechanism and conflict prevention**

As an interpretation maxim and legitimate basis for multilateral intervention, the "Sustaining Peace Approach" is fundamentally compatible with Dubler and Kalyk as well as Cassesean foundations: Whenever tensions and conflicts arise between the prohibition of use of force (peace), sovereignty (non-prohibition of intervention) and human rights (development and human security), the human rights doctrine represents the most striking validation of the UN Charter. From this stance, a conflict prevention imperative of the International Community as well as an obligation to intervene are to be regarded compelling.

Following the ICC formula and recent assumptions of the ILC (2019), the International Community continues to be moving in this direction. However, the failure to apply R2P in Sri Lanka 2009, Darfur 2006, Libya 2011, Myanmar 2017 or current developments in and around Syria evoke the fragility of the argumentation.

Again, the question arises whether this is an end or the beginning. Antonio Cassese's construct of a "restricted multilateralism" as permitted to counter crimes against humanity (Cassese 2005) is not covered by the concept of human security, which contrasts the focus on the individual with an equal concentration on UN mandating, uniquely representing individuals as collective entity. But how can the "Cassesean gap" be repaired? In line with the proposal in this article, a differentiation of the previous peace and security architecture and practice could result from revising Article 42 of the UN Charter to establish "Rapid Neutral Intervention Force", which can be provided regionally and, in the event of imminent threat, acts on the basis of PSC's assessment and decision as the preliminary mediator and de-escalator, with mandatory and immediate subsequent treatment of the issue by the UNSC (interpretative modification of the UN Charter; independent of the conclusion of bilateral treaties).

The normative basis of a responsibility to protect as an instrument of the International Community as a whole must in any case be upheld in the light of human security (Joubert in Rioux 2001: 337). It could otherwise be assumed that the era of the UN and thus the claim to universality with regard to responsibility for world peace would have come to a normative and practical end (for instance, only "notary function" in the Kosovo conflict 1999 and total silence in the Chechen war 2008 and the outbreak of the COVID-19 crisis 2020).

For this reason, it is proposed that the term "intervention" be replaced by the narrower term "peace protection mechanism in fighting for humanity" in the exercise of protection of civilians. Instead, intervention should be used as neutral term as relevant to the whole spectrum of "Sustaining Peace". Ideally, this argument should also facilitate discussion on the P-5 veto waiver in cases of crimes against humanity.

9.3.3 *Visualisation of Proposals Track 2*

In summing up, a merger of argumentation founded in track one and two offers the proposal in Fig. 9.2 (Werther-Pietsch 2021: 127-151).

9.4 Keeping Up Universality

The central reform idea in this book is the interposition of a regional level between parties to the conflict and consultation of the UNSC while keeping up universality by strengthening *ius cogens*. The neutralisation of a partner in a given region and the self-interest in long-term stabilisation of other partners makes regional cooperation a promising concept for global peace and security. Nevertheless, to come up with a functional order with a view to global peace, a common roof of human-centrism, the fight for humanity intervention formula, is required. This intertwined vision of regionalisation with a universalism element crystallised against an analysis of the state of geopolitics, geostrategic constellations and lessons from international engagement in hot spots and protracted crises. These aspects could boost innovation in the current model of conflict resolution with the given short time horizon of mandates under the UN Charter. The region affected and the PSC to be active in a given context is sub-continental by nature—a "regional public good" from the perspective of the geographical outreach of the crisis. Global attacks, wars in outer space or big international cyber-attacks over nations should rest with an exclusive handling by the UNSC itself.

It seems that in order to reach sustainable solutions, strategic thinking on the basis of new premises—new post-WW II positions and overcoming the ascertained "westlessness" (Munich Security Conference 2020)—can only be dealt with accordingly in a regional geographical setting. The Arab League, for example, had an eminently important function to play in the Arab world in 2011 (Bothe 2012). Decisive responsibility in this context will never be left by any Arab party to the US or Russia alone. And states like Turkey would be obliged to participate along its real power. The model of the PSCs as executive regional "subsidiary bodies" (or wing, or satellite) of the UNSC also draws on existing regional integration processes in security or economic terms, such as those of the AU or SCO. This means ultimately the strengthening of a "clearing of influence spheres" at the level of regions—not the G2 or G1 level (Natalie Tocci, How coronavirus will upturn the global order, linkedIn 10 April 2020).

Regional Peace& Security Councils
A new institutional set-up for global peace and security

Set-up:

For the sake of enhanced multilateral means and instruments to maintain peace & security, the establishment of permanent regional "wings" of the UNSC with monitoring and preliminary decision-making functions is proposed. Equipped with decentralised enforcement capacity within the UN, these "Regional Peace & Security Councils" (PSCs) should have the right to act autonomously under the co-chairmanship of a rotating regional presidency, a P-5 member and the UN Secretary-General (UNSG). Regular briefings of the UNSC should maintain steady information and learning loops between centre and wings, constantly pressing for harmonised common standards of action.

Format:

Preferably, the PSCs' composition should be adaptive to regional particularities in order to counter systemic blockades of political solutions from the outside. The regional bodies should be able to perform their tasks in a "depoliticised" manner by drawing on civilian expertise. Supported by corresponding science-based advisory bodies, escalation of conflicts could be faced and managed by systemic early warning and timely decisive action before, as well as peace talks and sustainable development after conflict.

Mandate:

1) "Fight for humanity" – a renewed intervention imperative

- *PSC plenaries*: Prepare and coordinate political reaction to "crimes against humanity", ultimately by robust means, as core task in order to duly meet time constraints in urgent cases of threats to peace according to Article 39 UN Charter – this could serve as a temporarily limited incentive for appeasement before final decision by the UNSC;
- *Implementation capacities*: Establish regional pools of civilian and military personnel with immediate deployment troops and for complex missions in crisis areas in the medium term, in collaboration with DPPO, DPO, PBSO, UNDP and other subsidiary UN bodies. They should follow a holistic lens according to the HDP nexus, starting from a rapid reaction mechanism;
- *Scientific advisory bodies*: Regional hubs of expertise for monitoring and obligatory assessment, including for robust action, in the institutional setting of "Peace Centres of Excellence". Such future "Hammarskjöld", "Ban" or "Guterres" P-COEs should also be responsible for training in regard to an effect-based comprehensive approach in International Crisis and Conflict Management, like the "Kofi Annan International Peacekeeping Training Centre" (KAIPTC) in Accra/Ghana.

2) Division of labour in a comprehensive spectrum:

PSCs should:

- take preliminary decision on a violation of Article 39 of the UN Charter, in cases when human rights violations amount to "widespread or systematic attack directed against any civilian population", a legal clarification according to Article 7 of the ICC Statute that emanated from practice in jurisprudence[41] - this decision would obligatorily be based on the Peace COEs recommendations and ideally reinforced by a corresponding veto-ban when action is confirmed at UNSC level (see II.3);
- remain directly subordinated to the UNSC's final decisive invocation to be realised within a sharp time limit;
- develop operational expertise and resources in the entire continuum from conflict prevention to establish post-conflict peace & security;
- foster progress in a whole-of-system response as reflected in UNSCR 2282/2016 (World Bank 2018) by an all-inclusive peacekeeping, peacebuilding and statebuilding concept for regional force action such as the African stand-by force of the AU, the SADC brigade for manoeuvres in Southern Africa or EU battle groups;
- The tasks can be summarised in four responsibilities of the International Community on the whole, namely "responsibility to prevent, mediate, react, and rebuild", to be derived from findings of the current peace & security discourse by each PSC-COE thereby substantially improving the modern intervention logic.

3) Synergies through institutional networking:

- Coordination with the UN Human Rights Council in the field of early prevention of massive, systematic human rights violations;
- Coordination with the Peace-building Commission in the whole spectrum of prevention, mediation, peace-building and state-building, benefitting from civil society action on regional level.

Fig. 9.2 Model of regionalisation of peace and security architecture (own source)

9.4.1 Recast the UN Peace and Security Architecture

The "division of labour" between PSCs for immediate/temporary action and UNSC for medium-term/final decision would allow for the argued greater sustainability and objectivity—even without changing the right of veto, as desirable as it may be. As a result, this flexibilisation—two-tiered rapid "peace protection mechanism" with obligatory successive responsibility of the UNSC—appears to be important for the quality of decision-making in "fight for humanity" scenarios, with regard to the continuum from observation to stabilisation, giving also more voice to eminent non-state actors of civil society. With regard to the operability of the proposal, it is undoubtedly advantageous to point to the arduous path to majority decisions in the CFSP within the EU or to the question of a European army or an EU Security Council (Ursula Werther-Pietsch, Der Standard 18 February 2020). Nevertheless, a focus on "strengthening collaborative regional orders" is for the first time internally expressed in the 18-month Programme of the EU Council by the presidencies of Romania, Finland and Croatia in implementing the 2016 EU Global Strategy (Council of the European Union, Doc No 14518/18 of 30 November 2018).

A condition *sine qua non* for the success of the model is that—as discussed—sufficient consideration is given to the progressive definition of massive, systematic human rights violations, initially specified in the sense of international crimes of humanity, as well as to the time factor, i.e. the comprehensive ability to react quickly, measured from the occurrence of the anticipated situation to an authoritative initial assessment and mobilisation of suitable resources by the respective PSC: According to former SG Javier Solana on 25 March 1999, NATO's motive for the Kosovo mission was "*to halt the violence and to stop further humanitarian catastrophe*". Similarly, the then Commander-in-Chief Wesley Clark justified NATO's 1999 military operations as a "*response to the deepening humanitarian tragedy unfolding in Kosovo as Yugoslav military and security forces continue and intensify their attacks on their own people*" (quotes from Thürer 2000, 60:3–4 Zaörv 823). Findings in the same direction by the ILC 10 years later are promising that work streams come to an end and operationalise the established formula.

9.4.2 Next Steps and Projection into Future

Finally, how to go forward? Massive, systematic human rights violations as preconditions for intervention in the Cassesian spirit would have to be explicitly anchored in or attributed to Article 39 of the UN Charter as a "threat to peace", or alternatively, the four elements of crimes against humanity could expressly be inserted for reasons of legal security. A third option would consist in introducing common articles into the regional rapid intervention rules of procedure. In the meantime, progress through "dynamic interpretation", which does not necessarily require any change of the Charter at all, is particularly effective and recommendable. Advancement in this direction was made at the occasion of the Munich Security Conference 2020 when Carnegie Europe tabled the idea of an EU Security Council. Scholars could pick up the issue by approaching the UNGS jointly with an initiative for a new political leitmotif of global peace and security.

The far-reaching proposal of regionalisation under a common global roof is certainly to be looked at with caution, but it primarily serves as a vision. Whether the influential world powers would embrace this, quickly can be explored with formative events like the COVID-19 crisis. It can be concluded that the focus of the strategic debate could indeed propel a strong cooperative ICCM and reinvent the multilateral peace and security architecture. What is required is

- *Upgrading of independent watching and reporting* to frontload preparedness ("Centres of Excellence for Peace),
- *Balance between collaborative regional orders and global levels of action* (principle of equidistance; "quadruple responsibilities" package),
- *Normative landing of "fight for humanity"* as the common denominator of collaborative regional orders and human-centrism as intertwined cornerstones of future external intervention.

A two-tiered track, together with the human perspective could frame the conditions for the new triad between USA, China and the new "multilateralism bloc".

9.5 Modern Intervention Logic

9.5.1 The Need for a New Consensus

Overcoming fragility as a context-specific goal has been priority for external engagement for decades (Feichtinger 2014). Lessons learned of this period are sustainability, resilience, conflict transformation, and coordinated action. In summary, after the analysis of history and the detection of the need for innovation in peacekeeping, it can be stated that the "achievement of resilient systems of socio-political order and alliances of security resilience at regional level" is the most promising of all new approaches to sustainable peace in the implementation of UNSCR 2282/2016. Having said this, and as an invaluable prerequisite, this is only true with strict adherence to a joint division of labour. This makes "Collaborative Crisis and Conflict Management (CCCM)" a multilevel game. Number of strategic and operational observations and challenges prove this thesis.[2]

---

[2] The following explanations are based on the author's deliberations in ÖMZ Austrian Military Journal 02/2019.

9.5.2 "Starters"

After the historical, geopolitical and normative analysis, listing incentives for new intervention principles looks like the following.

Strategic insights and incentives

- What could be interpreted as a "retreat" from a strategically weak multilateralism is a stronger emphasis on "enlightened self-interest", which not only puts the partners of the ICCM in each other's service, but also, conversely, absolves external actors of their sole responsibility for the desired success.
- This also applies to the thesis of R2P. There too, is a de facto averting of closed mandate-loyal enforcement of values and/or interests of the International Community. The premature regime change discussion in the Libyan case has certainly accelerated this collapse.
- In addition, international commonalities ("values") and the resulting "principled pragmatism" of the actors, such as those of the EU, are breaking apart.
- "Over-connectivity" may lead to a stronger focus on long-term goals based on self-interest, which detects and prevents "unintended consequences". This strengthens the view of regional implications and the recognition that the International Community has only limited influence on political processes.
- New cutting-edge technologies, Emerging Disruptive Technologies (EDT), Artificial Intelligence, cyber space, outer space activity create new methods of warfare (US Interim National Security Strategic Guidance, March 2021: 21).

Operational insights and incentives

- A major reform push with the character of a response to the observed changes is that the roles of the individual actors in the ICCM are perceived more precisely and more sharply—a specialisation in scenario technology.
- This is the basis for the willingness to introduce tools based on context-specific analysis, and to always have a long-term perspective in mind when applying them. The result is more flexible piecemeal mandates with different components (Starlinger in Werther-Pietsch 2017: 208; "capability-driven comprehensive approach").
- Grey area of peace actors: Constructive inclusion means inclusion of "bad actors". Only extremism that insists on the intention of enforcing its goals by force must be excluded. That can also be an entry point for the start of joint negotiations among the other parties to the conflict.
- As the example of Kosovo shows, the "endstate" discourse has shifted to process-oriented ways of attaining increased resilience. In order to realise peaceful and inclusive societies, the (international legal) principle of self-determination must be built in state-building processes.
- It also became clear that fragile situations in which conflict is part of everyday life require a preventive strategy.

- All the more, new cutting-edge technologies gain ground and challenge the national sovereignty of all parties involved.

An extension of capabilities for a renewed "capability-driven comprehensive approach" could therefore look as follows (European Forum Alpbach, 2018 Seminar 05; Fig. 9.3).

How do these resilience factors affect key principles of international peace operations? And what specific conclusions can be drawn for the Comprehensive Approach?

9.5.3 Looking Ahead

In 2016, the UN provided a solution that unspectacularly advocates deepening "common interests", i.e. hitting the heart of functioning multilateralism. In the 2018 A4P Declaration, the approach was further developed and approved by the UNGA. The Pathways for Peace study of the World Bank and UNDP 2018 shows the empirically proven and favoured model of "simultaneousness" (Werther-Pietsch and Ritzer 2013; ICRC President Maurer and Werther-Pietsch, Humanitarian Space—Triple Nexus, *TDHJ Podcast*, 19 Feb 2021, "Videos UWP", https://youtu.be/zdu4itayH6o; see Fig. 9.4).

All actors in the Triple (HDP) Nexus should therefore recognise the following principles:

1. Support for *legitimate policies* through a *process-oriented approach* as a priority (contemporary interpretation of the non-interference ban),
2. Readiness for *simultaneous action* with a *long-term perspective* in mind,
3. *Primacy of local solutions.*

The International Community is faced with a balance of forces to be redefined: When overburdened, large-scale missions are replaced, the interaction and the "right time"—as recommended by the resilience approach—is particularly important for each individual actor carrying tasks under the mandate. Strong political backing at a high level (UNSCR) cannot replace speed, precision, or perseverance, but it can reinforce a division of labour, often only make it possible.

It will therefore be crucial to create an overarching joint code of conduct for external engagement as a framework to ensure the quality of interventions ("Draft Principles for Responsible Peacebuilding and Statebuilding", Werther-Pietsch and Reinprecht in Nowak and Werther-Pietsch 2014: 232–33). Such a code of conduct would, in line with the trend towards voluntary commitments, also take account of the flexibilisation of rules-based international relations and attract the state's willingness to participate. And, it would prepare the quadri-fold responsibilities model.

Resilience factors - requirements for a revised ICCM			
Principle	**Conceptual Basis**	**Methodological Basis**	**Political Implication**
Resilience and culturally sensitive conflict transformation as overall goals	principled realism Holistic approach including all stakeholders and external actors Triple (HDP) Nexus: Unity of effort required, better understanding of "good & bad" actors	Rules-based engagement; readiness to solidarity and mutual assistance 3(4)C approach of coordination, complementarity, coherence and communication Early warning Focus on prevention	Draft Principles for responsible and inclusive Peace-building and State-building (proposal) Focus on indirect causes of conflict (non-hostility sphere>> SDGs) Reform of multilateral institutions in the light of prevention
Enlighten self-interest as driver of negotiations and the establishment of post-conflict institutions	Changed legal reasoning for missions: inclusive reference frame for ethical choice toward an "endstate" in a certain context New model of partnership (neither instrumentalisation nor unilateral ownership)	Strive for international alignment on a robust „*do ut des*"-base	Open dialogue; freezing out extremists/spoilers Bringing in women's voice as parts of society, actors and negotiators Engagement only when clear arguments and added security or wealth for country or region "Turn to the local" Initiative
Long-term thinking; no fix timelines	Flexibilisation of mandates Flexibility on the ground, capacity planning in head quarters Attentiveness to "windows of opportunities"/"ripe moments"	Instrumental, components-based approach Choosing distinct issues in engagement Divison of labour "niche philosophy"	Accompanying genuine processes, fostering inclusiveness Prioritisation of capabilities & capacity building at national level Start of mission & flexible adjustment of mandates until "success" is given
Regional impact and outreach	cross-border issues	Enlarged communication & coordination	Involvement and strengthening of sub-regional organisations
Joint and regular assessment of expected outcomes "on the way"	Rationalisation of motives for intervention Unintended implications ("do no harm")	Communication strategy on the ground	Not to be the "occupier"
Robust reaction as a matter of last resort, dialogue prevails	Redefinition of "necessity" (ILC Draft Articles) Negotiations underpinning the whole peace process	Reform of international order, formally, in using "soft law" track and jurisprudence; new rules to include new actors, open-up matters of self-determination or legislation for cyberspace	Stick to universal values of the international order &own legitimacy Remedy for eroded multilateralism

Fig. 9.3 How to intervene in fragile situations-state of the art (own source with the perission of participants of the seminar

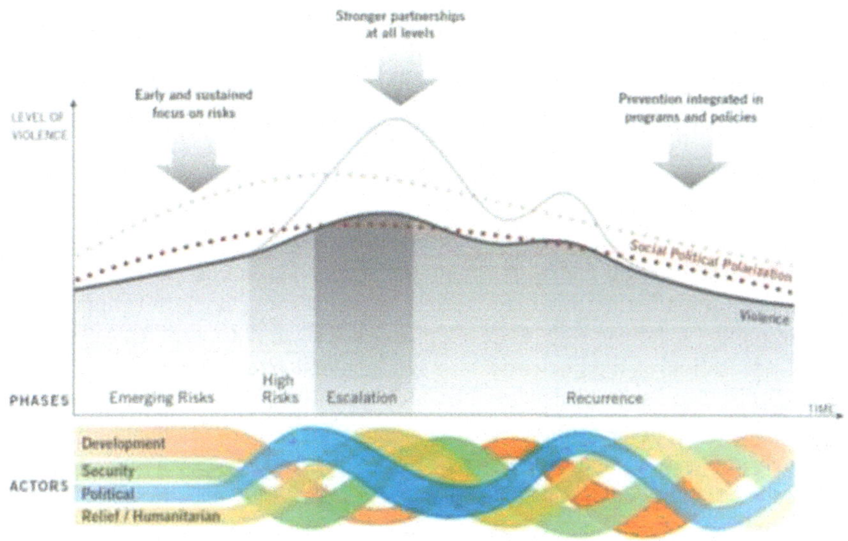

Fig. 9.4 "Sustained Approach to Peace" *Source* World Bank, and UNDP 2018. *Pathways for Peace*

Options for the UN in peace and security—The "future mission"

Future missions will have to be capability-driven and specific in profile to be successful.

Sven Bernhard Gareis and Johannes Varwick (2014: 410) conclude their book on the UN with a critical outlook on "muddling through", with the two poles ultimately defining the spectrum of both "world without UN" and "UN as world government". COVID-19 after initial stumbling blocks concerning the role of the WHO will certainly contribute a lot of solidarity in multilateral action and perhaps a new understanding of interconnectedness. It also signals rigorously sharp confrontation when it comes to hegemonic rivalry between super-powers. Furthermore, and not at least, armed groups will capitalise from the overall vulnerable situation, as NATO Secretary General Stoltenberg pointed out at the end of March 2020.

This evaluation positively identifies three ways forward, first, the "moderate and setback trend towards a 'monopoly on the legitimisation of the use of force'" in the peacekeeping sector, second, a strategic alliance with non-state global researchers and opinion-makers in order to avoid a loss of significance, and third, the change from forum to actor. What makes the UN indispensable for the stability of the international system is its claim that individual states or groups of states do not decide alone on the admissibility of the use of force. The old global governance concepts of delimitation and connection have in the meantime given way to "club governance", which has introduced a more active role for non-democracies and a more interest-based multilateralism (e.g. g7 + observer status at the UN since October 2019). This has resulted in confusing forms of cooperation with so-called output legitimacy ("messy multilateralism", Richard N. Haas, The case for messy multilateralism. In Financial Times, 5 October 2010), which seeks solution-oriented and flexible answers to concrete problems without institutional superstructure.

None of these "power bases" exhibits the rules-based comprehensiveness of the UN but can set the tone for international political and economic relations in various technical fields and thus make the UN one of several instruments for solving transnational state problems. This calls for an active approach by the UN to knowledge and decision-making hubs and cooperation if it is to maintain its function and authority in agenda setting. To this end, it must maintain the mandate of the member states and set clear priorities that enable them to lead. A critical instrument for this will be a convention on the human right to development (Geneva; draft as of 23 April 2020).

The realisation of the necessity of a fundamental reorientation can be a valuable impulse for a substantial "*supranationalisation*" of the UN: For example, steps towards the lifting of the prohibition of intervention in internal affairs by renouncing the veto in the case of stated crimes against humanity, genocide, or ethnic cleansing, as well as the prohibition of an unlimited war using fully autonomous weapons ("Lethal Autonomous Weapon Systems", LAWS) are strategic goals that would give diplomacy of even small, democratic countries a signal function and particular strength of action in foreign policy. A constant mainstreaming of such conceptual objectives would contribute to not falling into high-flying reform initiatives, but to taking the right steps forward.

Tips for procedure

The challenge is to renegotiate the issues at global level and influence regions. This runs counter "alliances of democracies" but opens strategic autonomy of regions. In order to test the practicability, these points as reflected in the Key CCCM Principles would have to be brought together under the leadership of the UNSG/UNDPO in an inclusive debate over the coming years:

- *Launch* of the elaboration of a comprehensive cooperative crisis and conflict management system ("UN-CCCM") by the UNSG based on the Sustaining Peace Approach, the Triple (HDP) nexus, the Brahimi and HIPPO Recommendations, together with the regional organisations NATO, EU and AU as well as relevant scientific institutions (IPI, New York University, Columbia, Georgetown, Harvard, Stanford, Oxford, Cambridge, Hamburg, Berlin, London, Paris, Tokyo, Vienna, EPON, SIPRI, to name a view), which could nurture this process
- *Deliverables*: Finding/defining *Peace Consensus* on regionalisation of the peace and security structure, intertwined with a commitment to fight for humanity; as well as negotiating Key Principles of CCCM
- *Communication strategy* for the project as a forum of inclusive governance in the area, open to the scientific community and civil society.

Appendix 1—Key CCCM Principles

Key Principles of Cooperative Crisis and Conflict Management (CCCM)
Revised version by seminarists of the Deutsche Bundeswehr University Munich and students at University of Graz[3]

- With a view to the overall goal of building resilient and inclusive societies (SDGs, 2015, UNSG Report on Peace-building in the Immediate Aftermath of Conflict 2009);
- Recalling that stabilisation and development are political processes and need local ownership and inclusion;
- Dedicated to the new nexus and multilateral system thinking in fragile situations;
- Willing therefore to establish Regional Peace and Security Councils and Peace-Centres of Excellence under the auspices of a reinforced *ius cogens* and intervention logic;
- Furthering a culture of an international "responsibility to prevent, mediate, react and rebuild";
- Building on legitimate external action and a transparent division of labour between all actors engaged;
- Advocating better long-term sensitive mandates in this regard;

We deserve attention to a broad spectrum of actors and capabilities in Cooperative Crisis and Conflict Management (CCCM), guided by the intertwined paradigm of equidistance and human-centrism:

1. **Crisis preparedness by "Resilience Networks"**

Overall lesson learned from the COVID-19 polycrisis is a new alert-sensitive and forward-looking governance model including all sources of information and knowledge generation of society, the model of anticipatory governance. Hand in hand with comprehensive planning exercises, "resilience networks" will automatically emerge. The proposal of Peace Centres of Excellence shall manage this critical observer function for early warming and action.

2. **Focus on resilience and conflict transformation in a regional setting**

All peace processes are processes of increasing self-determination and should be used as a chance to foster legitimacy and resilient in-country progress. Poor sustainability of international engagement can result not only in setbacks but also in loss of prior achievements in this endeavour. Instead of focusing on conflict stabilisation, the International Community needs to prioritise conflict transformation with a view to obtaining self-sustained security and development.

3. **Method of working: Specialised and targeted mandates, comprehensive perspective**

Om the basis of UNSCR 2282/2016, common goal setting and coordination are vital to increase the efficiency and credibility of international stakeholders sur place. This includes joint assessments of expected outcomes to build common ground (SWOT analysis, division of labour). Furthermore, the impact of international presences on local societies should always be checked for innovative solutions in procurement, recruitment, fair access to services, as well as confidence possible measures and reconciliation. The new method should furthermore focus on specificities in fields of new warfare (use of drones, etc.) and, to be successful, stick to small, manageable and more precise mandates.

4. **System-wide action under the HDP nexus thinking**

In the context of the recognised need for sustainable and long-term international engagement, it should be clear that external actors are only "guests" in the respective conflict country. Especially the military acts under time pressure, also in its effort to achieve local trust. In fact, a common understanding of simultaneousness of action, synergies and do no harm, should be guiding external players on the basis of the Triple ("HDP") nexus.

5. **Legitimacy of international action**

For the future of the International Community as a community of solidarity and peaceful societies, international action needs a legitimate basis in international law, at best a UN Security Council mandate. The proposed Regional Peace and Security Councils (PSCs), for reasons of their vicinity to the root causes of conflict, shall be involved in first instance. As a guiding line applies that peaceful settlement of conflicts prevails, whereas robust action always remains *ultima ratio*.

6. **The Art of diplomacy and mediation**

Political dialogue is crucial when it comes to reconcile groups after conflict or bolstering social cohesion in a given fragile setting. Often chances to prevent conflict lie in experienced, cautious but determined mediation structures at all levels (Tracks 1–3). Similarly, after an armed conflict ends, transitional dialogue platforms for inclusion in political processes have to be sought. Training for mediation facilities and rosters for eminent mediators can help being in a position to rapidly respond to needs.

7. **Reality-check: Avoiding too high expectations**

Management of expectations specifying opportunities and possibilities but also limitations and risks of international interventions needs to take place continuously, not only before a mission starts. Unmet expectations can result in mutual frustration and loss of confidence in international and local actors.

Prior to taking the decision to deploy a CCCM mission, international actors need to have a picture whether certain preconditions are in place. This is best done by all representatives on the ground who should be mandated to report regularly so as to be prepared if a crisis occurs (Centres of Excellence for Peace [P-COEs]). The conflict situation, success probability of an intervention as well as the availability of human and financial resources need to be judged in a realistic manner.

8. **Necessity of robust action in the fight for humanity**

In situations of *widespread or systematic attack directed against any civilian population*, military means might become necessary in support of international political engagement and mediation—as response to humanitarian emergencies and endemic violence as well as in the context of protection of civilians. NGO coalition for an advisory opinion of the ICJ on the ban of the veto right in the UNSC in those cases should be widely supported and the matter introduced into international law.

To fulfil its tasks seriously, robust peace support means all-inclusive capabilities including space and cyber defence at the disposal of missions. Military means cannot, however, replace civilian peace-building efforts and should embrace a transforming character.

9. **Democratic culture of inclusion, women's rights, and social cohesion**

The implementation of peace concepts can only be successful if these are not only supported but conducted and shaped by the respective local populations. In this context, resistance to peace efforts by spoilers—when local actors take political and/or economic advantages of the current conflict situation—needs to be overcome. Extremists are to be frozen out. Inclusion of women following the "WPS agenda" of UNSCR 1325 pays, since peace agreements last longer when women are included in negotiations and subsequent implementation measures.

10. **System-wide joint assessments and flexible exit-strategies**

High needs of resources, capabilities and assets and multiple challenges on the ground must result in increasing division of labour and coordination efforts between civilian and military actors. Here again, a turn to expressed needs and inclusion of local capacities is required to gain support and secure sustainability. This is to be done by joint situational awareness, a transformative approach and flexibility in implementing strategies. CCCM can only be limited in time, content and geographical space. It needs to incorporate transition challenges and adaptive exit-strategies including fair digitalisation, protection from hybrid threats, human rights-aligned PKOs and zero tolerance for discrimination. Clear goals of the external presence are a must for the sustainable development of the society concerned.

Appendix 2—Road Maps to Peace

The new notion of "sustaining peace" as stipulated in UNSC Resolution 2282/2016 and the 2030 Agenda of the United Nations translate processes of transition in legal terms. Four core elements assist in determining pathways to peace between all actors involved:

Human-centred system thinking in external engagement

0. [**Conflict prevention/intervention** (*ius cogens* with regard to crimes against humanity)]
1. **Commitment to democratisation servicing social inclusion and responsibility**:
   - Build responsive leadership and governance ("structural or built-in responsibility");
   - Establish fair access to power and resources;
   - Start with dealing with the past, mostly procedures of reconciliation; and
   - Mainstream broadly an overarching gender perspective.
2. **Contribution to the guiding principle of combining HDPS spheres** with the clear goal of reaching higher levels of self-determination:

[3] My gratitude to students of Universität der Bundeswehr Munich and University of Graz (2020/21) as well as Lukas Wank from the Think and Do Tank Shabka, who together with me and the 3C Net undertook an online questionnaire on the matter and assisted in formulating the theses from the view of a civil society organisation. Grateful also to Maria-Angela Brunner and Isabell Taxacher to have "translated" these principles in a full-fledged article in Werther-Pietsch, Ursula. 2021. *Powering Universalism*, 204–216.

- Unite political settlements for resilience;
- Create an environment that increases legitimacy;
- Follow a renewed human security doctrine in fragile situations;

  Focus on human dignity as the central objective,
  Put emphasis on root causes of the conflict,
  Reconcile peace-building with human security and transitional justice,
  Take conflict transformation and mediation as priorities,
  Promote non-discrimination at all levels,
  Protect vulnerable and marginalised people,
  Align with local priorities,
  Do no harm, with regard to other policies applied, and
  Concentrate on dialogue between all groups.

3. Support for a common understanding of resilience as a "joint end state" vision: Unite all actors around and build a win-win situation for all
4. Implementation of a "lex pacificatoria" anticipating measures for conflict prevention:

   - Negotiate inclusively but freeze out extremism;
   - Be gender-responsive (security issues DDR, SSR, IDPs, POC);
   - Take the essential question of migration on board;
   - Balance between transitional justice, amnesties and the fight against radicalisation;
   - Be accountable to partners; and
   - Collaborate comprehensively in planning and action ("Capability-driven Comprehensive Approach", CCCM Key Principles).

References

Bernhardt, Rudolf. 1983. International law as a legal order—International jurisdiction—Human rights. Festschrift Hermann Mosler, Contributions no. 81, Berlin.

Cassese, Antonio. 1995. *Self-determination of peoples: A legal reappraisal*. Cambridge: Cambridge University Press.

Cassese, Antonio. 2005. *International law*, 2nd ed. Oxford: Oxford University Press.

Commission on Human Security. 2003. *Security now*. Preface Sadako Ogata. https://humansecurity-chs.org/finalreport/. Accessed 8 Aug 2021.

Debiel, Tobias, and Volker Franke. 2008. Auf tönernen Füßen? In *Human security, Eine Welt*, vol. 21, ed. Cornelia Ulbert and Sasche Werthes. Text of the Development and Peace Foundation. Bonn

Deng, Francis M. et al. 1996. Sovereignty as Responsibility, Conflict Management in Africa, Washington DC. Brookings Institution Press.

Dubler, S.C.R., and M. Kalyk. 2018. *Crimes against humanity in the 21st century—Law, practice and threats to international peace and security*. Boston/Leiden: Brill.

Feichtinger, Walter. 2014. Between ambition and reality: International crisis and conflict management. An Inventory. In *Wege und Irrwege des Krisenmanagements, Internationale Sicherheit und Konfliktmanagement*, vol. 7, ed. Walter Feichtinger, Hermann Mückler, Gerald Hainzl, and Predrag Jurekovic. Vienna/Cologne/Weimar: böhlau.

Finnemore, Martha. 2003. *The purpose of intervention: Changing beliefs about the use of force*. Cornell University Press.

Gareis, Sven Bernhard, and Johannes Varwick. 2014. *The United Nations. Tasks, instruments and reforms*, 5th ed. Opladen/Toronto: Publisher Barbara Budrich UTB.

Hänggi, Heiner, and Vincenza Scherrer. 2007. Towards a common UN approach to security sector reform: Lessons learnt from integrated mission. Study No. 25, DCAF. Geneva.

Hobe, Stephan, and Otto Kimminich. 2004. *Introduction to international law*, 8th ed. Tübingen: Mohr Siebeck

ILC Report 2019. 2019. A/74/10 as of 20 August 2019, Report of the International Law Commission on the work of the seventy-first session (2019)—Advance version, French only (un.org)

Isensee, Josef. 1995. Intervention between Human Rights Protection and Great Power Policy, German Society for Foreign Policy 12.

Joubert, Jean Paul. 2001. Mutations in international relations: L' "intervention d'humanité", nouvelle jeunesse du jus ad bellum? with references of Serge Sur ["decentralized collective security"]. In *Human security*, ed. Jean-Francois Rioux. Harmattan Verlag

Paris, Roland. 2002. International peacebuilding and the 'mission civilisatrice'. *Review of International Studies* 28 (4).

Rioux, Jean-Francois. 2001. *Human security*. Harmattan Verlag.

Starlinger, Thomas. 2017. Creating a planning and operating mechanism—A stance by a military. In *Global peace and security. International crisis and conflict management*, ed. Ursula Werther-Pietsch, 176–209. Vienna: MANZ.

Taylor, Owen. 2004. Human security—Conflict, critique and consensus: Colloquium remarks and a proposal for a threshold-based definition. *Security Dialogue* 35 (3): 373–387.

Thalhammer, Andreas. 2018. 70 years of the "Universal Declaration of Human Rights" 1948–2018, Austrian MoD

Thürer, Daniel. 2000. Modern international law: A system in transition and growth, 4th scenario: NATO Intervention in Kosovo—Dilemma between state sovereignty and human rights, humanitarian justice commandment? *ZaöRV* 60 (3–4): 823ff.

Verdross, Alfred, and Bruno Simma. 1984. *Universal international law: Theory and practice*, 3rd ed. Berlin: Duncker & Humblot.

Von Arnauld, Andreas. 2009. Sovereignty and responsibility to protect. *The Peace Observatory* 84 (1): 11–52.

Werther-Pietsch, Ursula, and Astrid Reinprecht. 2014. Essentials, findings, implications. In *All human rights for all. Vienna guidebook on peaceful and inclusive societies*, ed. Manfred Nowak and Ursula Werther-Pietsch, 227–234. Vienna—Graz—Antwerp: nwv—intersentia.

Werther-Pietsch, Ursula, and Thomas Ritzer. 2013. PKOs and the new intervention logic. In *Strategy and security*, ed. Johann Pucher and Johann Frank, 87–98. Vienna: böhlau.

Werther-Pietsch, Ursula. 2009. Security and Development—Two Pillars of a System? Vienna: Series of the National Defence Academy in collaboration with DCAF Geneva, S/2/2009.

Werther-Pietsch, Ursula. 2019. Comprehensive approach 3.0: "Triple Nexus." *Austrian Military Journal* 02: 155–166.

Werther-Pietsch, Ursula. 2020. Brauchen wir einen EU-Sicherheitsrat? *Der Standard*, Vienna 18 February 2020: 27.

Werther-Pietsch, Ursula. 2021 (forthcoming). EU key for strategic autonomy—A proposal. In *AIES yearbook 2021*, ed. Clemens Fischer. Berlin: Springer.

Whineray, David. 2020. The pros and cons of a European Security Council. Carnegie Europe, 23 January 2020. https://carnegieeurope.eu/strategiceurope/80869. Accessed 8 Aug 2021.

Chapter 10
Reality Check: New Intervention Logic

10.1 Global State of Play

Higher levels of expressed self-interest, be it autocratic dominance or the outcome of "principled realpolitik", as well as rising economic and social inequality shows a world in profound change. It is questionable whether, in view of the changed conditions, consensus on how to build global peace and security can still be assumed at all. Relocation of security policy and legal discourses demonstrate new forms of political governance, diffusion of power and a need for adaptivity, contextuality and localisation. International Crisis and Conflict Management (ICCM) currently does not dispose of a "*coherent full spectrum force package*" (Biscop) of instruments.

During the last decades, internal conflicts have become internationalised, lines of internal and external security dimensions blurred. *Failed states* and *ungoverned spaces* emerged and are sadly there to stay. Non-state armed actors have stepped into the scene. Comprehensive efforts for "Road maps to peace" have increasingly expanded the ICCM's ratio and action. War crimes were further identified and perpetrators prosecuted and convicted; the International Community has acknowledged a subsidiary responsibility to protect civilians in fragile situations reflected in the changing conditions for intervention (Werther-Pietsch 2013). Cyber threats, emerging disruptive technologies (EDT) are further challenging military capabilities. In reaction, the ICCM made human security and a holistic approach the guiding principles of peace missions and, in the end, sometimes took over the international administration of post-war situations.

Expectations on the UN's potential for action have increased accordingly over the years—without at the same time solving the question of capacity and boosting the willingness of states to act. ICCM players themselves demonstrate less trust in each other, which leads to a remarkable decline in joint actions.

This slight disengagement, accelerated by the withdrawal from Afghanistan in August 2021, which will also shape the near future reorganisation of military capacities at the disposal of the UN in the aftermath of the COVID-19 crisis, took place due to a certain overstretching of what has been originally intended by the UN Charter.

U. Werther-Pietsch, *Transforming Security*, Global Power Shift,
https://doi.org/10.1007/978-3-030-87097-3_10

This can be discerned by the world's order is rooted in Cold War global conditions, which was certainly successful under the aegis of UNSG Dag Hammarskjöld (Kissinger 1996). At that time political, geostrategic influences and self-interests were perpetuated in two spheres, the East and the West. Despite this freezing, the UN was able to find a modus vivendi to manage the situation. It is true that such binary codes have to be reflected but obviously remain hostile to progressive normativisation and the creation of international rules for handling global frontier risks.

Geopolitical constellation is on the move—against the background of more or less repressive regimes building new categories of proxies. Chinese dragons, American bisons, and Russian bears along with keen Europeans with their "multilateral DNA" (Gu 2021) and catchy newcomers fight for a new balance on global stage, a movement the impact of which is at the core of this study.

10.2 Effects on International Law

The guiding framework remains the UN Charter of 1945 and its peace and security bodies, the Security Council, the General Assembly, and the Secretary General.

According to the new conditions however, Article 39 of the UN Charter, which can be regarded as the "roof top" of ICCM, must be seen as an open and adaptive norm. "*The assumption of a threat to peace was perpetuated, so to speak, until the peaceful reappraisal of a violation of international law.*" (Herdegen 2019). Inclusion of hybrid threats, a cautious extending of criteria for intervention, "individualisation" in the sense of human security in picking up the current *ius cogens* debate, and focus on core tasks in regional constellations belong to the most important theses for innovation in this regard, and will be looked at in-depth in this study.

10.3 Effects on ICCM

What has so far been learned by the International Community, continues to confront troop contributing states (TCC) *sur place* and leaves commanders on the ground with open questions when it comes to operational implementation:

- *Changes in mind-set, concept and objectives*
  "humanisation" > "securitisation" > "developmentalisation"
- *Change in the focus of deployment principles*
  "multidimensional" > "local" > "tool/effect-based/capability-driven"
- *Change in methodology of working together*
  "isolated" > "integrated" > "multipolar"

Key principles will be derived along the findings (Part III).

10.4 Effects on Joint Understanding of the Underlying Challenge

(1) Fragility and resilience: Failures to overcome

In a human-centred model, three categories (Stewart and Brown 2009) may be reiterated at this point serving as criteria for state fragility:

- → *Authority failures (survival functions of the state)*
- → *Service failures (expected functions of state engagement)*
- → *Legitimacy failures (political functions of legitimate government).*

State structures that fulfil these criteria are supposed to be resilient. The achievement of resilient systems of socio-political order combined with resilient security arrangements at the regional level can therefore be described as the integral guiding principle and desired endstate for all actors in ICCM missions. This adds on the positive side to the prevention of crimes against humanity and protection of civilians, as argued later.

Definitions, policy frameworks, orientation towards Triple ("HDP") nexus, interdisciplinary fields of action—the striving for an overall joint effort, the capability-driven comprehensive approach—are at disposal. ICCM actors show a lively commitment to work at high risk. The normative basis is however poor. Therefore, the ICCM should all the more be flexible to absorb different currents and to adapt to the conditions. Such a central element is UNSCR 2282/2016, which consolidates what has been thought and tested so far in the Sustaining Peace Approach.

(2) Building the framework—Sustaining Peace Approach / HDP nexusNnexus

It can be safely stated that peace, security, and development policy aspects must be pursued simultaneously in order to achieve sustainable peace on the basis of the comprehensive approach. Human security as common denominator for international players may have prepared the ground in this context. Therefore, cooperative ICCM and IL have to go hand in hand. Instruments of IL, however, to demand such action and governance yet appear to be weakly developed.

Tensions between strategic considerations become evident when power is not oriented towards welfare for all as reflected in the SDGs or, through potential opponents and weak institutions, cannot orient itself thereto. Aggravated by the COVID-19 pandemic, problems that have not yet been solved but play a role in human-centrism and multilateral system thinking show unanimously that

- number of actors are more strongly influenced by genuine local and societal customs and ties than by states and citizenship;
- state structures provide no longer exclusively for the welfare of the community but are complemented by non-state power houses, often acting in an under-regulated space; and

• **Peace-building vs. State-building**: The relationship has increasingly shifted to give peace-building priority over state-building, which corresponds to the values' structure of the UN Charter.	• **Inclusion vs. "spoilers only"**: Broad voluntary inclusion contrasts with destructive behaviour, which can be countered with socialisation, concessions through incentives, but also coercive measures when appropriate.
• **Institutions vs. grounded legitimacy**: In "hybrid political orderspeace must be built from bottom-up. " (Fukuyama, 2005, Clements, 2009, Rocha-Menocal, 2010, McGinty, 2011)	• **Local vs. global:** Embedding local structures permanently in changed institutional contexts (decentralisation; self-determination)
• **State vs. society**: Perception of legitimacy and existence of functional equivalents (Max Weber) unfold in a reciprocal, ambivalent tension relationship.	• **Realism vs. idealism**: A new concept with a stronger peace policy component in the form of the Sustaining Peace Approach (Triple "HDP" Nexus) attempts to mediate between this antagonism.

Fig. 10.1 Competing approaches, inspiring the principle of equidistane, human-centrism and a new balance-of-power doctrine (own source)

- peace in a socio-political sense against the background of radicalisation and extremism must be promoted and (re-)built "from the smallest cell" (Fig. 10.1).

In summing up, the balance between

- progress in development as a concern of the developing countries vs. dominance of the peace and security pillar; and
- the human rights versus sovereignty, in its wider comprehension as power orientation, which deeply shapes the UN since its foundation.

is a lasting characteristic of the current Collective Security System. It is however questionable whether this juxtaposition fully meets the challenges of the future or whether there has been a fundamental shift of the "global condition". Geostrategic power projection and a "technological neo-bi-polarism" between USA and China (Irene Giner-Reichl, Roundtable 27 May 2021[1]) interfered by non-state data power houses evokes new scenarios to be answered.

References

Werther-Pietsch, Ursula. 2013. Self-determination, Prohibition of the Use of Force and Peace-keeping Today. The Interface of Development, Peace, Security and Human Rights, Vienna-Graz: Neuer Wissenschaftlicher Verlag, Habilitation.

Kissinger, Henry A. 1996. The Reason of Nations. On the Nature of Foreign Policy. Berlin/New York.

Gu, Xuewu. 2021. Eine G3-Weltordnung. #TDHJ 03 21: 22—26.

Herdegen, Matthias. 2019. Der Kampf um die Weltordnung. München: C.H. Beck.

[1] https://youtu.be/7JylX_7LwkU. Accessed 28 May 2021.

Chapter 11
Multilateral System Thinking

11.1 "The UN Building"

Agenda-type policy documents, initiated by the UNSGs, are main points of orientation across UN policy fields. Besides normative advances in resolutions, conventions, and guidelines, they reflect knowledge gathered globally, global political consensus and willingness to take the means in hand and use them for the purposes of development and security. Agenda for Peace, together with the Earth Agenda (1992), Agenda for Humanity (2016), and Agenda 2030 for Sustainable Development (2015) with the Paris Agreement on Climate Change form the basis of the multilateral "UN building" in the twenty-first century, the real challenge lying in their full implementation. The UN Charter has thus been differentiated and deepened programmatically.

As an outcome of this huge policing progress, guiding ideas like human security, resilience and a human rights-based approach as emanations of multilateral system thinking evolved. And there is a new step in front, to avoid erosion of global peace and security in a new power environment, the paradigm of equidistance and human-centrism as intertwined cornerstones of future external engagement.

U. Werther-Pietsch, *Transforming Security*, Global Power Shift,
https://doi.org/10.1007/978-3-030-87097-3_11

11.2 The Geostrategic Future—Principle of Equidistance and Human-Centrism

A new paradigm of world politics may come up, *a maximum of influence in one's own region and a minimum of shared common goals to be managed at global level.* Global goals would be reduced to its lowest common denominator to remain manageable and close gaps of regulation in essential domains such as 5G, energy security, climate change, cyber sovereignty, space, and seas. At the same time regions acting under the rule of equidistance in global peace and security matters may be strengthened in the area of conflict prevention and solution by new responsibilities. This equally prepares for more strategic autonomy on regional level. Therefore, only a combined approach is feasible since it resembles a "*do ut des*" situation between world leaders and the International Community.

11.3 Nexus Thinking in ICCM—Compelling Lessons

Lessons learned comprise that peace-making and peacekeeping are interrelated: no development without security. Human rights and development are interdependent as well. Humanitarian aid, development, peace and security interact with each other. In line with such nexus concepts, multilateral system thinking begins to demonstrate its assets. When taking these lessons on board the new geostrategic constellation, implications for future external engagement could be identified (HDP nexus) and serve as basis for further discussion (Fig. 11.1).

Key milestones "in a nutshell"				
Agendas Time dimension Policy trends/ Frameworks	**Milestones identified** Country mark documents	**Key concepts/ideas** Goals, characteristics, new elements, Theory of change	**Key trends & conceptional lessons learned**	**Key implementation tools** Operationalisation in in practice
Peace-building Agenda 1992 –2000	• **1992 Agenda for Peace** • **1992 Earth Summit** (Rio follow up)	Development with a human face	Birth of the broad concept (concept of peace-building)	***From forum to actor:*** Somalia 1992 Rwanda 1994 Former Yugoslavia 1999 Afghanistan2001 Iraq 2003
Development Agenda 2000 – 2010 **Poverty focus**	• 2000 Brahimi report • **MDGs** • 2011 WDR Conflict, Security and Development	Growing perception of the institutional gap in peace-building	(Peacekeeping Reform) (POC first steps)	2001 9-11 2009 UNSG R2P (narrow but deep)
"Human Security Agenda" 2003 - 2015 **Individualised security**	• **2005 UN Reform Summit** • 2008 Capstone Doctrine • 2015 HIPPO Report • 2010 "New Horizons" (F/UK) • 2011 CivCap Initiative	Human security **Peak of multilateralism** (R2P attributed to UN mandate)	(PBC, HRC, R2P) ("integrated missions") (Peacekeeping Reform II) (Socio economic footprint of PKOs in C-34 Committee)	1325/1612/1894 2086 2003 UN Handbook on Multidimensional Peace Operations UNSCR 1970 and 1973/2011 1.x R2P under Chapter VII (Libya)
"Humanity Agenda" 2008 – 2016 **Era of joint engagement in fragile situations**	• **2016 Agenda for Humanity**	Integrated approach	**(Triple Nexus, Sustaining Peace Approach)**	**3D** **3C** **CA** **Capability-driven Comprehensive Approach**
Sustaining Peace Agenda 2016 – 2030 **SDGs** **Multilateral System Thinking** **COVID-19 crisis and the** **regionalisation of security**	• **2030 "Agenda for Sustainable Development"** • 2018 Pathways for Peace Study of the World Bank • 2017 Santos Cruz Report • 2020 Renewal of the WPS Agenda	Era of bilateralism *"do ut des"* partnership resilience concept Formation of concepts of "regional sovereignty" **Contraction and subsequent resilience at regional level**	(conflict prevention) (Tool-based ICCM) (Effect-based Comprehensive Approach/3C) (Draft HDPS Principles) **Fight for Humanity model** **Human-centrism**	***Both forum and actor:*** 2282/2016, **"A4P" Declaration 2018** 2254 and 2249/2015 (SYR, terrorism) **Regionalisation: Two tiered Peacekeeping** **Collaborative Crisis and Conflict** **Management – Key Principles**

Fig. 11.1 Overview on multilateral system thinking impulses in international agenda-setting (own source)

Chapter 12
Global Peace Mechanism 2050—Transforming Security

12.1 Back to Origins

The study resumes that the vision of the UN Charter to systematically unite the cornerstones of peace, security, and development leads to a novel intervention and prevention logic in a changed world.

The "milestones" analysis in Part II revealed instrumental and mandatory weaknesses and an underdeveloped comprehension and implementation with regard to the entire range of capability-based engagement in the sense of human-centrism. This analysis should propel action.

The transformative ideas lie with individualisation of security, institutional regionalisation, normative precision, and mutual trust.

12.2 Reform Proposals—Summary

(1) **Protection mechanism: the fight for humanity**

Building on this, it is first proposed to replace the term "intervention" with regard to the exercise of a responsibility to protect the civilian population under IL with the narrower term "protection mechanism" in order to politically neutralise action, connecting it to relevant questions of conflict prevention. This overall narrowing down of "must-intervention scenarios" should curb a renewed discussion on the veto waiver of the P-5. The concept of intervention itself, which of course remains intertwined, could again be opened up to its original outreach in a complementary way.

Specifically, further development of the System of Collective Security could be ensured by an intervention and prevention imperative of the International Community under the conditions of a two-tiered UN mechanism backed by a restriction of the right of veto in cases of crimes against humanity (Article 7 ICC Statute, UNSCR

U. Werther-Pietsch, *Transforming Security*, Global Power Shift,
https://doi.org/10.1007/978-3-030-87097-3_12

1973/2011 Libya). The recently intensified debate (NGO coalition for the ban of the veto right) shows that IL is advancing towards a core of *ius cogens.*

Since the entry into force of the Rome Statute in 1998, genocide, war crimes and crimes against humanity can be individually punished under international criminal law, regardless of the function in which the crime was committed. In the course of the negotiations on the ICC Statute from 1991 to 1998, and subsequent jurisdiction, a formula emerged on the intensity of the infringement as such: "*widespread or systematic attack directed against any civilian population*" (Article 7 ICC; Dubler and Kalyk 2018; ILC 2019). For these cases, through a unified practice, universality at the global level could be guaranteed. Politically, however, the questions of interpretation, often with an open outcome, remain challenging.

(2) **Regional Peace and Security Councils** "as first instances" of peace and security

In increasingly simultaneous conflict phases and scenarios, the responsibility of regional wings of the UNSC, the so-called Peace and Security Councils (PSCs) under the chairmanship of rotating regional presidencies, a P-5 member and the UNSG would be the way out. PSCs, acting holistically under a common roof, may be a powerful instrument to maintain and foster a rules-based global order in our times ("two-tiered peace and security responsibility").

A rapid reaction mechanism with obligatory successive responsibility of the UNSC is therefore suggested by the following schemes:

- Protection against imminent situations of acute life-threatening to a large number of people as a "regional public good", along joint key principles of CCCM on the basis of the five criteria (*recta auctoritas, recta intentio, iusta causa*, immanence, *magnitude* and proportionality) ("*responsibility to react*")

To this add further interrelated "*joint responsibilities*":

- Expansion and provision of stand-by mediation teams at regional level that are organisationally subordinate to the PSCs ("*responsibility to mediate*") (see also Interim Security Strategy of US Biden-Administration of 3 March 2021[1])
- Conflict prevention in the sense of regular and ad hoc consultation of the designated early warning mechanism on all security-relevant issues such as the development of security sector (system) reform, etc. ("*responsibility to prevent*") in the forefront of UNSC seizure
- Targeted support for the establishment of democratic regimes and economic development programmes in the reconciliation and reconstruction phase ("*responsibility to rebuild*").

This is to be operationalised by:

- Adaptive System of Collective Security

[1] https://www.whitehouse.gov/briefing-room/statements-releases/2021/03/03/interim-national-security-strategic-guidance/. Accessed 5 May 2021.

  - *Mandate*: Reconsideration and prioritisation of "*protection of civilians from massive or systematic attacks*" as the core of peacekeeping (*ius cogens* status; global reach)
  - *Localisation*: Two-tiered protective peace mechanism; differentiated peacekeeping through the introduction of regional Peace and Security Councils based on the "*cooling off*" instrument of the League of Nations
  - *Evidence*: Strengthening preventive dimension through broadening the knowledgebase in setting up UN-led Peace-Centres of Excellence (P-COEs) with observer function in the suggested peace and security mechanisms.

(3) Further reform needs: Certain framework conditions may further be conducive:

- Transforming the UNSC into a real "UNPSC"
  - *Tasks*: The formula "Peace and Security Council" should be extended to the UNSC creating a consistent state of the art understanding of means and goals of modern intervention logic. It can bring about political consensus for a holistic approach to a capability-based comprehensive approach in peace and security matters.
  - *Composition*: Continuation of the proposal of the "Group of Four" (Germany, Brazil, India, Japan—together with 23 other members) to strengthen Asian and African representation while maintaining the veto competence "narrow".
  - *Veto right:* Final adoption of the normative substance of crimes against humanity as the spearhead of IL in global peace and security, following the experiences of the twentieth century and the two world wars.
  - *Peace-building reform*: Acknowledgement that human rights and peace-building are mutually dependent. The stronger involvement of the PBC in peacekeeping relevant decision-making processes appears to be a quick means of increasing effectiveness. In the mid-term, PSCs should start performing their tasks in a cautious, experimental manner.

- Alignment of deployment strategies
  - The future of peace-making and peace-building will remain complex and multi-disciplinary (Gareis and Varwick 2014: 143). Thus, the factual change from interstate threats to the hybrid threat of terrorism took place in the strategic transformation from "no more deterrence by punishment" to "deterrence by denial" (US defence doctrine 2002), and remained so. The UN, too, must react to the perceived "irrationality" with an increased willingness to take risks, a changed logic of battle, management of hot conflict and institutional operability, only in emergencies through privatised standby forces and with equipment for electronic and digital defence methods, in order to create a new legitimising and attractive framework for TCCs.
  - Renew the support for peace processes using the know-how gained over three decades (HDP Principles): Besides continued service to non-controversial

issues in peace processes; elaboration and high-level adoption of relevant principles of mediating and negotiating as already initiated for peacekeeping in the 2018 A4P Declaration (see "Road Maps to Peace" as a starting point) and for which a rich practice exists. A work that could be done by the P-COEs.
- Joint guidelines for action: The vision is finally tailored and specified to an operable reform package reflecting the current state of development. The purpose of modern CCCM is to contribute to the achievement of resilient systems of socio-political order with complementary security arrangements for resilience at regional level. A to-do list for multidimensional, synchronised cooperation for the purpose of "protection of civilians", the common denominator of theoretical and practical analysis, provides the following basic instructions for corresponding progress of the capability-driven comprehensive approach (Sect. 9, Appendix 1).

The reform ideas of a collective CCCM model can be summarised in the vision of the UNSC as a "Peace and Security Council" with regional "satellites". These far-reaching proposals should certainly be taken with caution, but they serve as a vision. For reform steps it can thus be summarised that the focus of the debate should shift in order to revitalise multilateral core tasks:

- Objective systematic watching of trouble spots and streamed UN-owned reporting mechanism—upgrading UN-led think tanks
- Balanced "clearing" between regional and global influence spheres at the institutional level—two-tiered conflict prevention and intervention approach
- Normative bolstering of the "fight for humanity": Protection of civilians in cases of crimes against humanity as "common ground" for CCCM (Werther-Pietsch, Vienna Strategy Conference, 2019; Werther-Pietsch 2021: 143)

A *systematic nexus thinking*, the principle of equidistance as "code of conduct" in the framework of the new balance-of-power, and human-centrism as centres of gravity for a new "*Peace Consensus*" as presented in this study, intend to offer an entry point to this very discussion, which is urgent for maintaining a united global peace and security architecture: For the decades to come, we need to re-organise and transform security.

References

Dubler, SC, R. and Kalyk M. 2018. Crimes against Humanity in the 21st Century—Law, Practice and Threats to International Peace and Security. Boston—Leiden: Brill

ILC Report. 2019. A/74/10 as of 20 August 2019, Report of the International Law Commission on the work of the seventy-first session (2019)—Advance version

Gareis, Sven Bernhard and Varwick, Johannes. 2014. The United Nations. Tasks, instruments and reforms, 5th ed. Opladen—Toronto: Publisher Barbara Budrich UTB

Werther-Pietsch, Ursula. 2021. EU Security Structure Key for Strategic Autonomy—A Proposal. In AIES Yearbook, ed. Klemens Fischer. Springer, 127—151.

Printed by Printforce, the Netherlands